The Regulation of Air Tra

The regulation of modern civil aviation can be traced back to the later years of the Second World War. An intense debate about the future regulatory regime resulted in a compromise which to this day essentially dictates the structure of the global airline industry. Further progress towards 'normalising' the industry appears to be slowing down, and perhaps even going into reverse. Without an understanding of the development of regulation, it is not possible to understand fully the industry's current problems and how they might be resolved.

Many books have been written about the development of international air transport, covering deregulation, privatisation, the emergence of new business models among other things, but few if any have taken a broad view of the trends which have determined the industry's current structure. *The Regulation of Air Transport* charts the development of aviation from the end of the Second World War to the present day, following the key trends and disruptive forces. It provides an overview of what has determined the industry's current structure, the problems still facing the industry and the ways in which it could develop in the future.

This wide-ranging study is important reading for both professionals and academics within the aviation field, as well as anyone interested in the broader development of economic regulation.

Dr Barry Humphreys is an aviation consultant specialising in strategy and regulation. A former senior regulator with the UK Civil Aviation Authority and Director of Virgin Atlantic Airways, he subsequently chaired the trade body for UK airlines and was for several years a Non-Executive Director of NATS, the provider of air traffic control services in the UK. He currently chairs a start-up UK airline. In the 2016 New Year's Honours List he was made a Commander of the Order of the British Empire (CBE) for services to aviation and charity.

Managing Aviation Operations
Series Editor: **Peter J. Bruce**
Associate Editor: **John M. C. King**

The purpose of this series is to provide a comprehensive set of materials dealing with the key components of airline and airport operations. To date, this innovative approach has not been evident among aviation topics and certainly not applied to operational areas of airlines or airports. While more recent works have begun, in brief, to consider the various characteristics of operational areas, the *Managing Aviation Operations* series will expand coverage with far greater breadth and depth of content.

Airlines and airports are devoid of specific topic knowledge in ready-made, easy-to-read, creditable resources. Tapping into industry expertise to drive a range of key niche products will resource the industry in a way not yet seen in this domain. Therefore, the objective is to deliver a collection of specialised, internationally sourced and expertly written books to serve as readily accessible guides and references primarily for professionals within the industry. The focus of the series editors will be to ensure product quality, user readability and appeal, and transparent consistency across the range.

Airline Operations Control
Peter J. Bruce and Chris Mulholland

Aviation Leadership
The Accountable Manager
Mark Pierotti

Strategic Airport Planning
Mike Brown

The Regulation of Air Transport
From Protection to Liberalisation, and Back Again
Barry Humphreys

For more information about this series, please visit: www.routledge.com/Aviation-Fundamentals/book-series/MAO

The Regulation of Air Transport

From Protection to Liberalisation, and Back Again

Barry Humphreys

LONDON AND NEW YORK

Designed cover image: © Getty Images

First published 2023
by Routledge
4 Park Square, Milton Park, Abingdon, Oxon OX14 4RN

and by Routledge
605 Third Avenue, New York, NY 10158

Routledge is an imprint of the Taylor & Francis Group, an informa business

© 2023 Barry Humphreys

The right of Barry Humphreys to be identified as author of this work has been asserted in accordance with sections 77 and 78 of the Copyright, Designs and Patents Act 1988.

All rights reserved. No part of this book may be reprinted or reproduced or utilised in any form or by any electronic, mechanical, or other means, now known or hereafter invented, including photocopying and recording, or in any information storage or retrieval system, without permission in writing from the publishers.

Trademark notice: Product or corporate names may be trademarks or registered trademarks, and are used only for identification and explanation without intent to infringe.

British Library Cataloguing-in-Publication Data
A catalogue record for this book is available from the British Library

Library of Congress Cataloging-in-Publication Data
Names: Humphreys, Barry, author.
Title: The regulation of air transport: from protection to liberalisation, and back again / Barry Humphreys.
Description: Abingdon, Oxon; New York, NY: Routledge, 2023. | Series: Managing aviation operations | Includes bibliographical references and index.
Subjects: LCSH: Aeronautics, Commercial–Government policy. | Aeronautics, Commercial–Deregulation. | Aeronautics, Commercial–Law and legislation.
Classification: LCC HE9777.7 .H86 2023 | DDC 387.7068—dc23/eng/20221013
LC record available at https://lccn.loc.gov/2022048531

ISBN: 978-1-138-32794-8 (hbk)
ISBN: 978-1-138-32798-6 (pbk)
ISBN: 978-0-429-44897-3 (ebk)

DOI: 10.4324/9780429448973

Typeset in Bembo
by codeMantra

Contents

Preface	vii
1 Introduction	1
2 The Beginning	11
3 Growth and Disruption: Charters and Bermuda 2	27
4 US Deregulation	46
5 European Liberalisation	57
6 Open Skies	81
7 The Low-Cost Revolution	108
8 Ownership and Control	130
9 Technology and the Environment	156
10 Airline Profitability	182
11 Air Traffic Management	192
12 Airports	213
13 Summary, COVID and the Future	233
Index	251

Preface

The origins of this book lie in a suggestion from John King that I contribute to a series of studies he and Peter Bruce were planning on the subject of air transport management for professionals. Unfortunately, it proved impossible, at least for me, to limit the contribution to what was required, and the book took on a life of its own. Nevertheless, I am immensely grateful to John for his guidance, advice and patience as I slowly completed the work. I am similarly grateful to numerous others who have commentated on various parts of the book or helped in other ways, including Mike Goodliffe, Peter Harbison, Edmond Rose, Jeff Shane, Erwin von den Steinen, Handley Stevens, Jonathan Wober, Sharon Dai and the late Mike Tretheway. Thanks also go to Guy Loft and Amelia Bashford of Routledge/Taylor & Francis Group. Finally, and by no means least, I thank my wife, Diane, for extreme patience and understanding through a process that took far longer than I had expected, and my three children for guiding their technophobe father through the intricacies of the computer. I can only hope that the results were worth it, but that is for others to judge.

The book focuses on the economic regulation of air transport, tracing developments from the Chicago Convention of 1944 to the present day and tentatively beyond. I make no apology for describing in some detail the origins of the regulatory regime under which aviation operates today. It is only by understanding how we got to where we are now that we can hope to address the challenges which continue to face the industry and those which will certainly lie ahead. If this means starting the story several decades ago, then so be it. It was no less a person than Sir Winston Churchill, after all, who said that the longer you can look back, the further you can look forward.

I have also been influenced by the approach taken by the European Aviation Conference, for which I have served as a member of the Organising Committee for several years. This annual event has successfully brought together both academics and aviation professionals to address the problems facing the industry. The combination of the academic and specialist, with their different approaches and willingness to learn from each other, seems to me to be an excellent approach which deserves to be employed more widely. In addition, I have sought where possible to add the occasional light-hearted aside to what inevitably is a rather dry subject.

The book records the gradual, and intermittent, movement of the international aviation industry from being subject to a tight regulatory regime, where virtually nothing happened without the agreement of governments, to a more liberal environment, what I refer to as the 'normalisation' of the sector. The underlying assumption, supported by numerous studies, is that such reform has been beneficial for virtually all stakeholders, including consumers, governments and the companies involved. Unfortunately, while progress has been substantial, it has not been ubiquitous, with the result that in certain respects liberalisation seems to have ground to a halt. This has left the industry, and in particular the airlines, the very core of the sector, continuing to be subject to excessive government control and therefore unable to act as other 'normal' businesses do. Potentially of even more concern is the risk that regulatory reform is not only failing to progress further, but may even be going backwards.

The book was started before the appearance of the COVID-19 pandemic, which has had a devastating impact on the aviation industry. It is too early to judge with any certainty what the longer-term effects will be. On the whole, my approach has been to ignore the pandemic for most of the book, turning to its implications in detail only in the final chapter. There is little doubt that COVID has destabilised long-accepted economic relationships and made predicting what lies ahead all the more difficult. Some have argued that everything has changed fundamentally and the future will be very different. Others maintain that in fact the underlying principles which have formed the basis for the industry's success for many decades are still present and that some form of normality will resume eventually. We shall see who is right. In any event, hopefully, this book will make a modest contribution to understanding what will need to be done.

Finally, despite all the assistance provided by others in writing the book, the end result, with all its faults, remains my responsibility.

Dr Barry Humphreys CBE
September 2022

1 Introduction

Outline

In December 1903, the Wright Brothers made history with the first controlled, sustained flight of a powered heavier-than-air aircraft. Despite flying for a mere 120 feet/37 metres and lasting barely 12 seconds, the flight represented a truly momentous occasion. As Microsoft founder Bill Gates has noted: "The Wright Brothers created the single greatest cultural force since the invention of writing. The airplane became the first World Wide Web, bringing people, languages, ideas, and values together." Aviation has transformed the world, economically, socially, arguably even culturally. It certainly attracts more than its fair share of public attention and retains much of the allure and mystique first encountered over a 100 years ago. For most of those for whom flying has become mundane, a part of everyday life, there still remains that element of excitement as the tyres leave the tarmac. Given the industry's high profile, it is perhaps not surprising that terrorists have seen it as a way to gain maximum publicity for their activities. Aviation has also become a focal point for environmental campaigns aimed at reducing the world's carbon emissions.

Air transport today is, of course, vastly different from what it was during the early 20th century. It has become a significant industry in its own right. In particular, it has been transformed by technology, making it far safer, faster and more comfortable and greatly reducing the costs of flying. A recent report by the industry body Air Transport Action Group (ATAG)[1] illustrated the pre-COVID scale of activity:

US$3.5 trillion	- aviation's global economic impact (including direct, indirect, induced and tourism catalytic)
4.1%	- percentage of global GDP supported by aviation
35%	- proportion of world trade by value carried by air transport (less than 1% by volume)

DOI: 10.4324/9780429448973-1

In total, the industry supports over 11 million direct jobs, split as follows:

Airport operators	– 648,000
Other on-airport	– 5.5 million
Airlines	– 3.6 million
Civil aerospace	– 1.3 million
Air traffic control	– 237,000

Table 1.1 illustrates the geographical spread of air transport, and in particular the dominance of the Asia/Pacific, Europe and North America regions. The estimates quoted do not include other economic benefits, such as the jobs or economic activity that would not exist without air transport. Including these elements would increase the employment and global economic impact numbers several-fold. Above all, aviation is a *facilitating* industry, allowing other economic activities to take place.

Table 1.1 Geographical Impact of Air Transport, 2020

Region	Jobs Supported	GDP Supported	Passenger Numbers (2019)	% of Global Passengers
Africa	7.7 million	$63 billion	115 million	2.5%
Asia/Pacific	46.7 million	$944 billion	1.7 billion	37%
Europe	13.5 million	$991 billion	1.2 billion	26%
Latin America/the Caribbean	7.6 million	$187 billion	356 million	7.7%
North America	8.8 million	$1.1 trillion	1.0 billion	22.7%

Source: Air Transport Action Group, September 2020.

The numbers are impressive by any measure, and there is no reason to assume that growth will not resume once much of the impact of the COVID-19 pandemic has disappeared. Historically air transport has doubled in size every 15 years or so. An industry group organised by the International Civil Aviation Organisation (ICAO)[2] in 2017 forecast that by 2034, passenger traffic by air will have grown from 7.1 to 14 trillion revenue passenger kilometres (an average growth rate of 4.5% per annum) and freight carriage from 205 to 466 billion freight tonnes kilometres (or 4.4% per annum). COVID has merely delayed the achievement of such growth, not put a total stop to it. A particular factor in the continued expansion of the industry is the increased affordability of flying around the world and especially in emerging economies such as China and India with their rapidly growing middle classes. On the negative side, such expansion will place considerable strain on infrastructure and raise concerns about its environmental impact, both of which will be discussed later in the book. Airbus has estimated (pre-COVID) that by 2037, an additional 37,390 jet passenger and freighter aircraft will be needed (Boeing forecast a slightly higher figure), including replacements for the current fleet, based on the assumption that by then no less than 56% of the world's population will be classified as middle class, with 60% living in cities.

The air transport industry has evolved to reflect changing technology and market innovation. This book seeks to trace that evolution with a particular focus on government economic regulation. Such regulation has changed considerably over the years, with near universal government ownership of airlines and airports being replaced by a strong trend towards privatisation and liberalisation, reflecting a greater emphasis on competition and the needs of the consumer rather than the protection of producer interests. The trend has clearly been towards treating air transport as any other *'normal'* business. Yet in certain respects, as we shall see, progress has been much slower than might have been expected and the industry has remained fettered by archaic rules which have proved extremely difficult to remove, notably but not uniquely in relation to national ownership of airlines. To a considerable extent, this has determined the ongoing structure and profitability of the airline industry. Furthermore, there is a clear danger that what might have appeared before to be an inevitable progression towards a more liberal global regulatory regime may have come to an end, or even risk being reversed, a development which government reaction to the COVID pandemic may have exacerbated. Of particular note, as Lumbroso points out, is that while air transport exists within "one of the most elaborate and complex economic regulatory ecosystems among major, civilian sectors of the economy, …[it] does not possess singular characteristics that would suggest the need for this special treatment."[3] In other words, there is no fundamental economic reason for the unusual regulatory regime under which air transport continues to operate.

Later in this chapter, we will briefly address safety regulation, the need for which very few would challenge, but the main focus of the book will be on economic regulation in its various forms. Regulation has been at the core of the aviation industry from its early days. As long ago as 1921, for example, President Herbert Hoover wrote to a member of the US Congress: "It is interesting to note that this is the only industry that favors having itself regulated by Government." The US Senate Committee on Commerce similarly noted at the time: "Congress has been denounced unsparingly for passing legislation regulating and controlling business. It is rather startling, to say the least, to have an industry … asking and urging legislation putting the business completely under Federal control."[4] Such an approach, which was replicated in other countries, was understandable in the circumstances of the time. Quite apart from the need to achieve acceptable safety standards, the fledgling airline industry was incapable of sustaining itself financially without government support. In the US, this mainly took the form of subsidised airmail contracts for private enterprises; elsewhere direct public ownership was usually the norm. Governments were prepared to support the industry because of its evident strategic importance, including its role in furthering military, imperial and commercial power. Winston Churchill's insistence in

1920 that "civil aviation must fly by itself; the government cannot possibly hold it up in the air" did not survive long.

What is perhaps more surprising is the fact that despite substantial growth and technical development, the lack of sustained airline profitability which required the original government support has essentially persisted to the present day. The airline business, unlike most other sectors of the aviation industry, has struggled to be profitable, and even today achieving their cost of capital is an objective which eludes most carriers. It is said that since the Wright Brothers' first flight, airlines have actually destroyed more capital than they have created, which is hardly a record to be proud of. As one commentator has aptly noted:

> It is that this huge, progressive, and highly sophisticated industry is hamstrung by a worldwide proliferation of trade barriers that would be considered simply unacceptable in most other sectors of commercial activity. What we have is the strangest of paradoxes: a global enterprise boasting some of the world's most advanced science and engineering that operates according to a set of anachronistic, mercantilist rules consciously crafted to impede efficiency and limit opportunity. It is the marriage of 20th-century technology to 18th-century economics.[5]

It would be a challenge to think of another industry that has failed so often and so dismally to produce acceptable returns for shareholders over such a long period. We will examine possible explanations for this situation, in particular whether there are fundamental economic reasons why it is so difficult for an airline to make a profit or whether the explanation can be found in an industry structure largely dictated by government interference.

Over the decades the airline industry has been subject to numerous disruptive forces which have repeatedly transformed it. To a large extent, these forces have reflected technological improvements which have led, first, to aircraft flying further and faster without the need to refuel, thereby changing airline route networks, and, second, to improved operating efficiency which has resulted in lower flight costs, generating additional demand. There is every reason to believe that further technological disruptions will emerge in future years; some are already on the horizon. At the same time, the airline business has also been subject to innovative market disruptions as new business models have emerged, such as code sharing, alliances, low-cost carriers and the growth of mega-hubs. We will consider all these developments, and others, focusing on how they have been influenced by the industry's underlying regulatory regime, and indeed on how that regime has itself been impacted by disruption in the industry.

Despite the repeated transformations which the aviation industry has gone through over the years, far from everything has changed. Some elements in the industry's structure have proved difficult to reform. We have already mentioned the struggle to achieve sustainable profitability, surely a key factor in establishing industrial maturity. Similarly, the continued involvement of governments, even where public ownership has been abandoned and deregulation pursued, remains a common feature, as only too clearly illustrated during the COVID-19 pandemic. The close, even cosy, relationship between governments and airlines and airports has not disappeared and creates its own problems for the industry's development in many countries. Finally, the structure of the industry remains essentially nationalistic. The ICAO group referred to above noted that "aviation is one of the most 'global' industries: connecting people, cultures and businesses across continents."[6] Yet despite this, the fact remains that there is not a single truly global airline in the world, an omission found in very few other sectors even without aviation's international reach. (Consider, for example, the shipping and telecommunications industries, which both share several international features with air transport, but have managed to develop global companies.) The main reason for this shortcoming is to be found in the archaic ownership and control rules which continue to be applied to airlines, albeit often less overtly than in the past. Until these rules are subject to extensive reform, the industry will continue to be held back and prevented from becoming '*normal.*' We will examine how likely this is to happen.

Today every industry is subject to extensive regulation in most countries, designed in particular to protect consumers and maintain a competitive environment. Every industry probably also regards itself as 'special' in some way, different in certain respects from other sectors. However, air transport is both exceptionally highly regulated and really *is* different. It is virtually unique in having its own international regulatory regime, for example, wholly separate from bodies such as the World Trade Organisation. As Dawna L. Rhodes has commented in her study of international airlines: "The aviation industry has long been treated as a special case in international business, subject to different rules and held to different standards."[7] There were several reasons for this special treatment, particularly during the industry's formative years, including defence considerations, the perceived link between national airlines (the so-called *flag carriers*) and national achievement and pride, and the need to protect a fledgling sector seen as a key driver for other economic activity but with a far from secure financial base. The very term *flag carrier* reflects the special role allocated to airlines, promoting a country's power and influence around the world, although the term has also been applied to ships. The result, as we shall see, was a highly protectionist international regulatory regime which lasted for several decades and served, to a large extent, to determine the industry's global structure and viability.

It took a long time to break down the barriers to competition created at the end of the Second World War, and in many respects, some of those barriers persist in part or whole to this day. The clear trend, however, has been for old-style protectionist regulation to be replaced by rules designed to safeguard the interests of consumers. In practice what this has meant is that the much-publicised '*deregulation*' of the industry is really a misnomer. What has actually happened, first in the US, then in Europe and Australia/New Zealand and then increasingly elsewhere, is that one form of economic regulation has been replaced by another, so that overall the industry remains as highly regulated as ever. In addition, and as already noted, airlines continue to be organised essentially along national lines, with the right to operate international air services being traded on a bilateral basis between sovereign States.

The origins of this mercantilist approach lay, as we shall see, in the agreement reached in Chicago in 1944, between groups of countries led on the one hand by the US and on the other by the United Kingdom. This compromise agreement created the ICAO under the auspices of the United Nations. Ever since, ICAO has overseen the development of the industry, particularly in relation to safety and more recently security and environmental issues. Most importantly, the Chicago Convention reinforced the principle of the complete and exclusive sovereignty of States over the airspace above their territories, as well as stipulating that no international air service may be operated in the territory of a State except with that State's explicit permission or authorisation. Fundamentally, this remains the basis for the regulation of international aviation around the world to this day. Incredibly, the fear of being bombed from the air, prophesised so accurately by H. G. Wells in his 1908 book *The War in the Air*, has had an impact on one of the world's major industries far beyond what the pioneers could have envisaged.

Thus, particularly since the 1940s, States have formally 'traded' rights to operate specified international air services on a reciprocal, bilateral basis, then allocated use of those rights to air carriers established in (and generally owned by nationals of) their territory. Such agreements tended to be illiberal, with a focus on restricting competition and protecting the interests of incumbent, usually State-owned carriers; consumer interests barely featured. Today, according to one estimate,[8] there are over 7,000 so-called Air Services Agreements (ASAs), linking the vast majority of countries. (The precise number is unknown as not all ASAs are registered with ICAO.) While the fundamental principle, as enshrined in the Chicago Convention, of requiring agreement between States or groups of States before international air services may be operated remains in place, the contents of such ASAs have changed dramatically over the years as more and more countries, though still far from all, have turned from overt protectionism to a more liberal, pro-competition approach. This has usually been accompanied, or sometimes preceded, by a change to the regulatory regime applied domestically in the countries involved, as well as by increased privatisation. These regulatory trends had a major impact on the structure and fortunes of the aviation industry and will be described in detail.

Safety Regulation

As already explained, this book will focus on the *economic* regulation of air transport. However, it is worth spending a little time on safety regulation, which has itself undergone considerable change over the years. While one should never be sanguine where safety is concerned, the overwhelming conclusion from any study of the aviation industry must be that safety regulation has been an outstanding success. It goes without saying that sending sometimes several hundred passengers through the air in a metal tube (today increasingly likely to be carbon fibre) at over 500 miles per hour, and bringing them safely back down to earth, is an inherently dangerous and challenging activity. Even when aircraft were smaller and flew more slowly, danger was always present; indeed, more so judging by the safety statistics of the time. The early history of air transport was marked by frequent crashes and fatalities. The fact that this is no longer the case is something of which the whole industry can be very proud, and the whole world grateful. It is one of society's great ironies that were all aircraft grounded for a lengthy period, more people would die as the intrinsically more dangerous road traffic would inevitably increase. The way in which aviation was transformed from a dangerous to a very safe mode of transport sheds interesting light on how the industry has been run and regulated.

There are, of course, many ways of measuring aviation safety, but all of them point to a substantial improvement since the early pioneering years, an improvement which has continued to the modern era. One measure often used, at least for general purposes, is the so-called '*fatality risk*.' This measures the exposure of a passenger or crew member to a catastrophic accident where at least one of the people on board the flight is killed. It is usually expressed as '*fatality risk per million flights*.' The average fatality risk ratio over the five-year period 2016–2020 was 0.13, meaning that on average you would have to travel by air every day for 461 years before experiencing an accident in which at least one person was killed. The chance of *you* being killed is even less, of course. On average, you would have to travel every day for 20,932 years to experience a 100% fatal accident. Necessarily, at this level of incidents there is bound to be significant percentage variations year on year, and indeed the period after 2017 (a particularly good year for global aviation safety) has seen a modest deterioration, but the overall record and direction are clear (see Tables 1.2 and 1.3).

Table 1.2 Jet Hull Losses by Region (per million departures)

Region	2018	2020	2012–2016 (average)	2016–2020 (average)
Africa	0.00	0.00	2.21	0.28
Asia/Pacific	0.32	0.62	0.48	0.30
CIS[a]	1.19	1.37	1.17	1.20
Europe	0.00	0.31	0.14	0.14
Latin America/Caribbean	0.76	0.00	0.53	0.39
Middle East/North Africa	0.00	0.00	0.74	0.34
North America	0.10	0.00	0.10	0.03
North Asia	0.19	0.00	0.00	0.03

Source: IATA.
[a] Commonwealth of Independent States.

Table 1.3 Turboprop Hull Losses by Region (per million departures)

Region	2018	2020	2012–2016 (Average)	2016–2020 (Average)
Africa	1.90	13.02	7.38	4.93
Asia/Pacific	0.58	0.00	7.38	0.58
CIS*	7.48	0.00	20.59	13.75
Europe	0.00	0.00	0,73	0.00
Latin America/Caribbean	0.00	2.35	1.55	0.73
Middle East/North Africa	5.86	0.00	3.42	1.44
North America	0.00	0.00	0.98	0.30
North Asia	0.00	0.00	8.73	0.00

Source: IATA.
[a] = Commonwealth of Independent States.

Such improvements have not come about without a great deal of work. There has never been any serious challenge to the need for close government supervision of aviation safety standards, at both the multilateral and national levels. Few would be prepared to rely on market forces alone to achieve the same objective, despite the strong self-interest among airlines to operate as safely as possible. As long ago as 1969, for example, the so-called Edwards Report into the future of British civil aviation noted:

> It is true that in the long run a good accident record would serve an airline well commercially, but it would be unthinkable to most people that government should abandon the principle of prevention based on regulation and certification and wait for an airline to disqualify itself through its accident record from the confidence of its customers.[9]

Like economic regulation in the early years of civil aviation, safety regulation was an accepted, indeed welcome, part of the industry's structure and has remained so to this day.

Immediately after the Second World War, ICAO was charged with setting global safety standards, but the implementation of those standards was left largely to national governments, which inevitably led to variations in compliance levels. One significant trend over the following years was the creation of separate regulatory bodies in most countries, appointed by governments but with a large measure of independence. Finance for such organisations varies considerably; some continue to receive funding from the taxpayer, while others earn all or much of their income by charging those regulated for their services. A multilateral version of safety regulation below the ICAO level is seen in the EU, where the European Aviation Safety Agency (EASA) sets standards EU-wide, although again the implementation of the agreed rules is left mainly to national authorities.

However, an important part of the improvement in aviation safety is accounted for by the steps which the industry itself has taken. Airlines and regulators have worked together to maintain high standards, and occasionally the industry has launched its own initiatives. One notable example was the introduction in 2003 of International Operational Safety Audits (IOSAs) by the International Air Transport Association (IATA), the global airline trade body. IATA describes IOSA as an "internationally recognised and accepted evaluation system designed to assess the operational management and control systems of an airline." Previously airlines tended to audit each other. While in most cases this worked effectively, there was growing concern in the industry about regional disparities in safety standards, highlighted by the relatively poor safety records in Africa, the Commonwealth of Independent States (CIS, made up of a group of post-Soviet republics) and China. Eventually, compliance with IOSA was made a requirement for IATA membership, but such has been its success that as of June 2020, 139 (32%) of the 437 airlines on the IOSA Registry were non-IATA members.

The all-accident rate for airlines on the IOSA Registry was nearly four times better than that of non-IOSA carriers in 2017 and had shown an almost three-times improvement over the 2012/16 period. IOSA does not in any way replace government regulation. It is, however, an example of how an industry initiative can support and reinforce the underlying safety regime founded on ICAO principles. The success can be illustrated by reference to regional safety data (see Table 1.2). In 2012/16, the average jet hull loss rate in Africa was 2.21, far above any other region; by 2016/20, it had fallen to 0.28 and was actually zero in 2020. (Obviously, there was less flying in 2020, as a result of the COVID epidemic, with total flights reduced by over 50%, which may have distorted the statistics.) Similar, if less spectacular, improvements were seen in the Asia Pacific region and the CIS and in the turboprop hull loss rates (see Table 1.3).

European and US governments have also taken the lead in seeking to improve aviation safety levels around the world, in addition to any activity in ICAO. They have adopted different approaches, but with the same objective. The EU focuses on individual airlines, producing a regularly updated list of carriers which, in the view of the European authorities, fail to meet satisfactory safety standards. These airlines are banned from operating to EU Member States. The US, on the other hand, audits national safety authorities. All airlines from States whose regulatory regimes are found to be wanting are refused permission to serve the US with their own aircraft, although they can use equipment wet-leased from a State that has obtained US approval. It is difficult to identify which regulatory approach has been more successful, but the fact that in both cases those subject to action, whether airlines or regulatory authorities, usually strive to improve their performance and have themselves removed from the lists, suggests both have an impact, and may even complement each other.

Notes

1 ATAG: 'Blueprint for a Green Recovery.' Geneva, September 2020.
2 ICAO, with ACI, CANSO, IATA and ICCAIA: 'Aviation Benefits.' Montreal, 2017.

3 Alain Lumbroso: 'Aviation liberalisation: What headwinds do we still face?' *Journal of Air Transport Management*, Vol. 74, 2019, pp. 22–29.
4 Nick A. Komons: *Bonfires to Beacons: Federal Civil Aviation Policy Under the Air Commerce Act, 1926–38*. US Department of Transportation, Federal Aviation Administration, Washington DC, 1977. Reprinted in the Smithsonian History of Aviation and Spaceflight Series, Washington DC, 1989.
5 Jeffrey N. Shane: 'Challenges in International Civil Aviation Negotiations.' Speech before the Wings Club, *New York City*, 26 February 1988.
6 Ibid.
7 Dawna L. Rhodes: *Evolution of International Aviation. Phoenix Rising*. Ashgate, Aldershot, 2003.
8 Lumbroso, op cit.
9 'British Air Transport in the Seventies. Report of the Committee of Inquiry into Civil Air Transport' (The Edwards Report). HMSO, 1069, London.

2 The Beginning

The Second World War had an enormous effect on air transport, most visibly of course with the collapse in demand and the cessation of normal air services. A longer perspective, however, might highlight technological advances as the most important outcome, with the ground being laid for what today we recognise as the modern aviation industry. As Peter Lyth has commented:

> The Second World War revolutionised air transport… It brought forth new radio and navigational aids, as well as bigger four-engined aircraft like the Douglas DC4 and Lockheed Constellation with higher wing loadings, more powerful engines, nose-wheel undercarriages, and pressurised cabins…. These innovations meant that more passengers could be carried further and, for the first time, on a commercial basis.[1]

He might have added as well that the seeds of the jet age had already been sown. At the same time, the turmoil created by war also had a major impact on the regulation of the industry, establishing principles which have, to a significant extent, continued to be applied to the present day. This Chapter will describe those beginnings and how they influenced the structure of the industry for the next 70 plus years.

The Chicago Conference

Attempts at multilateral international regulation of air transport pre-date the Second World War by some way. As early as 1910, the French Government convened a conference, attended by 19 European countries, to draft a 'Convention on Air Navigation.' Unfortunately, fundamental disagreements between the key players meant that the conference ended in failure. While, Germany and France, for example, argued in favour of a regulatory regime based essentially on sea transport experience, with extensive commercial freedom, the UK favoured tighter government control over national airspace. The failure of the French initiative was quickly followed by unilateral UK action in 1911, with the adoption of the British Aerial Navigation

DOI: 10.4324/9780429448973-2

Act. The UK became the first country in the world to claim full sovereignty over the airspace above its territory. With the approaching World War, other nations soon followed. Thus was established probably the most important single principle in the regulation of international air transport, one that survives to this day and which has had a major impact on the development and structure of the industry, namely a State's absolute sovereignty over the airspace above its territory.

With the end of the First World War, attempts to negotiate a multilateral regulatory regime were resumed, but with only limited success. The Paris Peace Convention of 1919, reiterated the principle of a State's complete and exclusive sovereignty over its airspace and went on to deal with such issues as the national registration of aircraft, rules for airworthiness and the licensing of pilots. It created the Paris-based International Commission on Air Navigation (ICAN), eventually ratified by 26 countries, to consider further progress in multilateral regulation. However, both the US and Russia, who were entering a period of isolationism in international affairs, refused to join. In 1928, the US did sign the Havana Convention, but this embodied a very different approach to that being followed by most European States, particularly in rejecting the establishment of uniform international standards.[2]

The Second World War necessarily interrupted any further developments, but the scene was clearly set for the negotiation of a post-war regulatory regime. The war had, of course, affected countries in different ways. Virtually the whole of Europe was devastated. Its industry, including that in the UK despite the absence there of a successful mainland invasion, was severely weakened if not actually destroyed, and even where operational it was focused wholly on the war effort. The US, on the other hand, had a booming economy and had largely escaped the physical damage to infrastructure and industry seen in Europe. There was no doubt where the economic power lay in the immediate post-war world, and this was as true in aviation as more generally. While in Europe at the outbreak of war almost all air services had been either abandoned or used solely to support the war effort, in the US commercial air transport had continued to grow, as had the production of aircraft suitable for commercial air services.

This imbalance in readiness to take advantage of the opportunities emerging after the Second World War directly influenced the approach pursued by States in seeking a post-war multilateral aviation regulatory regime. As has continued to be the case up to the present day, the prevailing principle in international air services negotiations was self-interest, in practice if not necessarily in the public rhetoric adopted by those involved. As the Second World War came to an end, the two sides of the aviation debate were led by the US and UK, two of the three major pre-war aviation leaders, France being in far too weak a position to play a prominent role. The US strongly favoured open competition, with a minimum of regulatory restraint. The UK, on the other hand, as it had in 1910, sought tight control over routes, capacity and prices and safeguards to protect more exposed countries. Each side had its supporters among other States, but the US found itself relatively isolated. As Betsy Gidwitz has noted:

> Anxiety was felt by nearly all ... [States] toward US attempts to impose its will on other countries, a will backed by enormous American strength in both aircraft and general economic power ... The spectre of the American colossus, untouched by war devastation and well supplied with aircraft, dominating international civil aviation, was feared by many countries.[3]

It might seem odd today that informal discussions between the US and UK about a future regulatory regime for air transport began as early as 1943, well before the end of the war, but such was the perception of the likely future strategic importance of the industry. These contacts led directly to the Chicago Conference in November 1944, described by one commentator as "the single most important aviation conference of the era";[4] indeed, one might say, of any era. The conference lasted six weeks, with 52 countries attending. As Jeffrey Shane has noted:

> It is impossible to overstate the magnitude of what was achieved in Chicago... The Chicago Convention is civil aviation's charter; it is our constitution.... [The negotiators] somehow were able to see beyond the terrible fog of war and understand the contribution that civil aviation would make to peace and prosperity in the years ahead.[5]

From one perspective, the Conference was far from a success. The US failed to persuade a majority of delegations that unrestricted international competition based on market forces was the way forward. Equally, the UK's proposal for a global regulatory body controlling market access and prices did not find universal favour either. Australia and New Zealand even suggested a single United Nations organisation to own and manage all long-range international air service, despite the fact that the UN did not yet even formally exist. The UK then floated the idea of a single Commonwealth airline with exclusive traffic rights in British and other Commonwealth territories. (It was to be called 'All-Red,' reflecting the colour of the British Empire shown on maps.) None of these proposals, or others, proved to be acceptable to a sufficient number of delegations, and a compromise proposed by Canada seeking to bridge the US and UK positions was no more successful.[6]

The US may have had considerable economic power in the post-war world, but the UK was not completely defenceless. In particular, Britain still had extensive territories around the world, an empire 'on which the sun never set.' Given the operational limitations of even the latest long-range aircraft, there was a need to land frequently to refuel. Control of key landing facilities, therefore, served to strengthen the UK's negotiating hand, despite its weakened economic position. This, combined with a fear on the part of several countries of the newly emerging dominance of the US in civil aviation, was sufficient to create a stand-off between the UK and US, resulting in the failure of the Chicago Conference, in this respect at least. There was to be no general multilateral consensus on a regime for the post-war economic regulation of international air transport. Instead, final agreement on the rules governing air services was left to bilateral negotiations between pairs of States, to be negotiated after the end of the Conference.

In many other ways, however, Chicago was a great success. Most importantly, the delegates agreed to create a Provisional International Civil Aviation Organisation in 1945, to be replaced once ratification by 26 States was completed in 1947, by the International Civil Aviation Organisation (ICAO), a United Nations body. The Convention which emerged from the Conference, which today has a total of 193 signatory States, contained 96 Articles covering the many aspects of air transport without which international operations would have been extremely difficult, if not impossible. Although the history of ICAO since its inception has been marked by repeated failures to formulate widely acceptable economic policies for international air transport, in the areas of safety and navigation standards, later supplemented by environmental and security measures, it has played a key role in the development of the industry. It is difficult to exaggerate the importance of ICAO in the creation of the safe and reliable aviation system we have today.

One important economic principle which did emerge from the Chicago Conference was the agreement on the so-called Five Freedoms of the Air for international scheduled services. As defined by ICAO, these were:

First Freedom – The right or privilege granted by one State to another State or States to fly across its territory without landing.
Second Freedom – The right or privilege granted by one State to another State or States to land in its territory for non-traffic purposes.
Third Freedom – The right or privilege granted by one State to another State to put down, in the territory of the first State, traffic coming from the home State of the carrier.
Fourth Freedom – The right or privilege granted by one State to another State to take on, in the territory of the first State, traffic destined for the home State of the carrier.
Fifth Freedom – The right or privilege granted by one State to put down and take on, in the territory of the first State, traffic coming from or destined to a third State.

In this respect, at least, the focus of the negotiators was solely on international scheduled services. Little attention was paid to non-scheduled operations, which were to become far more significant in later years. As a result, charter carriers were subject to a different regulatory approach, although far from always to their benefit. Similarly, approval of cabotage services, flights within a country by a foreign airline, were dismissed out of hand.

The first four Freedoms of the Air originated in Canada's attempt to negotiate a compromise between the US and UK positions in Chicago. However, the US insisted on the inclusion of fifth freedom rights, seen as a critical requirement to operate long-haul multi-stop services. Many countries regarded fifth freedom services as a direct attack on a State's ability to protect its own airlines. As a commentator at the time noted, one person's fifth freedom is someone else's third and fourth freedoms. David Mackenzie, in his essay on Anglo-American aviation relations, comments: "To grant fifth-freedom rights was, in effect, giving a foreign operator the right to compete with direct international services. The problem, of course, was how to negotiate this right without endangering domestic airlines."[7] Improved aircraft technology has made fifth freedoms far less valuable, especially for passenger services, but they retain a symbolic importance even today. They are a key element in the open skies strategy promoted by the US, as we shall see, and the EU's insistence on restricting them has resulted in at least one country refusing to sign an Air Services Agreement with it.

Of the five Freedoms of the Air tabled at the Chicago Conference, only the first two were formally adopted. They were incorporated into the International Air Services Transit Agreement (IASTA) and accepted by most of the States present. Just 16 countries indicated a willingness to accept all five Freedoms, with the result that broader market access issues were left to later bilateral negotiations. The number of signatory States to IASTA has grown over the years to 133 today and the Agreement is seen as a success. Of those countries which still refuse to join (and geographically they cover a large part of the globe), Russia has probably been the most controversial. It has used control over the trans-Siberian route, critical today for flights between Europe and the Far East, as a means of earning substantial transit fees. (Since Article 15 of the Chicago Convention makes such transit fees illegal, Russia insists instead that airlines overflying its territory enter into commercial arrangements with the Russian flag carrier, Aeroflot. The effect, of course, is the same.) The broader political significance of these transit rights was only too clearly illustrated following the recent Russian invasion of Ukraine, when Russia took retaliatory action against many countries by banning their airlines from its territory. Ironically, Canada, which remains the home of ICAO and in Chicago had tabled the first two Freedoms of the Air that formed the basis for IASTA, later withdrew from the Agreement in an attempt to apply pressure on the UK during particularly difficult bilateral aviation negotiations. The tactic failed, but Canada has never re-joined the Agreement, although it does not follow Russia's example of charging for airspace access.

Only the first five Freedoms of the Air have been officially recognised, but since the Chicago Conference others have been added to the list, referred to by ICAO as 'so-called' Freedoms:

> Sixth Freedom – The right or privilege of transporting, via the home State of the carrier, traffic moving between two other States.

Seventh Freedom – The right or privilege, granted by one State to another State, of transporting traffic between the territory of the granting State and any third State with no requirement to include on such an operation any point in the territory of the recipient State, ie the service need not connect to or be an extension of any service to or from the home State of the carrier.

Eighth Freedom – The right or privilege of transporting cabotage traffic between two points in the territory of the granting State on a service which originates or terminates in the home country of the foreign carrier or (in connection with the so-called Seventh Freedom of the Air) outside the territory of the granting State.

Ninth Freedom – The right or privilege of transporting cabotage traffic of the granting State on a service performed entirely within the territory of the granting State.

Sixth Freedom services are, of course, simply a combination of two sets of Third/Fourth Freedom rights and are therefore rarely negotiated separately, although this has not prevented them from being highly contentious in many cases. The other Freedoms have become far more relevant in recent years. For example, they have all been incorporated into the EU's internal aviation market and formed a core part of the proposals made by the EU in negotiations with the US and Canada. We will return to this subject in a later Chapter.

The International Air Transport Association

One particularly significant outcome of the Chicago Conference was the formation of a trade body, the International Air Transport Association (IATA), to represent the interests of the world's major airlines. Agreed by airline executives present at the Conference as observers, but with the strong encouragement of their governments, IATA held its first meeting in Havana in 1945, attended by 51 members from 31 countries. Its Articles of Association stated that the organisation's aims were:

- to promote safe, regular and economical air transport for the benefit of the peoples of the world, to foster air commerce, and to study the problems connected therewith;
- to provide means for collaboration among air transport enterprises engaged directly or indirectly in international air transport service; and
- to co-operate with the newly created International Civil Aviation Organisation and other international organisations.

It is evident that from the beginning IATA's role was seen as going far beyond that of a normal trade body, in many respects effectively doing work normally undertaken by governments. There had been an earlier IATA, the International Air Traffic Association, formed in 1919 to set various technical standards, but the new organisation quickly established a special place in the regulation of international civil aviation. As a trade body, IATA has been exceptional in the way in which it has re-invented and transformed itself, often in the face of fierce external attack, to remain almost as relevant and important today as it was in its early years. It has been described as a 'quasi-public' or 'semi-governmental' organisation, which seems appropriate.[8]

For many years IATA was most closely associated with the setting of international fares and freight rates. The governments attending the Chicago Conference failed to agree on a common means of determining airline prices, but there was a consensus, supported even by the US, on the need to avoid what was termed 'excessive competition.' Fares, it was argued, should follow a 'coherent and orderly system'; they should be uniform, depending on the distance travelled, and all airlines serving the same route should charge the same price. It was not a surprise, therefore, that the first bilateral ASA signed by the UK and US in 1946 (see below) included a provision that fares and rates on the relevant routes should be agreed in IATA, subject to final approval by the two Governments (which in practice was usually little more than a rubber stamp of what the airlines had negotiated between themselves). IATA established a mechanism comprising three Tariff Conferences, each covering a different geographical area of the world, which met twice a year to fix seasonal fares. There were separate Conferences to fix freight rates. This was, of course, blatant collusion and price fixing which would not normally be acceptable under most countries' competition laws, where such laws existed, even in the early post-war decades. It was a sign of how 'special' and different air transport was regarded that governments were prepared to exempt airlines from competition law so comprehensively, and the US was no exception.

Perhaps the most surprising aspect of the IATA tariff-fixing arrangement was that it survived for so long. The agreement by the UK and US Governments to recognise IATA's role was replicated in most subsequent ASAs around the world, at least for a number of years. It is difficult today to comprehend the extent of IATA's control, which even included a Compliance Office to enforce Tariff Conference decisions. Airlines were fined if found to be charging unofficial fares, or even offering additional unapproved services, although the system was far from universally successful and occasionally broke down, leading to disputes. For example, a 'sandwich war' erupted when the Scandinavian national airline, SAS, began serving a sandwich which, according to competitors, amounted almost to a full meal. SAS countered by arguing that Scandinavian sandwiches were larger than those found in other countries. Similarly, the Czechoslovakian Government insisted that its national airline should be allowed to serve beer with meals even in Economy Class, something strongly opposed by the carrier's competitors.[9] These examples may seem ridiculous by modern standards, but they do reflect a common truth about this type of regulation, namely that to be fully effective it is almost invariably the case that gradually more and more intervention is necessary to close loopholes, as those regulated seek ways around the rules. The noted economist and 'father of airline deregulation,' Fred Kahn, wrote extensively about such 'regulatory creep' in relation to transport. Often this results in the rules themselves eventually being abandoned as it becomes increasingly evident that the costs of regulation exceed the benefits.

It is worth noting as well the sheer hypocrisy of the IATA carriers, who while publicly seeking to enforce their agreed fare levels, were at the same time all discounting many of their own fares with a vengeance, despite the efforts of the IATA Enforcement Office. The almost surreal 1974 case in the US of the so-called 'Money Socks' incident illustrates this clearly. An employee of the Belgian flag carrier Sabena was caught entering the US with US$80,000 hidden in his socks. Thinking initially that they had uncovered a major drug scandal, the authorities eventually ascertained that the individual was actually carrying money to pay certain US travel agents who had been rebating a portion of each ticket's fare, which was illegal. Furthermore, it emerged that every major airline was engaged in the same activity, even the US flag carriers despite their initial protests that the incident reflected attempts by foreign sixth freedom airlines to attract traffic. Estimates at the time were that fare rebates ranged from 5% to as much as 50% of the face value of tickets, on top of the normal travel agent commission rates of 7–11%. The rebates were paid to the agents, who in turn reduced the fares to customers. This led to criminal charges against all the trans-Atlantic airlines, most of whom pleaded 'no contest' and escaped with a relatively small fine. The rebating was suspended for a while but soon re-emerged.

Rebating had increased significantly as a result of growing competition on trans-Atlantic routes, particularly following the introduction of the Boeing 747, which came into conflict with the highly restrictive system of government-approved price fixing. Eventually the system was bound to disintegrate. An added factor at the time in encouraging government action was the lack of enthusiasm on the part of President Ford's administration to bail out Pan Am and TWA, both of which were experiencing financial difficulties in the face of increased competition. Action against foreign airlines was seen as an alternative way of supporting the US flag carriers. The Department of Transportation estimated, for example, that an end to rebating would increase Pan Am's income alone by some US$25 million. This was before, of course, the full involvement of the US airlines in the kick-back schemes became evident.[10]

For a long time, IATA membership did not include a number of rapidly growing airlines, especially in the Far East, although this slowly changed. In 1978, tariff co-ordination came under particular attack from the US Civil Aeronautics Board (CAB), which issued a so-called 'Show Cause Order' arguing that IATA was an illegal cartel on routes to and from the US. This challenged the very existence of IATA, and indeed much of the basis for the way in which international aviation was regulated, and caused close to panic in many countries, especially in Europe. In total, 45 governments made formal submissions to the US authorities, virtually all strongly opposing the CAB's action. While the CAB received support from the US Department of Justice, the State and Transportation Departments were far from pleased, fearing the diplomatic repercussions. Eventually a face-saving compromise was agreed. A Memorandum of Understanding was signed between the US and the European Civil Aviation Conference (ECAC), whose membership included most European governments, allowing for the continuation of IATA fare fixing on the North Atlantic subject to some additional flexibility, with so-called 'zones of reasonableness' around certain fares to allow an element of price competition between airlines, if they wanted to take advantage of such freedom.

The CAB's action was therefore successfully seen off, at least for the time being, despite a growing feeling that times were slowly changing. The industry was still characterised by an absence of real competition. It was common for airlines to share costs and revenues with other carriers on the same route, normally the fellow national carrier of the country being served. Even in the absence of IATA involvement, governments were rarely prepared to allow foreign airlines to charge prices which differed significantly, if at all, from those of their own State-owned carriers. To take the example of the London–Paris route, the normal process was for British European Airways/British Airways to file fares with the UK authorities on behalf of both itself and Air France, while Air France would reciprocate with the French authorities. An attempt as late as the early 1980s in ECAC to negotiate a European-wide arrangement to permit, say, British Airways to file its own fares in Paris, still subject to government (and in effect Air France) approval, was deemed to be far too radical.

Gradually, however, IATA's tariff-fixing role was diminishing. When the UK/US ASA was renegotiated in 1976, the reference to IATA was omitted, and increasingly other bilateral agreements did the same. An Australian Government report[11] in 1994, identified five reasons why IATA tariff coordination was dying:

- The growth and success of non-IATA airlines from newly developed countries, particularly in the Asian market, such as Singapore Airlines, Thai International and Cathay Pacific.
- Deregulation of US domestic air services, followed by European liberalisation.
- The increase in charter services, especially in Europe.
- The growing number of liberal ASAs.
- The increased adoption of competition policy in several jurisdictions and its application to aviation.

There are still a few old ASAs in existence which prescribe a tariff-fixing role for IATA, but nowhere is this enforced. The industry became less of a cartel and more competitive, a trend greatly helped by the increased involvement of competition authorities in the US, Europe and elsewhere, as we shall see in later chapters. The pressure to change resulted in new IATA membership rules being adopted in 1978. For the first time, airlines were able to join the organisation as a trade associate without being party to tariff co-ordination. This created a two-tier body and enabled IATA to become more global. Other tariff reforms included more flexibility to charge non-IATA fares, less restrictive conditions of service and more open and public co-ordination conferences. This really marked the beginning of the end for IATA tariff co-ordination as it had been. Today such co-ordination is tiny compared to the early post-war years, limited to a few specific interlinable fares, although some one hundred airlines still participate.

IATA's other activities, however, remained relevant, and if anything increased in importance as the industry grew. One key role, of course, is to act as a global trade body for international airlines, lobbying governments and regulators, as well as other aviation stakeholders such as airports and air traffic management companies, to promote and protect the interests of its members. Membership is open to any carrier licensed by an ICAO-member State and has now reached 290 airlines in 120 countries, representing some 83% of global air traffic. The days of IATA being primarily a northern hemisphere body are long since gone. The membership now covers all significant international airlines and increasingly also encompasses regional and low-cost carriers. We have already seen in Chapter 1 how IATA has worked to improve air safety, particularly by means of the IOSA programme. Much of its other work revolves around the standardisation of procedures, for example:

- passenger tickets and cargo waybills, and more recently electronic tickets
- the legal relationship between airlines and travel agents
- the carriage of hazardous materials
- airport slot allocation
- airline and airport designations.

This is just a small selection of the functions which IATA carries out, without which either the industry could not operate or governments would have to play an even larger role than they do already.

Finally, mention should be made of the role played by the IATA Clearing House, a key part of the international air transport system, albeit one largely hidden from public view or attention. The Clearing House carries out a settlement procedure which facilitates the cross-selling of airline products in different markets and currencies. For example, a passenger might buy a London to Sydney ticket, travelling from London to Dubai on British Airways, from Dubai to Singapore on Emirates Airlines, from Singapore to Perth on Singapore Airways and finally from Perth to Sydney on Qantas, paying a single fare in sterling. Each of the airlines involved in that journey needs to be sure that it will receive its share of the total ticket price in its own currency. That is what the Clearing House does. As described by IATA, it

> provides fast, secure and cost-effective billing and settlement services in multiple currencies for the air transport industry. It enables the world's

airlines and airline-associated companies 'suppliers' to settle their passenger, cargo, UATP and miscellaneous/non-transportation billings by applying the principles of set-of/netting, thus reducing cost and risk and increasing speed.

The importance of the Clearing House for the whole industry is reflected in the fact that many non-IATA carriers also participate. There are now over 430 companies involved, mostly but not wholly airlines. The annual turnover of the organisation is some US$56 billion. Failure of an airline to pay its Clearing House debts on time is a very serious matter. Few carriers are able to continue to function effectively if suspended from the organisation, and some form of bankruptcy usually follows quickly. In the case of bankruptcy, the Clearing House acts on behalf of members to secure any debts owed. In North America, there is a separate organisation known as the Airline Clearing House (ACH), which performs a similar role to its IATA counterpart for those carriers based in North America which tend not to operate beyond this geographical area. All major US airlines with international service are also members of the IATA Clearing House. The ACH has a membership of some 350 companies and an annual turnover of US$14 billion.

The Bermuda Agreement

The failure of the Chicago Conference to reach agreement on a multilateral regime for the economic regulation of international air transport meant that it was left to the two principal protagonists, the UK and US, to address the problem. They did this during negotiations in Bermuda early in 1946, although with some reluctance on the part of the UK. The substantial gulf between the economic power of the two countries, evident in the earlier debate in Chicago, was still present of course, added to which in bilateral talks there were no other countries, especially from the Commonwealth, to support the UK. Perhaps most important of all was the fact that the exchanges in Bermuda coincided with negotiations between the two countries on a financial settlement, essentially a bail-out of the bankrupt, war-torn UK, following the abrupt termination of the Lend-Lease Agreement. A financial deal was critical for the future of the UK, as the US was only too well aware, and certainly took precedence over aviation interests. The US was not slow to connect the two sets of negotiations. Against these multiple US advantages in Bermuda, the UK could muster only its extensive list of territories around the world needed for aircraft refuelling. (Ironically many of the strategic air bases in British territories had been built by the Americans during the war.) It was not an even battle.

The positions of the two sides reflected closely the ones taken at the Chicago Conference, as one might expect. The US pursued a 'wide open door policy,' in the words of a British diplomat at the time, while the UK sought tight control over airlines' operations, regarding the US approach as "an attempt to use its superiority in aircraft to monopolise the North Atlantic air service."[12] In particular, the US resisted any control over frequencies and capacity, while the UK's opening position was that all traffic between the two countries should be split on a 50/50 basis, with each side limited to 500 seats per week. It was an inauspicious start by any measure, with the two countries so far apart, but agreement was eventually reached. Pricing was settled early, with both countries willing to accept a role for IATA, as we have seen, combined with so-called 'double approval' government sanction. ('Double approval' required that any tariff needed to be approved by both governments before it could come into effect.) On the key frequency and capacity issues, the UK really had no choice but to give in to US pressure, although it did insist on a post hoc review mechanism.

The agreement specified broad principles to be followed, namely:

- "That there shall be fair and equal opportunity for the carriers of the two nations to operate on any route between their respective territories ... covered by the Agreement and its Annex;
- That, in the operation by the air carriers of either Government of the trunk services described in the Annex to the Agreement, the interest of the air carriers of the other Government shall be taken into consideration so as not to affect unduly the services which the latter provide on all or part of the same routes."[13]

A similar approach is seen in the agreement's following paragraph, which noted the general principle that capacity should be related:

(a) to traffic requirements between the country of origin and the countries of destination;
(b) to the requirements of through airline operation; and
(c) to the traffic requirements of the area through which the airline passes after taking account of local and regional air services.[14]

This can hardly be said to be setting the scene for free and open competition, despite the advocacy by the US of a more market-based system, although the US did achieve its objective of including fifth freedom rights in the agreement. 'Controlled competition,' with a high degree of producer co-operation, might be a better way of describing the way the two governments saw the development of the airline industry. All airlines were more or less guaranteed a share of the market; under many subsequent ASAs, this often amounted to a 50/50 split, with revenues and profits (or more likely losses) shared evenly by means of various so-called 'pooling' arrangements.

Not surprisingly, the US Government quickly approved the deal its negotiators had achieved in Bermuda. The UK Government, however, was more reluctant, despite the growing pressure over the financial settlement, the main cause for concern being fifth freedom rights. Granting extensive fifth freedom rights was bad enough, but the real problem was an associated clause covering so-called 'change of gauge' rights. This is the ability of an airline to change the size of an aircraft at an intermediate stop on a route, or even to add several smaller aircraft connecting numerous additional points. A UK Cabinet memo at the time summed up the perceived threat:

> If we agree to change of gauge, a United States operator running a service, say from New York to Paris, would be able to bring a load of passengers to this country in a trans-ocean aircraft and thereafter carry on those who wished to proceed to Paris or elsewhere in one or more smaller aircraft. The fear expressed at the cabinet was that this would enable the American operator to run an unlimited number of smaller aircraft from this country to Paris or elsewhere in competition with our air lines, and thus virtually establish an advanced base here.[15]

It seems strange today that the UK Prime Minister and his Cabinet colleagues should spend time discussing the intricacies of a change of gauge clause in a bilateral ASA, but such was the fear of US domination in post-war aviation. In the event, the UK only agreed to the US proposal if fifth freedom services had an 'adequate volume of through traffic,' combined with a provision forcing the smaller aircraft to wait for the arrival of the larger aircraft before departing. ("It is understood ... that the capacity of the smaller aircraft shall be determined with primary reference to the traffic travelling in the larger aircraft normally requiring to be carried onward.")[16] Such restrictions were thought sufficient to protect local services and became an accepted principle in other ASAs.

The Bermuda Agreement stipulated that each side should designate which of its airlines should be allowed to operate on the specified routes. The other party reserved the right to refuse to accept such designations unless the carriers in question were majority owned and controlled by citizens of the designating State. This has been a key article in almost every subsequent ASA, and is even reflected in multilateral agreements such as that establishing the EU internal aviation market. One benefit of the provision was that it helped to prevent 'free loaders,' airlines of States not party to an ASA, from taking advantage of the rights negotiated. It also served to restrict the emergence of flags of convenience carriers which, some have argued, has adversely affected the development of the shipping industry, especially in areas such as safety and employment conditions. However, as we shall see in later chapters, restrictions on national ownership have also held back the aviation industry by curtailing its ability to engage in cross-border mergers and take-overs. As a result, the industry remains essentially nation-based and has not followed other sectors in creating truly global businesses. Of all the basic tenets of economic regulation of civil aviation established during the immediate post-war period, the airline ownership and control provisions (along with cabotage rights) have probably been the most difficult to reform, with only limited progress made so far.

The UK/US Bermuda Air Services Agreement is important for a number of reasons. It was a compromise between two opposing views of the future global aviation regulatory regime, but a compromise strongly favouring one side. The UK's relatively weak position was evident for all to see, and unsurprisingly the US took full advantage of it. In many ways, the agreement was symbolic of a wider change in the balance of power. This was perhaps not the best of starts to the largest bilateral aviation relationship in the world, and some of the disappointment on the UK side was to fester for many years and eventually contribute to the decision to terminate the ASA. Nevertheless, the Bermuda Agreement was a model which others quickly followed and which remained relevant for a long time. When France, for example, agreed to a new bilateral ASA with the US shortly after the UK, it was closely based on the Bermuda agreement. Within two years the US had negotiated a further 24 similar agreements, and by the end of 1947, over 100 ASAs had been signed around the world, predominantly following the UK/US precedent.

Unlike the US, initially the UK sought more restricted bilateral agreements with aviation partners, which led to further disagreement with the US, who feared the emergence of an alternative model ASA. However, later in 1946, and after more bilateral consultations, the two countries agreed to a joint statement saying that "both parties believe that in negotiating any new bilateral agreements with other countries, they should follow the basic principles agreed at Bermuda."[17] Combined with the Chicago Convention, thus was created the basis for the post-war regulatory regime for international air transport.

Final Comments

In his study of the negotiation and evolution of the Bermuda Agreement's successor, Bermuda 2, Handley Stevens[18] lists three factors which characterised the post-war development of international air transport and which all stemmed from the early regulatory regime agreed by governments, as a compromise, in 1946:

- The industry developed around the concept of the national flag carrier airline, reinforced by 'a heady brew of patriotism, wealth, adventure and romance.'
- The close partnership between governments and airlines in the management of the business, illustrated in particular by the role granted to the airlines' trade body, IATA.
- The distinction between different types of service, catering separately for cargo and passengers, and distinguishing between scheduled and charter services. This resulted both in the application of different degrees of regulation to these various sectors and in a willingness on the part of

governments to be less restrictive than in the regulation of the core sector of scheduled passenger services, which lay at the heart of the flag carriers' operations.

All these factors led to the creation of an industry often referred to as a cartel, dominated by national, government-owned airlines with only the crumbs left for any emerging competitors to feed off.

The Preamble to the Chicago Convention reads as follows:

> WHEREAS the future development of international civil aviation can greatly help to create and preserve friendship and understanding among nations and peoples of the world, yet its abuse can become a threat to the general security; and
>
> WHEREAS it is desirable to avoid friction and to promote that co-operation between nations and peoples upon which the peace of the world depends;
>
> THEREFORE the undersigned governments having agreed on certain principles and arrangements in order that international civil aviation may be developed in a safe and orderly manner and that international air transport services may be established on the basis of equality of opportunity and operated soundly and economically.

One can see the impact of world war in this statement, but the core message has survived to the present day. The economic regime established in the immediate post-war period to regulate international air transport reflected a fledgling industry still unable to support itself, one with extensive government ownership and interference, one where producer interests were given priority over consumers, and one where competition was severely limited. Essentially, the history of the industry since then has been a gradual move away from these principles, albeit with occasional backward steps, combined with a reduction in the influence of the US as first Europe and then Middle and Far Eastern countries became more prominent. This has not been easy, as we shall see, and much still remains to be done if the objective is to 'normalise' airline activity. Those apparently innocuous words in the Chicago Convention Preamble, "equality of opportunity and operated soundly and economically," no doubt the result of lengthy negotiation and compromise, proved to be open to wide interpretation and became the basis for many inter-government disputes.

Notes

1 Peter J. Lyth: 'Air transport'. *Studies in Transport History*, Scolar Press, Aldershot, 1996.
2 Dawna L. Rhoades: *Evolution of International Aviation. Phoenix Rising*. Ashgate, Aldershot, 2003.

3 Betsy Gidwitz: *The Politics of International Air Transport*. Lexington Books, Lexington, 1980.
4 David Mackenzie: 'The Bermuda Conference and Anglo-American aviation relations at the end of the Second World War'. *The Journal of Transport History*, Vol. 12(1), 1991.
5 Jeffrey N. Shane, Airlines, April 2019.
6 David Mackenzie, op cit.
7 Ibid.
8 Betsy Gidwitz, op cit.
9 Ibid.
10 I am grateful to Paul Mifsud for his recollections of these events. See also Robert Lindsey: 'Airlines Admit to Paying Travel Agents Kickbacks'. *New York Times*, 21 December 1974.
11 Bureau of Transport and Communications Economics: *International Aviation. Report 86*. Australian Government Publishing Service, Canberra, 1994.
12 David Mackenzie, op cit.
13 Handley Stevens: *The Life and Death of a Treaty. Bermuda 2*. Palgrave Macmillan, London, 2018.
14 Ibid.
15 David Mackenzie, op cit.
16 Ibid.
17 Handley Stevens, op cit.
18 Ibid.

3 Growth and Disruption
Charters and Bermuda 2

Regulatory Stasis

We have seen in Chapter 2 that the period towards the end of and immediately after the Second World War saw the establishment of a regulatory regime for international air transport characterised by controlled competition, with a high degree of producer co-operation. Such a regime was to remain more or less intact throughout the 1950s and 1960s and much of the 1970s. This was a time of rapid growth for airlines, with the beginning of the jet age and the democratisation of air travel. The transformation was probably seen most clearly on the North Atlantic, where new technology, especially long-haul aircraft such as the Boeing 707, enabled the more efficient operation of non-stop routes between Europe and the US. This in turn meant that previously strategic re-fuelling airports such as Shannon in Ireland and the Azores in the Atlantic, and the associated fifth freedom bilateral rights, became far less important. In 1948, twice as many passengers crossed the Atlantic by sea as by air; by 1958, for the first time, airlines carried more passengers than the shipping companies, and by 1970, aviation dominated the market with a 97% share.

The cost of international air travel, while still high by modern standards, became more affordable, generating increased demand. According to ICAO statistics (which at the time excluded the USSR and China), in 1950 some 31 million passengers travelled by air globally; by 1960 the total had grown to 106 million and by 1971 to 328 million, an annual average rate of growth of 11.9%. The corresponding figures for passenger-kilometres were 28 billion (1950), 109 billion (1960) and 408 billion (1971), an annual average increase of 13.6%, indicating that not only were far more people flying, but on average they were also travelling further.

Under the Chicago Convention, the Nation State became the key factor in determining the structure of the industry. From the ruins of post-war Europe, national flag carriers emerged to join North American airlines serving the world's principal cities. Before long they in turn were joined by carriers established in Africa, the Middle and Far East and the Pacific. European and North American airlines actively assisted in the creation and management of new operators in developing countries, often acquiring significant shareholdings. Outside of the US, the norm was for each national market to be dominated by a single State-owned airline. Even those few countries which supported more than one national carrier, such as the UK and France, usually created *spheres of influence* to ensure that they served different markets. Direct scheduled competition between airlines from the same State was very much an exception.

It is worth noting that in the UK, where limited private sector competition with the flag carriers BOAC and BEA was allowed, the influential Edwards Committee report into the future of the nation's civil air transport industry actually found it necessary, as late as 1969, to defend the whole concept of competition in the sector, and even then only "regulated competition within a system of licensed entry and its consequential controls" was envisaged.[1] By any measure, this was some way short of an open market free-for-all. It was only in the 1960s that any stirrings towards significantly less regulation of scheduled air transport began to emerge, focused initially in the US. The domestic and international aviation policies adopted by virtually every country until then reflected the need to nurture and protect the developing airline industry, especially the established national carriers.

We have seen how the Bermuda agreement became a model for many other ASAs. The key paragraphs dealing with the exchange of traffic rights, as outlined in Chapter 2, gave a clear indication of the regulatory principles at the heart of the agreement, speaking not only of the opportunity for 'fair and equal' operations but also ensuring that the airlines of one side take into account the interests of carriers of the other side "so as not to affect unduly the services which the latter provide on all or part of the same routes." These are not words designed to allow, let alone encourage, airlines to compete freely. In fact, as the 1950s and 1960s progressed, even the Bermuda model came to be viewed as too liberal by many countries. In particular, a trend emerged towards a regime of predetermination, so that not only did there need to be agreement in advance on which routes could be operated, in line with the provisions of Bermuda, but also on the frequency of service and even in some cases the number of seats and the aircraft type to be provided. The designation of a single airline from each side also became more common. This approach contrasted with the *ex post facto* review principle provided for, at the insistence of the US, in the Bermuda agreement. The Edwards Committee of 1969 divided European countries into three groups with respect to international aviation policies:

- those applying Bermuda principles (Belgium, the Netherlands, Denmark, Norway, Sweden, West Germany and the UK)
- those with a predetermination philosophy (France, Italy, Spain, Portugal and Greece)
- those where capacity was even more highly controlled, in some cases requiring that it be shared between the two designated airlines in a so-called *pooling* agreement (the USSR and several other Eastern European countries).

As Edwards noted: "These conditions in Europe are repeated even to a greater extent in some other parts of the world; there are restrictive countries in Africa, Asia and South America."[2]

Pooling agreements between airlines, which became increasingly common, removed the last vestiges of competition even where the relevant bilateral ASA permitted some. Eventually, they came to dominate scheduled air transport throughout much of the world, with the notable exception of the US. A pool usually involved a joint agreement between the two (or very occasionally more) carriers operating one or more routes, covering tariffs, schedules, capacity and promotion and in many cases even the sharing of revenues and profits/losses. One important example, quoted by Edwards, was that between the UK's BOAC, Air India, Australia's Qantas, Air New Zealand and what was then Malaysia-Singapore Airlines, applicable to services between the UK and Australia via both the Kangaroo (flying east out of the UK) and Pacific (west) routings. BOAC's sister company, BEA, operating within Europe, similarly had pool arrangements with most of its direct competitors, covering some 60% of its total revenue; in 1953, it had had only two such agreements.

There is no doubt that pools were anti-competitive, that was their whole purpose, but they reflected the ethos of the time and were widely supported by governments. It is notable that in many respects the pools formed between State-owned carriers during the 1950s and 1960s were similar to the airline alliances created in later decades. The major difference is that originally most countries did not have effective, or indeed any, competition law, and if they did, it was rarely applied to aviation. Today, alliances require anti-trust immunity and are subject to close scrutiny by the competition authorities in most jurisdictions and approval often entails having to make concessions to preserve competition on individual routes. Nevertheless, almost invariably they are eventually approved.

In the remainder of this chapter, we will address two key regulatory developments which affected and disrupted air transport in the period from the end of the Second World War to the end of the 1970s: the growth of charter services, and the renegotiation of the UK/US Bermuda agreement.

Inclusive Tour Charter Services

The dominance of the major, almost wholly State-owned airlines in the post-war period cannot be doubted, but they were not unchallenged, and it is worth considering the role played by the large number of private carriers, often referred to as Independents, which sprang up at this time. There were literally hundreds of these companies, encouraged by two factors in particular: the many individuals who had been taught to fly during the war, had become committed to aviation and now found themselves in the labour market; and the disposal of thousands of surplus aircraft at very low prices by the Allied Governments. For example, by the end of 1946, France had some 30 registered charter carriers, mostly operating to North Africa and the UK.

The UK itself had 72 private sector carriers registered in April 1949. The Civil Aeronautics Board (CAB) later estimated that about 3,600 airlines were established in the US over this period. The US Government alone disposed of more than 4,000 DC-3s, as well as a large number of DC-4s and thousands of bombers capable of conversion to civilian use. In the UK, it was possible to buy a Halifax bomber for between £100 and £1,700.[3]

Most of these independent airlines were, of course, small and poorly capitalised. Not surprisingly, therefore, few remained in business for long. One commentator described pre-war British airlines as "flitting like brief shadows across the scene," and the description applied equally to their post-war successors, in the UK and elsewhere. However, there was work available, including from the scheduled flag carriers, many of whom struggled initially to meet the demand for new air services. Help came also from the provision of services to governments and their agencies around the world as reconstruction and recovery got under way, such as the two major operations in 1947 between India and Pakistan to move displaced citizens and the carriage of large numbers of refugees in 1948 between Hamburg and Montreal. Of particular note and importance was the Berlin Airlift in 1948/49, "the greatest and largest air supply operation ever attempted or ever likely to be attempted again,"[4] as the official British history recorded. Although most freight to Berlin was carried by the US and British air forces, the independent airlines also contributed substantially.[5]

The fragility of the independent carriers' existence continued for some years. According to one study, between 1945 and 1973, 208 private sector carriers were registered in the UK alone, and virtually every one of them failed, usually after only a short period of operation.[6] Inevitably the odds were strongly stacked against such airlines. At best they could hope for only a few crumbs from the table of the major carriers; at worst, they were actively discriminated against by governments determined to protect their mostly State-owned flag carriers. However, despite these hurdles, the private sector did play a pivotal role in the development of inclusive tour charters, which in turn had a significant impact on the whole aviation industry, especially in Europe. (Note that the description which follows focuses mainly on experience in the UK, where the concept of the inclusive tour (IT) charter was first fully developed, but other countries experienced similar growth.)

It is difficult to exaggerate the significance of IT charters both in establishing a viable private airline sector in Europe and in influencing broader social trends. It has been said that the first 30 years after the end of the Second World War saw two great explosions – the H-bomb and holidays abroad. Certainly, one should not under-estimate the economic and social impact that mass international tourism has had in many countries, and the IT charter is an integral part of that story. A 1971 US survey of European charter airlines noted that the inclusive tour charter, "having established its respectability beyond question, will be recorded by future historians as characteristic of the standards of life in Europe which evolved during the third quarter of the twentieth century."[7] An inclusive tour has been defined as "a trip undertaken for recreational purposes, planned in advance in all details (itinerary, accommodation, excursions, etc.) by a tour promoter for an inclusive price, paid for entirely prior to the commencement of the tour."[8] On a small scale, they had been provided before the war in both the US and Europe, usually on scheduled air services, but real growth came with IT charters operated from the late-1940s, first in the UK and then spreading to other European countries, especially Germany and Scandinavia. They offered both convenience and lower prices. However, to do so they had to find ways around the restrictions put in place by governments to protect the scheduled airlines.

Although others have claimed to have organised the first IT charter, most commentators acknowledge that the pioneer was Horizon Holidays. Its founder, Vladimir Ritz, advertised in the Nursing Mirror in the UK a special air holiday to Calvi, Corsica, with accommodation

> in large tents fitted with beds and mattresses, two to a tent … the best sanitation … meals are taken out of doors … departures every Friday by Douglas Air Liner [a 32-seat DC-3] of the Channel Island Air Transport Company.

Horizon sold 300 inclusive tours in 1950, but lost money on the exercise, mainly because it managed to achieve an average aircraft seat factor of only 62.5%. Nevertheless, from such a modest beginning emerged a major sector of the aviation industry. By 1971, total UK IT charter traffic amounted to almost 2.7 million passengers, overwhelmingly carried by British airlines. Initially, independent carriers seeking to operate a series of IT charters had to negotiate an associate agreement with the State airline, BEA, but from 1952 they were actively encouraged by the Government to enter the market. BEA and BOAC were even prevented from retaining obsolescent aircraft which might have been suitable for charter services. Needless to say, however, there were safeguards in case the competition proved to be too fierce. In particular, the Terms of Reference given to the licensing body, the Air Transport Advisory Council, stipulated that the operation of IT charters was open to any airline "provided that such services are not likely materially to divert traffic which would otherwise be carried by any operator already authorised for the route," which normally meant BEA.

Thus, while there was an element of liberalisation, capacity controls remained very much in place. In addition, and as a second line of defence, minimum prices were established, known as Provision 1 and in line with an IATA Resolution (045), which restricted the total price of an inclusive tour to not less than the lowest fare on a scheduled flight to the same destination. This did not, however, prevent the continued growth of the IT charter market; by 1956 charters, overwhelmingly inclusive tours, accounted for some 27% of total air traffic from the UK to Spain, and had significant shares of the markets to Austria, Germany, France, Northern Italy and Switzerland.

Eventually, and inevitably given this rate of growth, the legacy carriers had to respond commercially, since clearly the regulatory restrictions were having only a limited effect. IATA airlines began to introduce IT fares of their own, available on scheduled services and offering significant discounts from standard tariffs. Such a strategy certainly had an impact, at least in the short term, so much so that by 1961, the British airline entrepreneur Freddie Laker forecast that IT charters would be virtually finished in Europe in ten years. He was very wrong.

One development in particular saved and relaunched the IT charter sector, namely the creation of a new type of airline. At the time, Universal Sky Tours was the largest promoter of packaged tours by air in the UK. As such it was adversely affected by the frequent bankruptcies of the airlines it chartered to carry its passengers. The solution Universal Sky Tours came up with, representing a new business model in the industry, was the creation of an airline with two particular characteristics:

- it would be wholly owned by, and therefore vertically integrated with, the tour operator; and
- it would operate only IT charters.

The new carrier was initially called Euravia, reflecting the UK's attempt at the time to become a member of the European Common Market, but was later renamed an arguably more patriotic Britannia Airways. Operations began in May 1962. Three years later the airline was purchased by Canada-based Thomson Industrial Holdings, an acquisition by a foreign company which seems unlikely to have been approved had the airline been a scheduled operator. Britannia Airways set the standard for IT charter airlines, with service levels comparable to those of the scheduled carriers, including a fleet of modern jet aircraft. It became the largest non-scheduled airline in the world, but others quickly copied the model, including Monarch Airlines, with its sister company Cosmos Holidays and also financed by non-UK interests, and Thomas Cook. Freddie Laker took a slightly different approach in establishing Laker Airways, described as a "contract carrier to the package holiday trade – a personalised airline," but the core concept of a specialist IT carrier remained the same.

The charter share of air traffic between the UK and Spain was 32% in 1962 and reached 58% in 1967 and 83% in 1971. (The corresponding figure for air traffic between Germany and Spain in 1967 was 79.7%, for Scandinavia and Finland 97.4% and for the Netherlands 83.3%.) UK airlines' IT charter traffic grew by an incredible 52% in 1964 alone and by 40% the following year. The share of British holidaymakers going abroad accounted for by packaged tours, overwhelmingly IT charters, rose from 30% in 1960 to 55% by 1972. These figures clearly indicated a radical social change. The regulators could not ignore the obvious popularity of this new phenomenon and eventually began to relax the restrictions on the sale of ITs. By the early 1960s, capacity licensing in the UK had been significantly eased, really only leaving in place price control via the Provision 1 rule. In 1968, even Provision 1 was relaxed, with larger discounts allowed during the winter season. This was to prove a particularly important break-through for the non-scheduled sector. Previously IT charters had operated almost totally during the summer months. (In 1967, for example, Britannia made only one revenue flight between Christmas and March.) Year-round operations meant that the airlines could greatly improve their aircraft utilisation levels, thereby reducing unit costs. Substantially lower off-peak prices for packaged holidays (with prices as low as £10 for a long weekend in Spain) acted as a major stimulus to the market.

Provision 1 was finally abolished in late 1973. Even before then, however, with regulatory protection clearly being relaxed, the scheduled carriers were again forced to respond commercially. IT fares on scheduled services were reduced significantly during the second half of the 1960s, and in 1969 BEA launched a charter subsidiary of its own, BEA Airtours, to compete head-on with the independent sector, a move which several other European legacy carriers soon matched. As has been repeatedly shown over many decades, faced with a severe threat from a new competitive model, most major legacy airlines have been able to adapt and respond in order to survive.

Long-Haul Charters

For a number of reasons, IT charters had only a very limited impact on long-haul air services. Instead, it was the affinity group charter concept which was to challenge the established long-haul carriers, especially in the largest such market between Europe and the North America. As with intra-European inclusive tours, affinity (or closed) group charters only really gained momentum during the second half of the 1960s, particularly following the launch of a new British airline, Caledonian Airways (which later merged with British United Airways to form British Caledonian, the so-called UK 'Second Force'). One explanation for the failure of IT charters to gain acceptance across the Atlantic, and indeed within the US, was the very restrictive approach taken by the US authorities, who were even more protective of the scheduled sector than their European counterparts. The CAB required that an inclusive tour must be at least seven days in duration and stop at a minimum of three cities, each over 50 miles apart. In addition, the total IT price had to be more than 110% of the lowest available scheduled fare for the same route.[9] In such circumstances, it is hardly surprising that IT charters to, from and within the US failed to match the popularity and growth seen in Europe.

Caledonian received its CAB foreign air carrier permit in 1963, and its success across the Atlantic soon led to other charter airlines entering the market, subsequently aided by the ready availability of relatively cheap long-haul aircraft such as Boeing 707s and Douglas DC-8s as the established carriers re-equipped with the new Boeing 747. The growth of charters led IATA to suggest that if the trend were to continue, the flag carriers would inevitably have to consider their future "and specifically whether they will be able to maintain a scheduled service operation on acceptable economic conditions." Their concern increased as the long-haul charter airlines began to enter other markets as well, such as Australia and South East Asia, albeit on a smaller scale than across the Atlantic. In fact, IATA's pessimism was exaggerated, as Table 3.1 shows. IATA scheduled airlines' share of the trans-Atlantic passenger market fell from 84% in 1963 to 68% in 1971, but the scheduled carriers themselves increasingly operated charter services. In 1971, for example, IATA airlines' combined scheduled/charter share of trans-Atlantic passenger traffic was 78% (of a rapidly growing market), still down from the 98% level achieved in 1963 but hardly as much of a disaster as IATA was suggesting. Furthermore, within a year there were signs that traffic was moving back from non-IATA charter services to the scheduled operations of the established carriers.

Table 3.1 North Atlantic Passenger Traffic Shares, 1963–72 (%)

	IATA Scheduled	IATA Charter	Non-IATA Charter
1963	84	14	2
1965	84	11	5
1967	83	9	8
1969	73	10	17
1970	74	8	18
1971	68	10	22
1972	72	11	17

Source: IATA.
Note: Does not include non-IATA scheduled services, amounting to 2.3% in 1972.

Affinity/closed group charters were able to take advantage of a loophole in the definition of a scheduled service, in reality blatantly and widely abusing the rules. In the UK, for example, a scheduled operation was defined by the licensing authority as

> one of a series of journeys which are undertaken between the same two places and which together amount to a systematic service operated in such a manner that the benefits thereof are available to members of the public from time to time seeking to take advantage of it.

The loophole was the phrase 'available to members of the public.' Passengers on affinity charters were required to be a member, for a minimum period of six months, of a club or society, the primary purpose of which was not simply to supply cheap travel to its members. Such restrictions were very difficult to enforce and easily circumvented by means of phony clubs and back-dated membership. One passenger, Mr White, was quoted in the press as saying: "We thought we were flying out yesterday. We were given forms to join the Park Preservation Society of America. We didn't leave because the flight was over-booked. So today we were told to join the Shakespearian Dramatic Society." Despite the occasional well-publicised raid by officials on both sides of the Atlantic, such illegal charters were widely advertised in newspapers and attracted considerable public support. Thus, one of the key barriers designed to protect scheduled services and the flag carriers which operated them was breached.

However, yet again the scheduled airlines proved to be resilient, responding in particular in two ways. Firstly, through IATA they agreed to a series of very low fares, such as special rates for those aged under 25. This took market segmentation on long-haul services to a new level. Secondly, as they had done in Europe, they established a number of non-IATA subsidiaries to compete with the charter carriers head-on. Some of these subsidiaries were new, separate units, such as Lufthansa's Condor, or the already established BEA Airtours, but others were paper companies hiring equipment and staff from parent airlines, such as BOAC's British Overseas Air Charter Ltd. The two-pronged response was largely a success and halted the expansion of the independent carriers. In addition, in 1973 the US CAB and the newly formed UK Civil Aviation Authority (CAA) reached an agreement designed to both satisfy the growing social pressures for cheap air travel across the Atlantic and at the same time stem the widespread abuse of affinity group charter rules. The agreement provided for the introduction of Advanced Booking Charters (ABCs), known as Travel Group Charters in the US. Any individual could purchase a seat on an ABC provided they did so at least 90 days in advance of the departure date and remained abroad for a minimum period of 14 days (ten in the winter).

ABCs were a success and quickly replaced affinity group charters. In a way they represented yet another small step towards broader liberalisation, but they still included measures specifically designed to protect the flag carriers. An attempt by the UK CAA to create a more balanced competitive environment with the introduction of Advanced Purchase Excursion (APEX) fares on scheduled services (as BOAC had already introduced on UK long-haul cabotage routes with its 'Earlybird' fares) was rebutted by the US CAB following protests from the US charter airlines. This was a rare case of the charter sector being protected by the regulators against the threat of increased competition from scheduled airlines. It would be some time before the US authorities relented, but eventually they did.

The introduction of low scheduled fares on the North Atlantic, and subsequently on other long-haul routes, may have helped to restrict the growth of the charter operators, but as so often, it came at a high price in terms of profitability. As IATA noted at the time:

> The North Atlantic is a route ... on which the extended use of special fares has reduced the average yield to a point where it is already below cost. It is an instance where the carriers may have been over-generous to the public and have gone beyond the economic constraints which must apply to scheduled services.

According to IATA's calculations, in 1972/73, the First Class average seat factor on the North Atlantic was 30% (down from 36% in 1965/66) compared with a break-even level (including a 'reasonable return on investment') of 59% (61% in 1965/66). The average seat factor in the Economy cabin was 54% (down from 57% in 1965/66), with a break-even level of 70% (52% in 1965/66). Apart from the very low seat factors achieved by modern standards, what stands out from the IATA announcement is the sense of entitlement which characterised the flag carriers at this time. They clearly believed that they had a right to exist, irrespective of their profitability, and that it was only their own generosity which provided the travelling public with relatively low fares. There was no suggestion that they might compete with the charters by reducing their inflated cost levels. It would be many years before such basic economics would penetrate the minds of the management of most legacy carriers.

The Emergence of Bermuda 2

As we saw in Chapter 2, the UK/US Bermuda agreement was a compromise between two different views of the post-war aviation regulatory regime, albeit one that mostly favoured the US' perspective. It survived for some 30 years, despite occasional friction. Its importance and influence reflected not only its status as a model for others to copy, but also the fact that it governed air services between the two principal aviation nations at the time. The market between the UK and US was, by some margin, the largest in the world, at least in terms of passenger miles travelled. The Bermuda agreement facilitated the growth of this market, but at the same time restricted it. After all, that balance between liberalisation and control ('controlled competition') was at the heart of the historic compromise struck in 1946.

However, such a compromise could not survive for ever. Increasingly the Bermuda agreement came under pressure. Dobson[10] lists several factors which eventually led to a break-down:

- the rapid expansion of charter services in the 1960s, as described above;
- the growth of third-world airlines to challenge the established carriers;
- the introduction of a new generation of jet aircraft, the Boeing 747, which was much larger than the aircraft it replaced; and
- the rise in the price of oil as a result of the Middle East wars of 1967 and 1973, impacting both airline costs and the demand for air travel as a result of economic recession.

All of these factors affected the profitability of the established airlines. At the same time, and more generally, this was a period when increasingly the prevailing Keynesian economic consensus began to be challenged, with a growing interest in more open markets and reduced regulation.

Thus, the air transport industry went through a period of considerable upheaval and disruption, which was probably felt more strongly in Europe, including the UK, than in the US. One particular incident reflected the breaking down of the post-war regulatory consensus which the Bermuda agreement represented. In 1970, a route between London and Miami was inaugurated by National Airlines, a carrier new to international air services, joining fellow US airlines Pan Am, TWA and Seaboard (an all-cargo operator) on trans-Atlantic routes. This in itself signalled the emergence of a more aggressive US international aviation policy, but was also seen by the UK as a worrying development in terms of excess capacity at a time of economic uncertainty. In the words of one commentator, the incident

> exacerbated a problem already perceived by the British who felt that their competitive position vis-à-vis the USA was being eroded by the introduction of more US scheduled carriers and more US charter operators, both of which added to the over-capacity on the Atlantic route, reduced load factors and increased the competition for BOAC.[11]

The proposal, in May 1972, to introduce a daily National Airlines Boeing 747 on the London-Miami route, only partly matched by BOAC, led to British protests and eventually to a unilateral UK restriction on the capacity provided by the US carrier. This broke the terms of the Bermuda agreement, which provided only for *ex post facto* review of capacity. The US took retaliatory measures, but as is often the case with agreements between sovereign States, if one side chooses to ignore part of the deal, there is little the other side can do other than terminate the whole agreement, which may be seen as an extreme, or even at times a counter-productive reaction. It was probably not a surprise, therefore, that later in 1972, a compromise settlement was reached. However, it was evident that this relatively minor incident reflected broader and more significant underlying pressures. The UK was increasingly concerned at the growing dominance of the US airlines on the North Atlantic and was prepared to stand up to the US in a way that its precarious financial position in 1946 had prevented it from doing. By the mid-1970s, it again had a serious financial problem, but this time was far less reliant on the US. Under pressure from the International Monetary Fund, from whom the Government had had to seek support, the UK's focus of attention was increasingly on its deteriorating balance of payments. As Handley Stevens has noted: "Securing an improvement in Britain's balance of payments became a key factor in British economic policy and this was the context in which … [a] review of the working of the Bermuda 1 agreement" was commissioned.[12]

The election of a Labour Government in Britain in 1974, with its predilection to protect the State-owned airlines, added to the general feeling that something had to change. In an article published later in the 1970s, Patrick Shovelton, who took over as leader of the UK delegation to renegotiate the Bermuda agreement, summed up the situation:

> For several years before 1976 the United Kingdom had been increasingly dissatisfied with the working of the Bermuda Agreement. That Treaty

had been a landmark in its day and its authors can be – and must be – proud that it stood the test of time so long. It had a profound influence on the development of post-war civil aviation and was the guiding light for numerous bilateral Air Services Agreements the world over. But by the early 1970s its wording – possibly intentionally imprecise in a number of places – had become increasingly out of date and the subject of contentious argument.[13]

Shovelton went on to point out that in 1975/76, US airlines earned nearly £300 million in total under the Bermuda agreement, whereas the earnings of British carriers were only some £130 million, of which £127 million came from North Atlantic routes compared to £180 million for US airlines. (The Bermuda agreement also covered services between the US and Hong Kong and British territories in the Caribbean.)

Despite the influence of the UK's weakened economic position and need for a US loan in the original Bermuda negotiations, normally the relative sizes and strengths of the two parties are of only limited relevance to the outcome of ASA talks. Both sides have sovereign rights and occasionally certain advantages (such as geographic position) to trade in any way they please. The history of aviation relations between the UK and US, particularly since the 1970s, illustrates clearly that no matter how large and dominant one party may be, it will struggle to impose its views on the smaller country if that country chooses to resist. The UK and US are extremely close allies in virtually all international arenas and conflicts, but as we shall see, in aviation the relationship has been far from convivial and at times has come close to open (proverbial) warfare.

The guiding principle which predominantly governs international aviation negotiations is that of *mercantilism*. This is often interpreted as being synonymous with protectionism, but this can be a misleading. Essentially mercantilism, in this context, means *self-interest*. The British Secretary of State for Trade during the negotiations to replace the Bermuda agreement, Edmund Dell, felt comfortable with being described as a mercantilist, which he defined as follows:

> A mercantilist believes that benefit will accrue to the nation from careful calculation of his nation's interests and the adoption of policies appropriate to those interests. Mercantilism does not in principle rule out freer trade or require protection. It requires only calculation of what is in the nation's interests.[14]

On this basis, it is not difficult to explain how, for the 30 years that the Bermuda 2 agreement existed, both the UK and US regularly threw insults at each other about the other side's protectionism and reiterated their own commitment to open markets. Superficially they could not both be right, but in fact all that was happening was that each was taking the moral high ground by promoting its own self-interests. Such is the nature of bilateral air services negotiations.

The growing concern about the health of the British aviation industry in the 1960s had led the Government, in July 1967, to set up an independent enquiry, the so-called Edwards Committee, chaired by Sir Ronald Edwards but strongly influenced by its Assessor, Stephen Wheatcroft. The Committee's mandate was

> to inquire into the economic and financial situation and prospects of the British civil air transport industry and into the methods of regulating competition and of licensing currently employed; and to propose ... what changes may be desirable to enable the industry to make its full contribution to the development of the economy and to the service and safety of the travelling public.[15]

It reported in May 1969, and was to have a substantial influence not only on UK aviation policy, but also on the broader debate about competition and restriction in the industry. In many ways, although focused on the UK, it represents one of the key break points in the evolution of aviation's international regulatory regime.

Among the Edwards Committee's recommendations, and there were many, were that: the UK Government should issue a public Statement of Policy on its aviation strategy; there should be a role for both public and private sector airlines; BOAC and BEA should be merged under a single holding company; the private sector should be encouraged to create a 'Second Force' airline with sufficient financial and managerial resources to be viable and able to compete with the State-owned carriers; and a CAA should be established independent of government but with policy guidance set and published by the Government of the day, with responsibility, *inter alia*, for the economic and safety regulation of UK air transport. However, perhaps the most telling recommendation was that "the primary long-term objective should be to satisfy the individual customer at the lowest price consistent with an economic return on the investment and a level of safety equal to the best in the world." This emphasis on the interests of the consumer rather than only those of the producer represented a radical shift in policy and certainly contrasted starkly with the positions taken at the time by the vast majority of governments around the world.

The UK Government of the day accepted virtually all of the Edwards Committee's recommendations.

> In setting these objectives for the industry, the Government consider that the minimum of restrictions should be imposed on it or the users of its services, and that arrangements which restrain competition or innovation should be tolerated only to the extent that they are necessary to achieve the main objectives of policy.[16]

This was certainly not deregulation, but it was a clear move away from the approach which had dominated the regulation of the industry for the previous 25 years or more. Along with developments domestically in the US, it set the seeds for what was to be a relatively gradual evolution, with the occasional setback, towards more open international aviation markets. What was perhaps particularly remarkable about the UK's policy shift was that it took place under Harold Wilson's Labour Governments of 1964–1970. However, when Labour returned to power in 1974 (they governed until 1979), first under Wilson and then James Callaghan, the political climate had changed and at least for a while, aviation policy began to tilt back towards a less liberal, more dirigiste position.

The problem was that the Government had created a rod for its own back in the establishment of an independent CAA. The Board members of the CAA were appointed by the Government, which as we have seen, was also responsible for issuing periodic policy guidance for the regulator to follow. An attempt in 1975 to be overly prescriptive (and restrictive) in such guidance was challenged successfully in the courts by the aviation entrepreneur, Freddie Laker, fighting to save his Skytrain project. As a result, the CAA was able, to a significant extent, to pursue its own, more liberal policies, which at times departed from those of the Government. Ministers still had responsibility for international aviation negotiations, but the CAA was certainly not without influence, both in the UK and more widely. This was an unusual state of affairs, seen occasionally also in the US with its multiple aviation agencies, and was to persist for some time until UK government policy caught up with that of the CAA. As a CAA Director commented, from 1974 to late-1976, "the CAA was digging its heels in and trying every way of preserving such liberalisation as had been achieved."[17] A biography of Freddie Laker put it even more succinctly: "In Whitehall parlance, neither its chairman nor its staff could be considered 'safe'. The CAA had a mind of its own."[18]

The Renegotiation

Thus, the reasons for the decision by the UK Government to give the required 12-month notice of termination of the Bermuda agreement were complex. Some reflected longer-term developments, some more immediate concerns. The UK's approach to the regulation of air services, both domestically and internationally, had undergone several gyrations, and there was a clear lack of consistency between the Government and its still quite new independent regulator on how liberal that regulation should be. Finally, and critically, the summer of 1976 saw the UK economy under considerable pressure, with the Government having to seek substantial international financial assistance, and a strong feeling that the US had not been as helpful as it might have been in this crisis. For a number of reasons, therefore, resentment against the US was not in short supply. The large imbalance of earnings under the Bermuda agreement attracted increasing attention at a time when so much of the public focus was on the UK's broader balance of payments problems.

In April 1976, the self-proclaimed mercantilist Edmund Dell was appointed Secretary of State for Trade and Industry, responsible *inter alia* for the UK's international aviation policy. Politically this cleared the way for the announcement on 22 June that the UK was terminating the Bermuda agreement and followed yet another bilateral dispute over capacity on North Atlantic routes. It set in train 12 months of intense negotiations between what were still the two largest civil aviation powers in the world. The US had reinforced its pro-competition approach in new policy statements in 1963 and 1970, although the objective fell well short of what today we would recognise as open skies. In particular, the US sought to maintain as flexible an interpretation as possible of Bermuda's capacity controls. The UK's opening position, on the other hand, was for the benefits of any new agreement to be far more evenly balanced, to be achieved by:

- single airline designation on all routes;
- capacity to be determined in advance by governments;
- new US gateways for UK airlines to increase their access to the US market; and
- the abolition of all US fifth freedom rights beyond London.[19]

However, it is a mistake to think that the UK and US approached the negotiations from completely opposite ends of the policy spectrum. The core argument was still about the extent of 'controlled competition' rather than deregulation. The 1970 US Statement on International Air Transport Policy, for example, which was certainly more consumer focused than UK government policy at the time, nevertheless argued that in practice the extent of competition should be determined on a case-by-case basis. Despite this, the bilateral negotiations were difficult and lasted the whole 12 months available, occasionally involving political intervention at the highest levels. Agreement came only at the eleventh hour, with preparations in place for the cessation of all direct UK–US air services. (In one of those human touches which can arise in even the most critical and serious of negotiations, at the very end of the 12-month termination period the wife of the leader of the UK delegation was dispatched to buy hamburgers in London to keep the teams going through the night, "not without some difficulty since the hamburger store had a policy of not serving lone women after midnight! The agreement was finally initialled at ten past five in the morning.")[20]

The new agreement, soon known as Bermuda 2, was inevitably a compromise in many ways, but arguably one tilted more towards the UK's preferred outcome. In other words, in this respect at least, it was the opposite of what had emerged in 1946. In his comprehensive review of the negotiations and subsequent evolution of Bermuda 2, Handley Stevens comments that it was very much to the credit of the chief negotiators on both sides that they kept their heads in the face of so much intense political pressure, arriving at an agreement which both sides could live with.[21] The recently elected US President Carter even wrote:

> The Agreement is one that reflects well on our two great nations. Its quality, its fairness, and its benefits to the consumer and to airlines should make it last as long as the original 1946 Bermuda Agreement. It continues our long and historic relationship with the United Kingdom.

Carter was right on one point; Bermuda 2 did indeed last as long as its predecessor, to the surprise of many. However, to imply that both parties to the agreement were equally pleased with it is a distortion of the truth. Virtually from day one, criticism of Bermuda 2 started to build in the US, and it was not long before replacing it became a core objective of US international aviation policy. Administratively it would have been relatively easy for the US to do what the UK had done and terminate the ASA within a short period of time. However, politically such a course of action was extremely difficult, which serves to highlight the magnitude of the UK's decision, as well as the fact that so many key elements came together in 1976 to facilitate what was widely seen as an aggressive stance against one of the country's closest allies. It was a gamble that paid off for the UK, albeit at the price of creating ill feeling on the US side that was to last for a long time. As Edmund Dell commented: "Britain secured more of its objectives than a cool assessment of the relative strength of the two contenders made probable."[22]

A brief look at the contents of Bermuda 2 is sufficient to indicate why the US might be unhappy with it. The new bilateral fell short of the restrictive agreement the UK initially set out to achieve, but it did retain double government approval for tariffs, limited the number of gateways which could be served in the UK and US, restricted the number of airlines which could serve each route, provided a seasonal capacity review with caps on frequency increases, reduced the fifth freedom opportunities available to US carriers and permitted only two named US airlines to serve London's premier airport, Heathrow. While as already noted, the US had not been seeking an open skies arrangement, a concept which in any case had yet to emerge as a serious proposition, it certainly would have preferred a more liberal regime. The signing of Bermuda 2 marked the beginning of a long campaign by the US to persuade the UK to allow more access for its carriers, in particular to Heathrow, which was only fully satisfied many years later with an EU-wide agreement. The US even attempted to bypass the UK by negotiating more liberal ASAs with Continental European countries, in the expectation that the loss of traffic would force the UK to be more amenable. It was a strategy which failed totally (as did a similar campaign against Japan), such was the attraction of the London market. When Bermuda 2 was finally set to one side, after some 30 years, the UK's share of the Europe–US market was little different from what it had been in 1977, but British airlines had a substantially larger share of UK–US traffic.

Bermuda 2 is important for a number of reasons. Some believed that it would become a model for other countries to follow, as its predecessor had been. This proved to be far from the case. Rather than representing the beginning of a new era in international aviation relations, Bermuda 2 might more accurately be regarded as the last major fling of the old system. It was a step back from the less restrictive Bermuda 1 approach, particularly with respect to capacity control, but at the same time was consistent with the type of ASA which many countries had been increasingly negotiating. The sheer size of the market between the UK and US meant that Bermuda 2 could not be ignored, and as we will see in a later chapter, it played a crucial role in the important aviation negotiations between the EU and the US which, for a time at least, seemed to offer the prospect of a truly radical reform of the whole bilateral process.

The new ASA may have been a retrograde step in the long journey from the Chicago Convention to a fully liberal aviation market, but in reality, it proved to be remarkably resilient. It evolved over the years to accommodate a changing and rapidly growing market. The UK's position as the dominant trans-Atlantic market from the US was never seriously challenged, despite the emergence of far more liberal ASAs between the US and several other major European countries. The UK and US Governments showed a willingness, admittedly often after difficult negotiations, to agree amendments to the bilateral which, while maintaining its core principles, nevertheless accommodated such potentially destabilising developments as the deregulation of US domestic air services, the privatisation of British Airways, the demise of Pan Am, TWA and British Caledonian, the rise and fall of Laker Airways and the rise of Virgin Atlantic, etc. As Handley Stevens comments, while Bermuda 2 was a child of its time, by 1995 its architects would scarcely have recognised the Treaty they had designed in 1977:

> A balanced assessment might perhaps conclude that for all its faults Bermuda 2 provided the two governments with what turned out to be a surprisingly flexible instrument for the regulation of air services over a period of some thirty years of rapid growth and change in a dynamic industry. Bermuda 2 was not designed to give airlines the extensive freedoms they ultimately enjoyed to set their own prices, to choose their own frequencies, to enter into alliances, or for British airlines in particular to compete with one another head-to-head on so many gateway route segments. But with good will on both sides ways were found for Bermuda 2 to operate with the flexibility that the changing market required.[23]

This evolution was helped by the fact that the UK itself adopted a far more liberal international aviation policy, with the CAA and the new Government of Margaret Thatcher pursuing the same approach. The UK became a leading advocate of reform in Europe and beyond, although this did not stretch to actually abandoning Bermuda 2.

One of the most surprising aspects of the period covered by Bermuda 2 was the frequent absence of the good will referred to by Handley Stevens, despite close UK/US political relations in other areas. Although agreement was reached on several significant amendments to the bilateral over the years, there remained a constant unhappiness on each side which affected the bilateral relationship. Initially, this was focused on the US side, as we have seen, leading virtually from the day Bermuda 2 was signed to strong criticism of the UK's apparent protectionism. Eventually, the UK responded with its own criticism, highlighting the less liberal aspects of the US aviation policy, especially the refusal to allow foreign airlines to operate domestic services within the US and to acquire controlling stakes in US carriers. These restrictions, the UK argued, put British airlines at a significant disadvantage when competing across the Atlantic and justified the ASA controls on US carriers.

Jeff Shane, once Under Secretary for Policy at the US Department of Transportation and previously chief US aviation negotiator at the State Department, described the UK/US aviation relations thus:

> Perhaps it is because our two peoples enjoy so strong and enduring a bond that the long-fraught history of Anglo-American civil aviation relations stands out in such stark relief. Allies standing shoulder-to-shoulder in respect of just about everything else, they have more often been eyeball to eyeball when it comes to the commercial flights that connect their two territories.[24]

This was almost always a surprise to UK Secretaries of State for Transport, arriving in their new posts. For a short period, they would believe that the problems could be sorted out relatively easily if only those pesky civil servants could be bypassed. One of them, Cecil Parkinson, went so far as to suggest that had it been left to UK and US aviation negotiators, the Third World War would have started by now. Parkinson's successor, Malcolm Rifkind, described the airline industry as combining the most modern state of the art with rules straight out of Byzantium.[25] Eventually, UK politicians, like their opposite numbers in Washington DC, came to realise that the problems were deeper and more intractable than they first realised.

The truth, of course, is that the prolonged negotiations and disagreements had little to do with the frequently changing cast of civil servants on either side. They reflected the substantial interests involved and the importance of the trans-Atlantic market, where routes between the UK and US were predominant. The rest of the world was certainly watching what the UK and US were doing, even if they were less inclined than previously to follow suit. Both countries were defending protectionist policies, but equally each believed that it had the moral high ground of support for less regulation and more open markets, although the UK arrived at such a position somewhat behind the US. Elsewhere in the world both countries were also among the leaders in pressing for the normalisation of air transport regulation. (There was even a suggestion at one stage that they should work together to seek to persuade the EU to adopt radical reforms of its internal aviation market, at a time when there was strong opposition to increased competition from most Member States.) In other words, what we see is an example of the mercantilist approach to aviation regulation which Edmund Dell defined so accurately. Self-interest was alive and kicking and showed no real sign of defeat.

Notes

1. Sir Ronald Edwards: *British Air Transport in the Seventies. Report of the Committee of Inquiry into Civil Air Transport.* HMSO, London, 1969.
2. Ibid.
3. Barry K. Humphreys: 'The Economics and Development of the British Independent Airlines since 1945.' PhD Thesis, University of Leeds, 1974.
4. Dudley Barker: 'Berlin airlift: an account of the British contribution.' HMSO, London, 1949.
5. Barry K. Humphreys, op cit.
6. Ibid.
7. Ibid.
8. Michael Peters: *International Tourism. The Economics and Development of the International Tourist Trade.* Hutchinson, London, 1969.
9. Alan H. Stratford: *Air Transport Economics in the Supersonic Era.* Macmillan, London, 1973 (Second Edition).
10. Alan P. Dobson: *Flying in the Face of Competition.* Avebury Aviation, Aldershot, 1995.
11. Ibid.
12. Handley Stevens: *The Life and Death of a Treaty. Bermuda 2.* Palgrave Macmillan, London, 2018.
13. W. Patrick Shovelton: 'Bermuda 2 – A discussion of its implications.' *The Journal of the Royal Aeronautical Society*, February 1978, pp. 51–54.
14. Edmund Dell: 'Independence and the judges: Civil aviation and antitrust.' *Journal of International Affairs*, Vol. 61(3), 1985, pp. 355–373. Quoted in Stevens, op cit.
15. Sir Ronald Edwards, op cit.
16. 'Civil Aviation Policy.' HMSO, Cmd 4213, London, 1969.
17. Quoted in Dobson, op cit.
18. Roger Eglin and Berry Ritchie: *Fly Me I'm Freddie!* Futura, London, 1980.
19. Stevens, op cit.
20. Ibid.
21. Ibid.
22. Edmund Dell, op cit. Quoted in Dobson, op cit.
23. Stevens, op cit.
24. Jeffrey N. Shane: 'Foreword' in Stevens, op cit.
25. Quoted in John Newhouse: 'A Reporter At Large. Air Wars.' *The New Yorker*, 5 August 1991.

4 US Deregulation

Background

1978 was a momentous year in the development of air transport regulation, marked by the US decision to deregulate its domestic market. The impact of the US initiative reverberated around the world and set in train a process which is still evolving to this day, well over 40 years later. As we have seen, in bilateral and multilateral negotiations the US had pursued a relatively more liberal approach than that of most countries, although with only limited success. The international policy of the US reflected primarily the strength of its airline industry, as well as its enormous home market, from which foreign competition was excluded. Limited moves towards a less restrictive approach to international airline regulation made (slow) progress, in particular during the Nixon administration, but was not replicated domestically.

The formal regulation of air services in the US can be traced back to the Civil Aeronautics Act of 1938, which created the Civil Aviation Authority. (It is a notable and unique fact that at the time of writing, the US has recently passed the landmark of its domestic air transport industry having existed for longer under a deregulated regime than under a tightly regulated one.) In 1940, the Civil Aeronautics Board (CAB) was created as a separate regulatory body, semi-independent of government and functioning in a similar way to a public utilities commission. The Civil Aviation Authority retained responsibility for safety oversight of the industry and the provision of air traffic control services, in 1958 becoming part of the newly established Federal Aviation Administration (FAA), which in 1966 came under the control of the Department of Transportation. It was the CAB, however, which remained the key economic regulator for domestic air services.

The regulatory regime which developed under the CAB was highly restrictive and bureaucratic, with tight control over route access (and indeed egress), new entrants, tariffs and overall competition. Airline tariffs were set to ensure a 12% profit while operating with a 55% seat factor, hardly a recipe for intense competition or entrepreneurial initiative. Shaw reflects the views of many commentators in describing the regime as "extreme … a burdensome system of regulation … a cumbersome and extremely slow bureaucratic procedure."[1] An Acting US Secretary of Transportation, speaking in 1977, called it "outdated, inequitable, inefficient, uneconomical, and sadly irrational."[2] For a period of five years in the early 1970s, the CAB refused to approve a single new route authority.

Typical of the problems encountered by those airlines seeking to introduce more competition was the experience of World Airways, which in 1967 applied to begin a low-fare route between New York and Los Angeles. The CAB studied the request for over six years before eventually dismissing it because 'the record was stale.' Similarly, Continental Airlines began service between Denver and San Diego eight years after its initial application only because a US Court of Appeals ordered the CAB to approve it.[3] Such examples of delay and bureaucracy were far from unusual. Furthermore, unlike the situation found in many other countries, especially Europe, charter operations were very tightly controlled, as we saw in Chapter 3, with direct ticket sales to the public and regular services not permitted and numerous other restrictions imposed. The Chairman of the UK CAA was even driven to comment, no doubt in the face of pressure from the US to increase competition on trans-Atlantic routes, that the CAA had been liberalising while the CAB was still measuring the margins of airline tariff filings.

The Nixon administration, which lasted until August 1974, had a predisposition towards more competitive markets, but in practice, regulatory reform of domestic air services made little progress, not helped by the appointment of a series of reform-resistant CAB Chairmen. Nixon was a moderate conservative on economic matters. However, as Dobson has argued, for regulatory reform and more competitive policies to be pushed forward with sufficient ruthlessness to succeed, "two different and somewhat incompatible political types" are needed, namely "the neo-conservative ideologues who shunned pragmatism and brought a moral fervour to the call for a return to the free market" and a more liberal approach "which did not feel a close identity with the business community in the way such feelings existed among Nixon's conservatives."[4] The neo-conservatives would arrive with the administration of Gerald Ford; the liberals under President Carter. Together they formed a relatively bipartisan movement to carry reform forward.

The Legislation

The Carter administration took up reform of aviation regulation as a key policy initiative, but the groundwork had already been laid, albeit in terms of debate rather than practical progress. Within weeks of assuming power, President Carter informed Congress:

> One of my Administration's major goals is to free the American people from the burden of over-regulation ... As a first step toward our shared goal of a more efficient, less burdensome Federal government, I urge Congress to reduce Federal regulation of the domestic commercial airline industry.[5]

This would involve the complete withdrawal of market access and tariff approval restrictions, with the industry in future subject primarily to generic competition policy, consumer protection and safeguards against predatory behaviour, although support for some loss-making community services via the Essential Air Services (EAS) programme was to be retained for a ten-year period. (In fact, the EAS is still in existence today, protected by politicians eager to maximise air service to their local communities.) Three Senators, Cannon, Kennedy and Pearson, took the lead in promoting legislation through Congress during 1976 and 1977.

It was air freight services which were the first to be deregulated, in 1977. Cargo reform has been far less contentious in many countries and in the US even attracted the support of the established all-freight airlines. However, it was a different matter when it came to passenger services. There was intense opposition to reform, particularly from trade unions and the existing major carriers. Many doubted the industry's ability to stand on its own feet without the protective wall of tight regulation. Deregulation was a leap into the unknown; nothing like it, certainly on this scale, had been attempted before. Of course, there were also those who were content to operate in a highly regulated environment and simply did not want to face more competition. Nevertheless, pressure to adopt a radically different approach continued to mount, especially from consumer groups who were able to highlight, for example, the success in terms of profitability, lower fares and improved service quality of airlines such as Pacific Southwest Airlines (PSA), which operated wholly within the State of California and therefore was not subject to CAB control. Interestingly, far less attention was paid at the time to another intra-State carrier, Southwest Airlines, which operated within Texas and was to become probably the main beneficiary of Federal deregulation. (Texas and California were only liberal in relative terms. Both awarded monopoly route rights for intra-State services, and California restricted pricing freedom.) The founders of Southwest copied many of PSA's innovations on the way to becoming one of the four largest US airlines (see Chapter 7). PSA itself never managed to be as successful on inter-State routes as it had been serving solely the California market and was merged into USAir in 1988.

The opposition of the principal carriers to reform was perhaps not surprising. In practice, few companies welcome increased competition, no matter what they say in public. A particularly vociferous opponent was Bob Crandall, renowned Chief Executive of American Airlines for many years. He claimed, often in colourful language, that deregulation would wreck the industry and not be in the interests of consumers. He regarded airlines as providers of essential services, like utilities, and therefore in need of regulation. (Ironically, American Airlines was among the first legacy carriers to restructure its operations following deregulation, not least because Crandall quickly realised what needed to be done in the new regulatory environment.)[6] However, the position of the major carriers was undermined when one of them, United Airlines, probably out of frustration at the CAB's refusal to grant it certain additional route rights, broke ranks and started to campaign for reform. This had the additional effect of neutralising the main airline trade body, which could not lobby on any issue unless it had the unanimous support of all its members. In the end, the momentum for change just proved too strong.

Particularly influential in the deregulation debate which preceded legislation were several academics who published studies highlighting the experience of intra-State air services and the costs associated with regulation. They provided critical intellectual backing for reform. It was probably not coincidental that two such academics, Alfred Kahn and Michael Levine, were appointed Chairman and Chief of Staff respectively at the CAB by President Carter. Mention should also be made of Elizabeth Bailey, who moved from AT&T to academia and served for a while as Republican Vice-Chair of the CAB. (Kahn was a Democrat, and this bi-partisan approach was a key factor in achieving political success.) This was an important change after a period during which senior CAB appointments had been a brake on progress towards reform. Kahn and Levine, both of whom had written extensively in academic journals and books on the subject of economic regulation,[7] were to be key players in promoting a new approach. As one person involved at the time has said: "All the right people in the right place at the right time delivering what I think was the most economically transformative event ever to occur through the removal of government regulatory oversight."[8]

Kahn was actually reluctant to take on the CAB role, a post which he held for just 18 months. He strongly supported deregulation but argued that he knew next to nothing about airlines: "I really don't know one plane from the other. To me they're all just marginal cost with wings."[9] His academic work had largely avoided aviation and focused on other transport modes. Nevertheless, his influence was substantial and it is no accident that he has become known as 'the father of deregulation.' (In 1979, he also coined the term 'open skies,' which has become synonymous with the international liberalisation of air services.) In later years he was less enthusiastic about the outcome of deregulation, particularly the absence of sufficient competition from successful smaller new entrant airlines and the way in which the legacy carriers were able to consolidate and maintain their dominance. It was the effectiveness of competition which he regretted, rather than the reduced number of competitors with, he thought, too much political interference in the market.[10]

The CAB under Kahn initially adopted a far more liberal approach to market access and tariff approval than had previously been the case, but within the existing legislation. There was always the fear, however, that such action could be challenged in the courts or even reversed by later administrations. Hence it was important to draft new legislation as soon as possible. The Air Transport Regulatory Reform Act was introduced in the Senate by Senators Cannon, Kennedy and Pearson and passed in April 1978. Approval by the House of Representatives, where opposition was stronger than in the Senate, followed and the Bill was signed into law by President Carter on 24 October 1978. Change to the regulation of the industry came quickly, but possibly just as important, especially symbolically, was the announcement that the existence of the CAB itself was to be time-limited. From 1985, its remaining regulatory responsibilities were to pass to the Department of Transportation. This so-called CAB 'sunset' provision was actually added to the deregulation legislation as a 'poison pill' by Representative Elliott Levitas, an opponent of reform. Unfortunately for him, it was never debated or deleted and so became law.[11] There was to be no going back.

The Impact

The deregulation of domestic air services by the US is often referred to as a 'Big Bang,' to reflect the sudden change towards a more open, competitive market. However, although initiated in a single piece of legislation, deregulation was not actually implemented overnight; the restrictions were relaxed over a period up to the beginning of 1983. Nevertheless, this was still far faster than the approach later adopted by Europe. Button and Johnson identify the pros and cons of these two approaches. As they point out, a Big Bang may have adverse short-term consequences because there can be what economists call 'stranded, quasi-sunk costs' that are technically sound but economically inefficient, and "because equipment de facto becomes obsolete as new types of personnel are required and as managerial experimentation takes place in the new economic environment." The alternative is 'gradualism,' with reforms phased in over a lengthy period, allowing airlines the time to adjust their fleets and operations to the new regulatory regime. "In [this] case ... there is the problem of potential capture of the system by those in it and by regulators who see their economic rents being dissipated."[12] Thus, both approaches have their potential shortcomings, although equally both aim for the same longer-term objective.

One immediate effect of the Big Bang approach was the substantial destabilisation of the market. The airlines previously licensed by the CAB expanded the scale of their operations rapidly, seeking competitive advantage before the onslaught of new entrants. At the same time, carriers which had been restricted to operating solely within an individual US State now found that they were free to enter inter-State markets, and even international routes if the bilateral rights were available. Finally, of course, there were new start-ups seeking to make their mark. Consumers were the clear initial beneficiaries as fares fell and route networks expanded but at the cost of financial losses for airlines and structural instability in the industry, including numerous bankruptcies. Eventually, however, a more stable environment emerged and it was possible to take a broader view of deregulation's successes and failures. One very obvious conclusion was that regulation, at least as practiced by the CAB, had not succeeded in replicating a competitive industry. In fact, there was ample evidence that there had been a substantial distortion of the market, for example, in under-pricing certain services relative to other operations. The problem was that such distortion inevitably favoured some stakeholders and disadvantaged others; deregulation simply reversed the winners and losers, albeit in an economically more rational and efficient way.

Most commentators have come down clearly on the side of deregulation being a success, especially for consumers. As Rhodes has argued, deregulation was "expected to improve service to the public, lower fares, allow carriers to achieve higher profits, and create a more competitive airline industry through the entry of new carriers as well as the freer regulatory environment afforded to existing competitors."[13] With a few caveats, this was achieved. Similarly, Button concludes that: "The experience of the US in liberalizing its domestic market demonstrated that regulation had stifled the development of the industry, led to excessive fares, fostered inefficiency and limited consumer choice."[14] An early and well-regarded economic study, by Morrison and Winston, estimated that air fares fell by 33% in real terms between 1976 and 1993, of which at least 20% was attributed to deregulation itself.[15] Several other studies have produced similar results.

However, not everyone agreed with such conclusions. One problem is that it is very difficult to separate the impact of deregulation from other factors affecting the airline industry. For example, air fares may well have fallen after deregulation, but they had been falling for some time before, mainly as a result of efficiency gains from improved technology. Academics such as Morrison and Winston tried to isolate the effects of deregulation, but inevitably there was room for debate. Not surprisingly, therefore, those who perceived that they were disadvantaged by the reforms, especially the labour movement, were far from slow in criticising them. The same was true of most of the incumbent airlines, who faced a major challenge to reduce costs and reorganise operations to meet the new competitive threats. Among academics, Paul Dempsey was, and remains, probably the most critical about the achievements of deregulation, arguing for example: "The case for a gain to consumers … is entirely vacuous, to put it charitably."[16] Similarly, David Dayen has commented: "Airline deregulation has been disastrous for workers, frustrating for travellers, and devastating for consumers."[17] As we shall see later, many of these arguments persist to the present day, not just in the US, and have led to pressure to re-regulate parts of the industry.

One important result of deregulation was the reconfiguration of airline networks away from point-to-point services, with the emergence of a series of major hub airports. Hubs were not new. In Europe, for example, what Burghouwt and de Wit have termed 'spatially concentrated networks' had been operated for many years, with airlines concentrating services at their national home bases as a result of the restrictions imposed by bilateral ASAs.[18] However, most of these star-shaped networks were not coordinated to maximise passenger connections, with any transfers which did take place tending to be a by-product rather than part of an underlying business model. They lacked the *waves* of flights spread over the day which were to become a characteristic of the new hub airports. This was to change as each of the major US carriers established a series of hubs across the country, competing with each other for connecting traffic. Previously, only Atlanta could be said to resemble what we now recognise as a major airline hub airport. (The old joke was that whether you went to heaven or hell, you had to change planes in Atlanta.) In the overwhelming majority of cases, a hub became dominated by a single airline, exploiting economies of scope to connect network spokes with other spokes via the central hub.

Many have argued that hub operations reflect the fundamental economics of air transport, the development of which had been held back by regulation. Michael Levine expressed this view picturesquely:

> Network airlines are nothing more or less than factories to manufacture route density. They assemble passengers in groups large enough to fill an airplane of efficient size. They take them to some place where they can mix with other people going on to some other place in enough numbers to fill another airplane and then take them there. And they choose customers willing to pay a combination of prices that covers total costs. The trick is to gather them and transport them together.[19]

This is what economists call *economies of scope*. Hubbing does not necessarily reduce costs; in fact, the reverse may be true, and it tends to increase congestion and overall travel time. In point-to-point markets from hubs, there is also clear evidence of a so-called 'hub premium' for fares, although its extent is hotly debated. However, hubs enable far more destinations to be served profitably, at higher frequencies using larger, more efficient aircraft. The fact that the concept of connecting hub airports has now spread throughout the world is a testament to the advantages they bring to airlines and passengers.

The development of US hub airports also had an impact on international services and competition. Traditionally, US international air services had been provided by Pan Am and to a lesser extent by TWA. This dominance had been under threat for some time, but was greatly exacerbated by deregulation as other carriers began international service, usually from their own hubs. TWA and especially Pan Am lacked the strong domestic networks to compete effectively with these newcomers. (Pan Am tried to overcome this problem by absorbing National Airlines, but with only limited success.) The result was the rapid growth of new gateways for international service and the relative decline of the traditional principal point of entry to the US, New York, where Pan Am and TWA were dominant. This was a significant factor in the eventual demise of both Pan Am and TWA.

An equally important result of the development of US hub airports was the impact on foreign airlines serving the country. Because most hubs were dominated by a single carrier, competing airlines found it increasingly difficult to access feed traffic there. This, it was argued, gave US airlines an unfair competitive advantage, which they were not slow to exploit. For example, a British airline flying between London and Atlanta, a route with a large proportion of traffic connecting at the US hub, would be forced to rely on its direct trans-Atlantic competitor, Delta Air Lines, for most feeder traffic. Even where services were provided by carriers other than Delta, they were likely to be to those airlines' own hubs with direct and competing services to Europe. Delta, on the other hand, had far more choice of connecting services in London, where because of the bilateral regulatory regime, most routes had a second airline happy to take Delta's feed traffic.

A similar problem was encountered in operating US routes from European regional cities. For example, UK airlines had always struggled to operate profitable trans-Atlantic services from Manchester, partly because of insufficient point-to-point traffic, especially business passengers, and partly because of the lack of feeder services at the UK airport. However, the first US airline to serve Manchester, American from its Chicago hub, discovered an instant success. The route quickly became American's most profitable international service with an average seat factor in excess of 80% (high at that time), primarily because of the number of passengers travelling to and from points beyond Chicago, usually in small numbers to each destination but adding up to a significant flow. It was this apparent imbalance in competitive opportunities, reflecting in particular the restrictions imposed by the US on the provision of cabotage services by foreign airlines and on investment in US carriers, which drove UK trans-Atlantic aviation policy for many years, despite strong US pressure for further liberalisation.

One irony of deregulation is that while it resulted in the rapid growth of hub-based networks, the most successful carrier to emerge was one that focused on point-to-point services. Southwest Airlines began commercial operations within Texas in 1971, with a fleet of four Boeing 737s serving just three markets. Today it is the fourth largest US airline (the largest in terms of domestic passengers carried) with a network covering the whole country and beyond. It serves well over 100 airports, employs some 60,000 staff and operates over 700 aircraft, still consisting wholly of B737s of various types, the world's largest B737 fleet. Its initial success lay in offering a very different type of service which quickly attracted consumer support, described by Beckenstein and Campbell as a single, simple, no-frills product, low costs achieved by having a fleet of just one aircraft type flown at high utilisation levels, high frequency, low fares, and a '*fun and friendly*' experience for its customers.[20] Perhaps most surprising of all was the fact that while virtually all the other major US airlines regularly lost money until relatively recently, Southwest's record was one of persistent profitability. Southwest may not have been the first low-cost carrier, but it became the iconic representative of the sector. It was the model others sought to imitate around the world, with varying degrees of success. We will take a closer look at the low-cost carrier phenomenon in Chapter 7.

Southwest brought a very different style of service to the deregulated US domestic market, but above all, it brought low fares. Every time it entered a new route, fares across the board fell and traffic volumes increased disproportionately. A 1993 study by the US Department of Transportation called this the 'Southwest Effect.' The name and the impact have both endured to the present day, with one recent study concluding that a new non-stop Southwest service still produces, on average, a fare reduction of 15% and traffic stimulation of 28%–30%.

> The Southwest Effect is alive and well. We find no evidence that [it] has been eroded or overtaken in significance or magnitude by other airlines … Our study finds that Southwest produces $9.1 billion annually in domestic consumer fare savings. One-way average market fares are $45 lower when Southwest serves a market non-stop than when it does not.[21]

Other studies have come to similar conclusions. Over the 40 plus years since deregulation, of course, the market has evolved and other airlines have succeeded in lowering fares and stimulating traffic growth, but none has had the impact that Southwest has had, both in the US and globally. This success would simply not have been possible under the old CAB-style of regulation.

Success?

So, what do we conclude about US deregulation? Has it been a success or not? Rhodes comments that the purpose of the Airline Deregulation Act was "to encourage, develop, and attain an air transportation system which relies on competitive market forces to determine the quality, variety, and price of air services."[22] To that extent, deregulation can be viewed as a success. However, in reality, the picture is far more complex. Many of the early proponents of regulatory reform in the US believed that the mere threat of competition would be sufficient to restrain any monopoly power and protect consumers from exploitation, what economists call *contestability*. That proved not to be the case in air transport. It has become apparent that deregulation in itself, without additional regulatory tools, is not sufficient to guarantee a competitive marketplace. After the initial rush of new entrants into the inter-State market, often with radically lower costs and innovative business models, the legacy airlines were forced to react in order to survive. They succeeded in matching the products of the low-cost carriers, which were clearly attractive to consumers, and narrowing the cost differences, although they failed for a long time to do so profitably. Gradually over the years more and more consolidation took place (sector concentration reached a low point in 1985, but by the early 1990s had reverted to its 1979 level),[23] until today just four airlines dominate the internal US market.

Increased market concentration may in fact be an inevitable and necessary part of *'normalising'* the airline industry, something to which we will return later in the book. Alfred Kahn himself had a realistic approach to deregulation, expecting its outcome to be more akin to the idea of 'workable or effective competition,'[24] rather than any idealised concept. His deregulation co-sponsor, Michael Levine, later commented that "the choice is between imperfect markets and imperfect regulation," and went on to identify many of the ways in which deregulation did not go quite as planned:

> We underestimated the determination and ingenuity that would be displayed by legacy airlines as they defended their business model against attacks by lower-cost carriers. Frequent flyer programs, corporate contracts, [Global Distribution Systems] and travel agency loyalty programs, highly differentiated fare structures, radical scope expansion, alliances, etc, all provided much more effective and enduring defences against competitors than we anticipated.[25]

Nevertheless, and despite the frequent criticism of service standards in the US domestic market, it is unlikely many consumers would welcome a return to old-style regulation. Regulation was shown to have substantially distorted the market and prevented the emergence of new business models far more suited to meeting consumer needs. Its removal released pent-up entrepreneurial initiatives, the outcome of which few foresaw fully. This is an experience which was to be repeated on numerous occasions around the world. At the end of the day, perhaps the real success of US deregulation can be seen in the fact that it set in train a momentum globally which, despite the occasional setback, for a long time proved impossible to stop. Imitation is, after all, the greatest form of flattery.

Notes

1. Stephen Shaw: *Airline Marketing and Management*. Ashgate, Aldershot, 2007. (Sixth Edition).
2. Jeffrey N. Shane: 'Air Transport Liberalization: Ideal and Ordeal.' Second Annual Assad Kotaite Lecture, Royal Aeronautical Society Montreal Branch, 8 December, 2005.
3. Kenneth Button: 'A book, the application, and the outcomes: How right was Alfred Kahn in *The Economics of Regulation* about the effects of deregulation on the US domestic airline market?' *History of Political Economy*, Vol. 47(1), 2015, pp. 1–39.
4. Alan P. Dobson: *Flying in the Face of Competition. The Policies and Diplomacy of Airline Regulatory Reform in Britain, the USA and the European Community 1968–94.* Ashgate, Aldershot, 1995.
5. Quoted in Dobson, op cit.
6. See Dan Reed: *The American Eagle. The Ascent of Bob Crandall and American Airlines*. St. Martin's Press, London, 1993.
7. See for example, Alfred E. Kahn: *The Economics of Regulation: Principles and Institutions*. John Wiley & Sons, New York, Volume 1, 1970, and Volume 2, 1971. Also, Michael E. Levine: 'Is regulation necessary? California air transportation and national regulatory policy.' *Yale Law Journal*, Vol. 74, 1965, pp. 1416–1447.
8. Personal exchange with Scott Gibson.
9. Button, op cit.
10. See, for example, William A. Jordan: 'Airline Entry Following US Deregulation: The Definitive List of Startup Passenger Airlines, 1979 – 2003.' 46th Annual Transportation Research Forum, Vol. 1, Washington DC, March 2005.

11 Robert W. Poole: 'If you can afford a plane ticket, thank deregulation.' *Reason*, June 2018.
12 Kenneth J. Button and Kirk Johnson: 'Incremental versus trend-break change in airline regulation.' *Transportation Journal*, Vol. 37, 1998, pp. 25–34.
13 Dawna L. Rhodes: *Evolution of International Aviation. Phoenix Rising.* Ashgate, Aldershot, 2003.
14 Kenneth Button: *Wings across Europe. Towards an Efficient European Air Transport System.* Ashgate, Aldershot, 2004.
15 S. A. Morrison and C. Winston: *The Evolution of the Airline Industry.* Brookings Institute, Washington DC, 1995.
16 Paul S. Dempsey: *Flying Blind: The Failure of Airline Deregulation.* Economic Policy Institute, Washington DC, 1990.
17 David Dayan: 'Unfriendly skies.' *The American Prospect*, Fall 2017.
18 Guillaume Burghouwt and Jaap de Wit: 'Temporal configurations of European airline networks.' *Journal of Air Transport Management*, Vol. 11, 2005, pp. 185–198.
19 Michael E. Levine: 'Liberalisation, Consolidation and the Struggle to Survive: What Future for Airlines? In Search of a Viable Airline Revenue Model.' Airline Leader, October 2010.
20 Alan R. Beckenstein and Brian M. Campbell: 'Public Benefits and Private Success: The Southwest Effect Revisited.' University of Virginia Darden Business School Working Paper No. 206, 2017.
21 Ibid.
22 Dawna L. Rhodes, op cit.
23 Peter B. Belobaba and Jan Van Acker: 'Airline market concentration. An analysis of US origin-destination markets.' *Journal of Air Transport Management*, Vol. 1(1), 1994, pp. 5–14.
24 Button and Johnson, op cit.
25 Interview with Michael E. Levine, Travel Weekly, 27 October 2003.

5 European Liberalisation

If US deregulation was the first major challenge to the post-Chicago consensus on the regulation of air transport, the liberalisation of air services within the EU was certainly the second. (Note that since its foundation the EU has gone through several different titles, as well of course as adding new members. The titles reflect political changes in the constitution of the Community, but here all are used interchangeably. See Addendum 1 to this chapter.) It has even been argued that the European initiative was a greater achievement than that of the US, despite the latter's pioneering role. While the US was a single country, requiring the agreement of a single legislature, the EU at the time was made up of 15 Member States, each fiercely independent as far as aviation policy was concerned. It is an understatement to say that reaching a broad consensus in those circumstances created its own challenges.

This was a period when the EU was focused primarily on creating a single market for goods and services, rather than the political integration which was to come later. However, while progress to establish a Common Market was made in almost all sectors, aviation was initially excluded. This meant that air services between Member States were treated as international and no different from services to and from non-EU countries. Most Member States were determined to resist reform of intra-EU aviation.

Pressure Builds for Reform

Kassim and Stevens describe the regulatory changes which took place in Europe as a "revolution in air transport." As they point out, and as we have already seen, before the creation of the single market in air services, European aviation was characterised by protectionism, collusion and fragmentation, just as it was throughout most of the world.[1] Each European country retained its own set of regulations, with some co-ordination via ICAO (especially on safety matters) and to a lesser extent the European Civil Aviation Conference (ECAC). The interests of State-owned national flag carriers were fiercely promoted and protected, and cabotage services were virtually unknown. The replacement of these protectionist barriers came about as a result of the confluence of several factors, although some were more important than others.

DOI: 10.4324/9780429448973-5

As one commentator put it: "The liberalization of air transport in [Europe], where entrenched national interests prevailed ..., took four decades to bring ideas to ripeness, feeding on American experience and on the emergence of marketing realities. It has been a cultural adventure."[2]

It was certainly the case that events in the US had an impact on Europe, provoking a debate about the role of regulation which in turn led to some questioning the status quo. Kassim and Stevens suggested that US deregulation created an environment which, for the first time, made EC involvement in aviation a genuine possibility,[3] but such influence was far from sufficient in itself to change the minds of most European Governments. While the UK and the Netherlands (later joined by Ireland) increasingly promoted a more liberal approach, the remaining Member States were essentially united in their opposition to reform. Of particular significance in this respect was the widely-held belief that Article 84(2) of the EEC Treaty (later Article 80(2)) required the approval of each Member State for Community intervention in aviation and shipping, which meant in particular that the EU Commission was unable to enforce unilaterally the competition rules of the Treaty of Rome. To do so required unanimous support among Member States, which was highly unlikely to be forthcoming.

Aviation reform is known as *liberalisation* in Europe and *deregulation* in the US, and the differentiation is significant. As we saw in Chapter 4, US deregulation took place over a relatively short period of time and initially resulted in substantial market destabilisation. In Europe, on the other hand, change came far more slowly, spread over several years in the form of three so-called *'packages.'* This gave the established airlines more time to adjust to the changing environment and therefore resulted in a more gradual transformation from tight regulation to an open internal market. Nevertheless, the final outcome in Europe was remarkably similar to what had occurred in the US, notably with the emergence of new entrant low-cost carriers to challenge the predominant market position of the legacy airlines. Similarly, in both Europe and the US, market access reform was only part of the picture. Other regulations, primarily designed to promote competition and protect consumer interests, also quickly emerged in both jurisdictions. Unlike the US, however, the EU faced two additional challenges: weaning airlines and airports off state aid in its various forms; and the appearance of privatisation initiatives.

The liberalisation of market access in the European airline industry took place over a period of some nine years, between 1983 and 1992, although initial debate began earlier:

The First package	– 1983–1987
The Second Package	– 1988–1990
The Third Package	– 1990–1992

As already indicated, at the outset only the UK and the Netherlands supported the efforts of the European Commission to introduce reforms.

The Commission's interest lay partly in a belief in the benefits of more competitive markets, but also in a wish to transfer significant control of the sector from individual Member States to Brussels, as had already taken place for most other industries. The UK had become a strong believer in international liberalisation, at least within certain broad confines, and had succeeded in persuading four EU Member States (the Netherlands, Ireland, Belgium and Luxembourg) to agree to what at the time were very liberal bilateral air services agreements, as well as reaching slightly more restrictive agreements with several other European countries. The Netherlands, with its small home market, a major international airline reliant on access to other markets and a history of entrepot trade, had long sought the removal of bilateral restrictions wherever possible. Ireland was to join the UK and Netherlands in seeking EU aviation reform with the emergence of a serious Irish challenger to the national flag carrier in the form of Ryanair. As ever in international aviation regulation, what united these reformers was essentially self-interest, albeit wrapped up in free market principles.

At the time of the creation of the European Economic Community and Euratom in the 1950s, the intention was to encompass all transport modes. Jean Monet certainly did not envisage any exclusions for aviation and shipping. In 1956, for example, the Spaak Report to the (Messina) Intergovernmental Conference, which drafted the Treaty of Rome, highlighted the importance of transport for the creation and success of the Common Market, drawing attention especially to aviation and the need to liberalise commercial traffic rights.[4] However, unanimous agreement among the six original Member States proved impossible to achieve, with France, Germany and Italy indicating particularly strong opposition to EU involvement in aviation and shipping. As a result, ambiguity was introduced, which succeeded in preventing any serious reform. Article 74 of the Treaty of Rome enjoined Member States to support a common transport policy, while Article 75 said that they should do so while taking account of the distinctive features of the industry. In particular, as already noted, Article 84(2) seemed to exclude air and sea transport completely from EU involvement in the absence of a unanimous decision by the Council of Member States.

This situation prevailed for many years. A few cracks appeared during the 1970s, with decisions by the European Court of Justice (ECJ) which, inter alia, raised questions about the legality of aspects of international air services agreements without coming to a firm decision. Also of relevance, albeit again with little immediate impact, was the creation in 1977 of a separate aviation unit within DGVII, the Commission Directorate responsible for transport policy. Similarly, the Single European Act of 1986, which introduced Qualified Majority Voting rather than unanimity among Member States in relation to most industrial policies, was eventually proved important in pushing through reform. However, the edifice of protectionism remained essentially unbreeched. An early official review of the application of the EU competition rules to air transport, in 1978, concluded that, given the extent of government intervention in the industry, agreements between airlines "were a matter of the governments of the member states...the governments are ultimately responsible for the setting of fares."[5]

There is no doubt that the UK played a particularly important role in reforming European aviation regulation, and in particular it was the election of the Thatcher Government in 1979 which marked the beginning of a major push to break down the old protectionism with a two-pronged attack, seeking more liberal bilateral agreements with individual European States while simultaneously pursuing multilateral negotiations within the EU. It is worth mentioning as well the role played by ECAC, a group covering virtually all European countries, not just those with membership of the EU, which although it had no real decision-making powers, nevertheless proved to be influential in moving the reform agenda forward. At the same time, external pressure for change began to emerge. For example, Freddie Laker, having established his trans-Atlantic Skytrain service after initial regulatory setbacks, turned his attention to Europe, with the inevitable associated publicity. He applied to the UK Civil Aviation Authority for licences to operate between (not just to and from) 36 cities in Europe at fares substantially lower than those charged by the incumbent carriers. (Laker actually had no idea how many individual routes (630) he had applied for. The author, then an Economic Adviser to the CAA, worked out the number for him as part of the licensing process.) The application was refused, as there was no chance of most other governments granting approval, but the publicity generated helped to launch a Europe-wide consumer campaign for a more competitive intra-EU aviation market. Thus, pressure for reform was mounting, with a number of developments coming together.

The Reforms

European liberalisation got off to a modest start in 1983, with the adoption of the Inter-Regional Air Services Directive, first proposed by the Commission in 1979. (The difference between a Directive and a Regulation is that the latter has the force of law automatically in all Member States, while the former requires each Member State to implement it by means of its own national legislation.) This removed market access restrictions for aircraft with less than 70 seats serving regional airports. In the overall scheme of things, the Directive was of only marginal importance, unlikely to affect the State-owned flag carriers very much. Perhaps of most significance was the fact that it was adopted while Germany held the EU Presidency, suggesting that opposition to reform might not be as insurmountable as many had thought (or hoped), especially when transport ministries are influenced, even over-ruled, by other political considerations.

A new European Commission took office in 1985, with Peter Sutherland of Ireland as Competition Commissioner. Mr Sutherland had a personal interest in and commitment to reforming the EU's air transport policy, but initially faced a more conservative Transport Commission (ironically headed by a British Commissioner). To the surprise of many, it was the courts which set change in motion. In 1986, a French travel agent (Nouvelles Frontières) was accused of selling KLM fares which had not been approved by the French authorities. The case was referred to the ECJ for a judgement on whether this action was inconsistent with Article 85 of the Treaty of Rome, which prohibits agreements which "directly or indirectly fix purchase or selling prices or any other trading conditions." As we have seen, the prevailing assumption had been that aviation and shipping were not covered by the EU competition rules, but the ECJ found otherwise. It concluded that agreements to fix airline fares were in fact prohibited under the Treaty and that the French authorities could not exempt them without the unanimous approval of the EU Council, which was very unlikely to be forthcoming given the reforming objectives of several Member States.[6] Now the Commission had a proverbial *big stick* to force the pace of reform.

It is difficult to overstate the significance of the Nouvelles Frontières case, described by Kyrou as "paramount to the episode of air transport liberalisation in the EC"[7] It came as a bombshell to the European aviation industry. Among other implications, it threatened the whole basis for IATA tariff co-ordination in Europe, for so long a fundamental principle of international air transport. Essentially, reform was now inevitable as any attempt to exempt fare fixing from the Treaty's competition rules would result in the Commission insisting on broader liberalisation. It was no longer a question of whether reform would come, but when. In mid-1986, the Commission launched legal proceedings against ten airlines for breaking EU competition law, but in fact there was no need to pursue the case. Everyone knew what was coming. For those Member States which had resisted change for so long, the focus of attention now switched to introducing reform in a controlled and hopefully lengthy manner to allow their national carriers sufficient time to adjust. They would continue to fight a rear-guard action, but the real power now lay with the Commission, which was committed to liberalisation.

In March 1984, the Commission submitted to the Council its so-called Memorandum No. 2. The adoption of the first set of new rules came 45 months later in December 1987, after intense negotiations among Member States and the Commission. As Handley Stevens has pointed out, it was a measure of the changing climate that the gap between proposal and adoption for the next two stages of reform was just nine months in each case. Even France, which had probably been the most resistant to liberalisation, adopted a completely different, and far more co-operative, approach. Stevens goes on to note:

> It is difficult to exaggerate the suddenness or the importance of the change which seems to have overtaken French policy… In less than two months, starting from a position where they appeared to be leading the resistance to even the relatively modest proposals put forward by the Commission

for the second stage, they presided over a Council meeting which committed the Community to complete liberalisation by 1 January 1993.[8]

This really was a different European approach to regulatory change.

It is usually accepted that reform came in the shape of three distinct 'packages,' spread over several years and eventually leading to full liberalisation. In fact, however, there were four separate elements in addition to the earlier Regional Air Services Directive. Full liberalisation of intra-EU freight services was approved in December 1990, between the adoption of the Second and Third Packages, mainly because of concern about the effect of European fifth freedom rights granted to US airlines. The key elements in the Packages are shown in Table 5.1.

Eventually, the EU internal aviation market would cover 28 Member States (now 27 with the withdrawal of the UK) and incorporate several neighbouring countries. It has created a market larger than that of the US within which virtually all the old bilateral restrictions on airline operations have been removed. It has been a remarkable achievement, not least because of the numerous sovereign States involved. (Although, of course, once it was decided that aviation was after all subject to the Treaty of Rome's competition rules, these countries discovered that in fact they were less sovereign than they had initially thought.) However, the Three Packages were only the beginning. They represent the start of the transfer of responsibility for the regulation of aviation within the EU from individual Member States to the European Commission.

The misnomer of 'deregulation' when applied to the aviation industry can be seen in Europe just as clearly as elsewhere. It is certainly true that the old bilateral restrictions were swept away with the Three Packages. No longer would States decide where airlines would fly, how often and at what fares within the EU, but at the same time a liberalised internal market saw the emergence of a long list of other regulations, mostly designed to promote competition and protect consumers. The end result is that the European aviation industry remains as tightly regulated as ever. The EU Commission also turned its attention to state aid to the industry, again because of its potential to distort the market. Gradually the Member States were forced to reduce and eventually stop most financial assistance to their nationalised airlines, increasing the arguments in favour of privatisation. This did not totally break the close relationship between the flag carriers and their governments (especially transport ministries), as the reaction to the COVID pandemic would illustrate only too clearly, but it certainly weakened it, to the benefit of new airlines such as the emerging low-cost carriers. The final significant post-liberalisation development related to the EU's external aviation policy. With the creation of the internal aviation market nearing completion, the Commission turned much of its attention to the negotiation of air services agreements with third countries on behalf of the whole EU, with varied success. We will return to this initiative in the next chapter.

Table 5.1 The EU Three Packages and the Creation of the Internal Aviation Market

Package	First	Second	Third
Tariffs	Automatic approval for discount and deep discount fares within certain 'zones.'	Further flexibility within zones.	Automatic approval subject to possible State or Commission intervention in the case of excessive or predatory fares.
Capacity	Shared between airlines 45/55% from 01/01/1988 and 40/60% from 01/10/1989.	Maximum share of airlines of each State increased from 60% by 7.5% per annum.	No restrictions.
Designation	Multiple designation on routes with more than 250,000 passengers per annum, reducing to 200.000 passengers in Year 2 and to 180,000 passengers in Year 3.	Route size for multiple designation reduced to 140,000 passengers from January 1991 and to 100,000 passengers from January 1992.	No restrictions.
Route Access	No restrictions on third/fourth freedom routes to hubs from regions. Fifth freedom access allowed for up to 30% of capacity.	No restrictions on third/fourth freedom flights. Fifth freedom access for up to 50% of capacity.	No restrictions on services between and within Member States.
Public Service Obligations	–	Subsidy and some protection permitted for new regional routes subject to EU-wide rules.	Certain protections for services in the Azores and between the Greek islands.
Airline Licensing	–	–	Common rules across the EU. Introduction of the concept of 'Community Carrier,' majority owned and controlled by EU nationals.

Selected EU Regulations

The list of EU Regulations and Directives which apply to air transport is contained in the Civil Aviation Section of the so-called *'acquis communautaire.'* It is long and continues to expand. Von den Steinen[9] categorises the legislation as following:

- Market Access and Ancillary Issues
- Air Traffic Management
- Aviation Safety
- Aviation Security
- Environment
- Social Aspects
- Consumer Protection
- Competition and State Aids
- Other Legislation.

The EU Civil Aviation Handbook separates legislation applicable to air transport into three parts: Regulations and Directives, Decisions and Case Law and International Agreements. Addendum 2 at the end of this chapter contains a full list of Regulations and Directives at the time of writing. Here, four representative examples have been chosen, each of which highlights particular aspects of EU aviation decision-making, namely:

Passenger rights, where the courts have greatly expanded the original coverage of the legislation.
Safety, especially the role of EASA, highlighting how technical co-operation backed by the force of law can benefit the industry.
Computer reservation systems (CRSs), where early regulatory intervention created a more balanced competitive market, but was relatively quickly overtaken by other developments.
Airport slot allocation, where the EU adopted industry standards, amended them in certain respects and to a large extent set the new global rules.

Passenger Rights. Rules governing how airlines should treat their customers in the event of disruption had existed for some time in many Member States, as they had in other countries, but there was a lack of consistency which was incompatible with the internal market principles. Many of these schemes were specific to individual airlines and did not have the force of law. In addition, there was widespread criticism that even where adopted, existing rules were not sufficiently comprehensive and had relatively low compensation levels. The public debate was further fuelled by the aggressive marketing approach of certain of the new low-cost carriers, such as Ryanair, which some argued, seemed to deliberately ignore the rights of consumers. The Commission sought to change all this by introducing common rules applicable across the whole of the internal market. As the Commission commented:

"... liberalisation is not enough. Other measures are needed to protect passengers' interests and ensure that they fully benefit from the single market." Some of the proposals in the broad area of passenger rights were relatively uncontroversial. For example, Regulation 2017/1997, amended by Regulation 889/2002, implemented the Warsaw and Montreal Conventions dealing with air carrier liability in the event of accidents. Regulation 1107/2006 established rules for how disabled passengers and persons with reduced mobility should be treated by airports as well as airlines.

However, Regulation 261/2004 (replacing Regulation 295/1991), covering denied boarding and flight delay compensation, was anything but uncontroversial and continues to be the subject of heated debate to this day. The Director General of IATA described it as a "confusing and poorly worded regulation that is adding cost to the European industry." Most would accept that some form of government intervention is justified in this area, which is why similar rules have been introduced in many jurisdictions around the world. Less obvious, at least to many airlines, is the justification for the levels of compensation contained in Regulation 261 and the circumstances under which it should be paid. The reduction in many air fares in Europe with the growth of low-cost carriers has meant that compensation for delayed flights can often amount to many times more than the original fare paid. However, there is very little chance of such compensation levels being reduced significantly; if anything, the trend may be in the opposite direction. Most industry concern has instead been focused on the reasons why compensation must be paid. One study of Regulation 261 by academics, undertaken for the UK Government, described it as offering "the most unambiguous and comprehensive consumer protection for air passengers in the world."[10] The Regulation may well be comprehensive, but it certainly was not unambiguous, at least judging by the way in which it has subsequently been interpreted by the courts. Many believe that the extent of its application has gradually been extended far beyond what was originally intended by making airlines responsible for flight delays over which they have little if any control.

This has created increased business for law firms, many of whom have earned substantial profits from encouraging passengers to seek compensation, with the result that Regulation 261 is now a major source of additional costs for all airlines in Europe. A study in 2012 found that the average number of complaints received per million passengers in Europe was 53.4, ranging from 218.7 in Portugal to 16.0 in Greece, indicating an absence of uniformity in the application of common rules across EU Member States. 38% of all complaints made under the Regulation concerned delays, a further 38% cancellations, 7% denied boarding and 15% were categorised as 'other.' The average financial cost to an airline was estimated by the EU Commission as between 0.6% and 1.8% of turnover, or approximately €1 to €3 per one-way ticket.[11] Additional costs at these levels in such a price-sensitive, competitive industry are not insignificant and are certainly capable of driving airline behaviour. In addition, of course, they will increase fares in the longer term.

Computer Reservation Systems. Aviation is a major user of computers. Without them, airlines, airports and air traffic control companies simply could not function, and indeed do not when computers break down even for a short period. For airlines, showing what services and fares are available on a route, taking a booking for a seat and issuing a boarding pass are relatively straightforward tasks and ones well suited to computerisation. This is what CRSs do, although they have also evolved far beyond such basic functions. Originally, booking systems were developed by individual carriers for their own services, which meant that a travel agent often had to consult more than one system to serve their customers. It was the deregulation of the US domestic aviation market, combined of course with advances in computers themselves, which provided the spur to develop more sophisticated CRSs, ones able to display the services and fares of all participating carriers. Michael Levine called these new systems one of the "unanticipated phenomena of the deregulated environment."[12] The scale of the task created by deregulation was highlighted by Geoffrey Lipman, who noted that the

> continuous adjustments in fares and conditions – reportedly as many as 100,000 in a single day for American Airlines – the need to track frequent flyer points, to control inventory or traffic mix on a daily basis to meet competition and to track performance of sales agents – all pointed towards enhancement and growth of CRSs.[13]

Another commentator, the Director of the MIT Flight Transportation Laboratory, put it more succinctly in 1989: "Aircraft technology was once the core of airline industry competition, but computer and communications technology determine today's victors."[14]

The new CRSs meant that travel agents could easily compare the prices and schedules of all airlines serving a route, including connecting services and codeshares. They became such a powerful marketing tool that most major airlines felt impelled to invest in them, either owning their own (such as American Airlines with its Sabre system) or jointly with other carriers, such as Amadeus (originally owned by Air France, Lufthansa, SAS and Iberia) and Galileo (British Airways, KLM, Swissair and Alitalia). A study in 1990 concluded that "it is difficult to exaggerate the impact these systems have had on the air transport industry, initially in the United States but increasingly elsewhere as well."[15] Unfortunately, the market power of the CRSs, especially their ability to influence consumer choice by, for example, giving display preference to the owning airlines' services, resulted in competitive distortions and quickly attracted the attention of the regulators.

> CRSs ... have been used to distort competition between airlines in a way which has created serious concern for the long-term competitive health of the industry. They have resulted in users being provided with incomplete and biased information about flight options and prices, effectively forcing them to choose flights or fares not best suited to their needs.[16]

In such circumstances, it is not surprising that demands were soon heard for regulatory intervention, first in the US, where wide-ranging rules governing CRS use were introduced in 1984, then in Europe. This was a time when EU jurisdiction over aviation was still in its infancy and responsibility for drawing up a European code of conduct fell to ECAC. Only subsequently, in 1989, was the code given the full force of law in the form of an EU Regulation. The new rules in Europe and the US, later followed elsewhere in the world, were a success. They removed most of the market distortions, especially those associated with screen display bias, by prescribing in detail how services should be shown and in what order. However, the rules were not perfect and soon problems began to emerge which provide lessons for regulatory intervention in such circumstances. For example, the technology behind CRSs was developing so fast, and the commercial advantages of exploiting that technology were so great, that it became necessary to revise the rules. Regulators were forced to intervene in more and more detail, leading some to question whether the costs of regulation were exceeding the benefits.

In addition, there was growing concern about oligopolistic pricing among the CRSs, expressed in particular by those airlines which did not own shares in one. Not only were booking prices high, but the competitive element of the market revolved around persuading travel agents to choose a system for their sole office use. Since most fees were paid by the airlines, CRSs had an incentive to reduce the charges to agents but increase them to their captive airline customers. CRSs were certainly highly profitable, far more so than their airline customers and owners. It proved more difficult for the regulators to control excessive pricing, if that is what it was (the CRSs denied that they were abusing their market position, of course), not least because of the complexity of the products provided by the systems. However, there was no denying the impact on the airlines. For example, in the ten years from 1989, at a time of falling real air fares, British Airways' cost of sales and distribution rose from £20 per passenger to £30, with much of this 50% increase attributable to higher CRS fees. BA, like many carriers, especially the new low-cost airlines, reacted by seeking to increase direct sales and reduce the role of intermediaries, with the result that BA's cost of sales and distribution had fallen to £15 per passenger by 2004.[17]

The fundamental regulatory problem created by CRSs was the fact that they were owned by airlines, thus potentially creating a clear conflict of interest. The owning carriers had a strong commercial incentive to ensure that their own services received preferential display treatment. Inevitably, pressure grew to enforce what was termed '*dehosting*,' the separation of airline ownership of and participation in CRSs. Levine, for example, was not alone in arguing that

> ... a good case could be made for the proposition that the method of resolving the [CRS] issue with least potential for damage through misplaced government intervention is simply to require divestiture of the CRSs by the airlines and accept whatever level of contestability is exhibited by the divested market.[18]

However, in the event such intervention proved to be unnecessary as gradually carriers sold off their shareholdings, often in order to raise finance for their other operations. It was far easier to sell stakes in a highly profitable CRS than in a barely profitable, or frequently loss-making, airline. Today airline ownership of global CRSs is far less common and most of the market distorting problems which emerged in the 1980s and 1990s have disappeared, although airlines still complain about CRS prices and profitability.

The CRS rules developed in the US and Europe were very similar in most ways, but there was one significant difference which resulted in a major trans-Atlantic dispute. The European rules for the way in which connecting services were displayed on the travel agent's computer screen were far more prescriptive than their US counterparts, following complaints by European carriers that the US rules permitted too high a level of priority to online (including codeshare) connections. The result, it was claimed, was discrimination against non-US airlines, which were not allowed to operate connecting US domestic services in their own right. For a European carrier to even enter into a codeshare arrangement to improve access to US cities behind the international gateways, it had to reach an agreement with a US airline which was often a competitor for trans-Atlantic passengers. The dispute lasted for some time, including several rounds of inter-government negotiations, and was never fully resolved. It reflected an underlying problem for non-US airlines: the difficulty in gaining access to the huge US domestic market in the absence of cabotage rights or the ability to acquire majority shareholdings in US carriers. This is an issue which has significantly affected international air services negotiations over many years, and governments are still some way from solving it, as we shall see in a later chapter.

The European Union Aviation Safety Agency (EASA). To a substantial extent, EASA has taken over most of the air safety policy formulation tasks previously performed by national regulators within the EU. It covers all aspects of aviation safety, such as airworthiness, operations, personnel licensing, aerodromes and air traffic control management, although the actual implementation of EASA rules is largely left to national authorities. There had been extensive co-operation between European safety agencies since the Second World War, led by the UK and France as the largest aircraft and engine manufacturers. This resulted in the creation of the Joint Airworthiness Authorities (JAA), beginning in the 1970s but more formally established in 1990. The JAA has been described as a pragmatic approach to achieving pan-European regulation, supported by most of the European aviation industry despite having a number of acknowledged shortcomings.

One of those shortcomings, which limited the JAA's ability to operate effectively, was its lack of legal authority. The extent to which it was able to harmonise standards across Europe was limited, with the result that its efficiency was reduced and the industry's compliance costs were increased. One expert group complained that "the JAA was frustrated by national habits, disparate languages and different adoption/implementation rules."[19] Pressure grew for the creation of an EU safety body with more powers and backed by Community law. This was achieved with the establishment of EASA in 2002, under Regulation 1592, initially empowered to develop and manage common EU rules for airworthiness and certification and for the technical maintenance of aerospace products, including aircraft, but subsequently extended to encompass all other aviation safety requirements.

There was a certain irony in the fact that despite its strong support for greater EU involvement in the regulation of European air services in general, the UK (and especially the Civil Aviation Authority) was initially reluctant to give up its sovereignty over aviation safety. For example, a 2006 report by an influential UK House of Commons Committee, chaired by an anti-EU politician, spoke of a

> significant challenge to the integrity of aviation safety within the UK… [EASA] brought into the certification and approval system a range of additional bureaucratic steps which meant that the improvement of safety regulations had to be slowed as compared to the system operated under the Joint Airworthiness Authorities, and that operations which had been completed by the CAA in days sometimes took EASA months, thereby imposing significant problems on industry.[20]

There may well have been some merit in these criticisms during the early days of EASA's existence, but they mainly reflected teething problems as the new organisation created a new management structure and recruited its own staff, rather than any fundamental difficulties. Eventually, EASA settled down and today there is broad agreement that not only does it operate relatively well, but it has also achieved significant cost savings for the industry compared to the previous JAA approach. EASA is now recognised, along with the US Federal Aviation Authority (FAA), as one of the two pre-eminent aviation safety regulators in the world. Most countries, for example, choose to apply either EASA or FAA safety rules. EASA is formally an agency of the EU, but unlike most such agencies, it is funded mainly by the companies it regulates. Some 26% of its budget is financed from central EU funds (2016); 8% of its income comes from other contributions such as third country charges and 66% from the aviation industry. It is reasonable to conclude that EASA has been a success, an example of EU co-operation in the regulation of aviation safety which has benefitted all stakeholders and that to achieve its objectives fully it required the backing of EU legislation. However, the withdrawal of the UK from the EU and EASA may have weakened Europe's overall safety regulatory regime. The UK, previously the largest contributor to EASA in terms of manpower and funding, has refused to participate in the organisation even as an Associate Member, despite support for such an approach from most of its own industry. Instead, the UK CAA has had to re-establish its old, independent regulatory regime, although it seems unlikely that this will differ significantly from the broader European approach.

Airport Slots. The definition of an airport slot, under EU legislation, is permission "to use the full range of airport infrastructure (runway, terminal, apron, gates, etc.) necessary to operate an air service at an airport on a specific date and time for the purpose of landing or take-off." There is a need to allocate landing and take-off slots at an airport only where capacity is in short supply, either because of the airport's success and growth or because of a failure to provide new infrastructure, or both. In the aviation industry's early years, slots were made available on a first come, first served basis, with no need for intervention by a regulator or the airport owner, and this is still the case at most airports today. However, as demand for air travel has grown and as building new airport capacity has become more difficult, particularly because of environmental concerns, many airports have experienced congestion and been unable to meet demand in full, especially at peak periods. Attention is usually focused on runway usage, but problems can also arise in relation to terminal capacity and gates.

It fell to IATA, the global airline trade body, to produce rules governing airport slot allocation, known as the Worldwide Slot Guidelines (WSG), which grew out of IATA's role in coordinating schedules. (IATA's Scheduling Procedures Guide was first issued in 1976. It is now produced in association with the Airports Council International and the Worldwide Airport Coordination Group.) The WSG are voluntary rules, widely accepted throughout the world, but with some notable exceptions, for example among most US airports. Airports are divided into three 'Levels,' with the most congested categorised as Level 3 and the least congested as Level 1. Globally in the summer of 2019, there were 141 Level 2 airports and 204 Level 3. Despite their widespread acceptance, the WSG suffered, like the JAA, from the lack of legal backing in many countries. As a result, the EU introduced its own legislation (Regulation 95) in 1993, subsequently amended in 2002 (Regulation 894) and in 2004 (Regulation 793), applicable throughout the European Economic Area. The original proposal by the Commission for an EU Slot Allocation Regulation was resisted by many Member States, who preferred to rely on the IATA rules. It was only when the Commission threatened to use EU competition legislation to achieve its objective that the EU Council reluctantly gave way, but even then it insisted that any EU slot rules should be negotiated initially through ECAC, where other stakeholders could more easily influence the outcome. It may not be surprising, therefore, that the EU Regulation which eventually emerged was based closely on IATA's WSG. However, it did introduce some innovative elements, particularly in relation to the priority given to new entrant airlines in order to encourage increased competition, which were later incorporated into the IATA Guidelines.

Airport slots are allocated twice each year, for the summer and winter seasons, primarily at two major conferences administered by IATA. Central to the IATA and EU rules is the concept of *'grandfather rights.'* While it has proved impossible to achieve a consensus view on who actually owns an airport slot, an airline is permitted to retain in perpetuity those slots allocated to it provided that it uses them for at least 80% of the time each season. Failure to meet this criterion, other than in exceptional circumstances, results in the relevant slots being returned to the 'pool' and re-allocated to other airlines. The slot pool is made up of such returned slots, plus those no longer needed and any new slots which might have been created, for example by means of improved ATC efficiency. Each season, 50% of the pool is offered first to new entry carriers at the airport. Any slots not taken up through this mechanism, plus the other 50% in the pool, are then allocated according to objective rules designed to ensure fairness among applicant carriers and administered by an independent body.

Slots at congested airports have a value, despite the fact that airlines do not pay for them when allocated from the pool, but there has been strong resistance in many countries to their sale. Most focus has been on so-called '*secondary trading,*' or the sale of slots already in the possession of a carrier. (In fact, the process is to swap a valuable slot for a less valuable one, with the transaction accompanied by a payment from one party to another, but in practice, this is little more than a subterfuge. The reality is that the slots are sold by one airline to another.) '*Primary trading,*' on the other hand, is the sale of new slots which have yet to be allocated. In 1999, a UK court found that secondary trading was legal under the EU Regulation. Although the EU Commission expressed its disagreement with this decision, it chose not to challenge it and the case remains the only guidance on the legality of slot sales in Europe. Secondary trading is now extensively practised in the UK, but less so elsewhere. The value of a slot depends on the demand for it and will be highest at the most congested airports during peak periods. At super-congested Heathrow Airport, for example, prices have been particularly high. In 2016, when 224 Heathrow slots were traded, compared with just 22 released from the pool, Oman Air set a new record by paying US$75 million for a pair of slots. The following year SAS sold a pair at the same airport also for US$75 million.[21]

Several studies of the EU Slot Allocation Regulation and the IATA WSG have concluded that while, on the whole, they work well, there may nevertheless be room for improvement. Airlines, however, are overwhelmingly resistant to significant change, partly because of the complexity of the whole process and partly because of the risk, or even likelihood, that the established carriers would lose out in any EU-driven reform, which would almost certainly focus on ways of increasing competition. One of the criticisms of the current system is that grandfather rights help to cement in place the established structure of the industry, making it more difficult for new carriers to enter the market. The allocation of 50% of pool slots to new entrants was intended to address this problem, but such an approach only works where the pool has a significant number of slots to distribute. At airports such as Heathrow this has clearly not been the case for some time. The system also incentivises airlines to hoard slots, resulting in a less efficient use of scarce resources. It is probably fair to say that the Commission has struggled to devise an allocation system which works for everyone, serving the interests of incumbent carriers and at the same time encouraging new entrants and increased competition. Various radical reforms were proposed at one stage, but the debate was overtaken by the crisis which followed the terrorist attack of 11 September 2001.[22] Since then the argument has resumed, but with little sign of a consensus emerging.

The EU Regulation and IATA's WSG are essentially designed to deal with the regular transfer of slots in relatively small packages. However, particular problems are created when a substantial number of new slots become available in a short period of time and where demand is likely to exceed even the new supply. Such a situation will arise, for example, when (if) a third runway is built at Heathrow. The problem is exacerbated if, as has been the case in the UK, the regulator favours the pre-financing of the new capacity, whereby airport charges are raised to at least partly pay for the new runway even while it is being constructed and before it can be used. This means that the current users of the airport will finance much of the new capacity, of which 50% will be allocated to new entrants without charge. In other words, the incumbent carriers will be cross-subsidising their future competitors. The benefits of pre-financing include lower overall costs; the downside, partly as a result of the rules governing slot allocation, is clearly a potential distortion of the market.

Among the solutions proposed to this quandary is the auctioning of the new slots, or primary trading. This, it is argued, would ensure that scarce slots go to those carriers which value them highest and avoid the cross-subsidisation of new competitors. Some have even suggested that a proportion of all slots at a congested airport should be re-allocated periodically by means of an auction. For example, every season 10% of each airline's slots could be returned to the pool and sold to the highest bidder.[23] Such an approach appeals to many economists as a way of improving the efficiency of slot allocation and encouraging more competition. However, there remains strong political opposition, encouraged by virtually all airlines, and the chance of radical reform of the rules in the near future remains remote. Even secondary trading, as we have seen, attracts only limited support in Europe outside of the UK, despite numerous studies concluding that on balance it improves economic efficiency.

The Benefits of Liberalisation

In a major study of the liberalisation of European air transport, published in 1998, just one year after the completion of the regulatory reforms, the UK Civil Aviation Authority concluded that:

> The effects of deregulation in aviation are analogous to that of other markets. It has brought steady growth to smaller and medium-sized airlines and a consequent fall in the market share of the national carriers. In particular, there have been major advances in competition in

the domestic markets of a number of larger EU states including France, Germany, Italy and Spain. On routes where significant new entry has occurred air fares have normally fallen, often quite dramatically. This however has not been true on routes where the national airlines have kept their monopolies.[24]

Broadly speaking, that conclusion still holds today. A more recent review, for example, has concluded:

> Within the space of a few decades, highly segmented and protected national aviation markets have opened to wide-ranging and mobile regional competition, while at the same time detailed rules have increasingly worked to establish uniform standards across the region. The Community has also assumed an increasingly significant role as a collective actor on the world stage.[25]

The creation of the EU internal aviation market has seen lower fares, more services, increased competition and a reduction in the stranglehold of the State-owned national flag carriers, who have been forced to adapt in order to survive. Under pressure from the European Commission, EU Member States have been weaned off public subsidies for their airlines (at least until the COVID epidemic struck) and embarked on widespread privatisation. Above all, as in the US after deregulation, EU reform has seen the emergence of low-cost airlines with new business models. As the UK CAA noted: "The spread of low-cost, no-frills carriers has been one of the most striking developments in airline competition in Europe in the last few years, and possibly one of the more significant for the longer term."[26] The low-cost revolution, which has done so much to transform the airline industry, would not have been possible under the old regulatory regimes. We shall return to this subject in Chapter 7.

Just as in the US, not everyone agrees that the results of EU liberalisation have been of overall benefit to society.[27] However, very few would argue in favour of a return to the restrictive regulatory approach which prevailed before the creation of the internal aviation market. While it is impossible to say with certainty what would have happened in the absence of reform, there are strong grounds for concluding that liberalisation's achievements have included:

- The complete removal of national restrictions on airlines throughout the EU, and to some extent beyond.
- Lower air fares as a result of increased competition, with more routes and more services.
- The creation of an even playing field with a single set of rules, to enable all airlines to compete freely.

74   *European Liberalisation*

- The gradual removal of airline subsidies, leading to the demise of some formerly State-owned carriers.
- Extensive airline and, to a lesser extent, airport privatisation.
- The creation of the concept of a 'Community Carrier' with ownership and control broadened to EU citizens rather than the nationals of any one State.
- A single EU-wide safety regulatory regime.

On the other hand, many challenges still remained, such as:

- Liberalisation applied only to intra-European air services. Air services to third countries were a different matter and not as easy to reform.
- Air traffic control services remained mostly nation-based and subject to only limited reform.
- Increased competition and privatisation required the introduction of new forms of regulation, covering airlines, airports and ATC companies, to protect consumers and avoid anti-competitive behaviour. Achieving the right balance between regulation and liberalisation is a challenge.

We will return to these issues in subsequent chapters.

One important area where a liberalised Europe has not followed the example of a deregulated US is the extent to which airlines have consolidated, especially among the legacy flag carriers. Between the Second World War and 2001, not a single national carrier disappeared. Subsequently, some were forced out of business, mostly smaller ones, but even the bankruptcy of Sabena and Swissair in 2001 was quickly followed by the emergence of two new airlines with, as one commentator noted, 'curiously similar names.'[28] (The same was subsequently true of Alitalia.) It is clear that three airline groups, Lufthansa, Air France/KLM and IAG, dominate Europe's airport hubs and intercontinental traffic, each having incorporated several smaller carriers. Yet, as IATA has pointed out, the European airline market overall remains highly fragmented, despite liberalisation. In 2019, 348 city-pairs in Europe generated 25% of total passenger revenues, compared with 167 in North America. 80% of the seats serving these city-pairs were provided by 28 airlines in Europe, compared with just seven in North America. Despite the fact that between 2007 and 2017, 84% of total passenger growth in Europe was provided by low-cost carriers, several of whom have managed to combine route and traffic growth with financial success, there remains what IATA has called 'a long tail of struggling' European airlines. To a significant extent, this disparity between Europe and the US can be explained by the impact of the global aviation regulatory regime, as we shall see in Chapter 8.

Finally, it should also be noted that while the potential emergence of the low-cost business model attracted only limited attention in the debate leading up to the creation of the EU internal aviation market, there was concern about the future of the large IT charter sector. The new EU legislation abandoned the historic distinction between scheduled and charter; now there were only 'airlines.' In the event, the former charter carriers proved to be remarkably resilient. Certainly, the sector saw significant consolidation and a number of bankruptcies over the following years, but many charter carriers adapted their business models to match those of the new low-cost airlines. They already, of course, had unit cost levels significantly lower than the legacy airlines. This was a further example of European experience differing from that in the US, where charters had never played as important a role.

Notes

1 Hussain Kassim and Handley Stevens: *Air Transport and the European Union. Europeanization and Its Limits.* Palgrave Macmillan, London, 2010.
2 Jacques Naveau, Preface to: *European Air Law. New Skies for Europe.* Institut du Transport Aèrien, Paris, 1992.
3 Kassim and Stevens, op cit.
4 Handley Stevens: *Liberalisation of Air Transport in Europe – A Case Study in European Integration.* The European Institute, London School of Economics, 1997.
5 Ibid.
6 Ibid.
7 Dinos Kyrou: *Lobbying the European Commission, The Case of Air Transport.* Ashgate, Aldershot, 2000.
8 Stevens, op cit.
9 Erwin von den Steinen: *National Interest and International Aviation.* Kluwer Law International, the Netherlands, 2006.
10 S. Ison, L. Budd and A Timmis: 'International Comparisons of EU Regulation 261 Enforcement.' Briefing note prepared for the UK Department of Transport. Undated.
11 Ibid.
12 Michael E. Levine: 'Airline competition in deregulated markets: Theory, firm strategy, and public policy.' *Yale Journal of Regulation*, Vol. 4(2), Spring 1986, pp. 393–494.
13 Geoffrey H. Lipman: 'The CRS Revolution – Promise and Pitfall.' Michael E. Levine: 'Airline Competition in Deregulated Markets.' Paper presented to the Air Transport Symposium, Monash University, Melbourne, Australia, August 1987.
14 Dr Robert Simpson, Director, MIT Flight Transportation Laboratory, quoted in 'Global Distribution Systems: Emerging Trends and Strategic Issues.' SRI International, 1989.
15 Barry Humphreys: 'The CRSs.' Institut du Transport Aèrien, Paris, 1990. See also Barry Humphreys: 'New Developments in CRSs.' Institut du Transport Aèrien, Paris 1994, and Barry Humphreys: 'Do Airlines Still Need To Own CRSs.' Avmark Aviation Economist, April 1994.
16 Humphreys (1990), op cit.
17 Fariba Alamdari and Keith Mason: 'The future of airline distribution.' *The Journal of Air Transport Management*, Vol. 12(3), May 2006, pp. 122–134.
18 Levine, op cit.
19 Royal Aeronautical Society: *Civil Aviation Regulation.* Royal Aeronautical Society, London, 2017.
20 UK House of Commons Transport Committee: *The Work of the Civil Aviation Authority.* UK House of Commons Transport Committee, London, 2006.

21 UK House of Commons Library: *Airport Slots. Research Briefing.* UK House of Commons Library, London, 2017.
22 Kassim and Stevens, op cit.
23 Barry Humphreys: 'Slot allocation; a radical solution.' In Keith Boyfield (ed.): *A Market in Airport Slots.* The Institute of Economic Affairs, London, 2003, pp. 94–106.
24 UK Civil Aviation Authority: 'The Single European Aviation Market: The First Five Years.' CAP 685, London, 1998.
25 Erwin von den Steinen, op cit.
26 UK Civil Aviation Authority, op cit.
27 See, for example, Peter Reed: *Railtracks in the Sky: New Labour, Air Transport Deregulation and the Competitive Market.* Spokesman, Nottingham, 2002.
28 Martin Staniland: "Surviving the Single Market: The dilemmas and strategies of 'small country' airlines." University of Pittsburgh, Graduate School of Public and International Affairs, Working Paper No. 4, February 2003.

Addendum 1
Membership of the European Union

1957	–	The Treaty of Rome created the European Economic Community
1958	–	Belgium, France, Italy, Luxembourg, the Netherlands and West Germany join
1973	–	Denmark, Ireland and the UK join
1981	–	Greece joins
1986	–	Portugal and Spain join
1995	–	Austria, Finland and Sweden join
2004	–	Cyprus, the Czech Republic, Estonia, Hungary, Latvia, Lithuania, Malta, Poland, Slovakia and Slovenia join
2007	–	Bulgaria and Romania join
2013	–	Croatia joins
2019	–	The UK leaves.

Addendum 2
EU Regulations and Directives

1. Air Transport and Market Issue.
   1A. Internal Market

   - Licensing of air carriers (Reg. (EC) No. 1008/2008)
   - Access for Community air carriers to intra-Community routes (Reg. (EC) No. 1008/2008)
   - Fares and Rates for air services (Reg. (EC) No. 1008/2008)
   - Insurance requirements for air carriers and aircraft operators (Reg. (EC) No. 785/2004)
   - Code of conduct for computerised reservation systems (Reg. (EC) No. 80/2009)
   - Statistical returns (Reg. (EC) No. 437/2003)
   - Implementing rules of statistical returns regulation (Reg. (EC) No. 1358/2003)

   1B. Relationship with Third Countries.
   - Air services agreements (Reg. (EC) No. 847/2004)
   - Protection against subsidisation (Reg. (EC) No. 868/2004)

2. Passenger Rights.
   - Air carrier liability (Reg. (EC) No. 889.2002)
   - Denied boarding cancellation or long delay of flight (Reg. (EC) No. 261/2004)
   - Rights of disabled persons Reg. (EC) No. 1107/2006)

3. Safety
   - Harmonisation Reg. (EC) No. 216/2008
   - Investigation of civil aviation accidents and incidents Directive 94/56/EC
   - Common rules – EASA establishment Reg. (EC) No. 216/2008
   - Occurrence reporting in civil aviation Directive 2003/42/EC
   - Rules for the airworthiness Com. Reg. (EC) No. 1702/2003
   - Continuing airworthiness Com Reg. (EC) No. 2042/2003
   - Safety of third country aircraft using Community airport Reg. (EC) No. 216/2008
   - Board of appeal of the EASA Reg. (EC) No. 216/2008
   - Community list of air carrier subject to an operating ban Reg. (EC) No. 2111/2005
   - Implementing rules for the banned air carrier list Reg. (EC) No. 473/2006

- Fees and charges levied by EASA   Reg. (EC) No. 593/2007
- EASA working methods for standardisation   Reg. (EC) No. 736/2006
- Collection and exchange of information on the safety of aircraft   Reg. (EC) No. 768/2006
- Common rules – EASA establishment   Reg. (EC) No. 216/2008
- List of banned air carrier   Reg. (EC) No. 1043/2007

4. Security
   - Common basic standards on aviation security   Reg. (EC) No. 820/2008
   - National civil aviation security quality control programmes   Reg. (EC) No. 1217/2003
   - Security restricted areas at airports   Reg. (EC) No. 1138/2004
   - Procedures for conducting inspections in the civil aviation security   Reg. (EC) No. 1486/2003
   - Civil aviation security   Reg. (EC) No. 300/2008

5. Environmental Protection
   - Limitation of noise   Directive 89/629/EC
   - Operation of aeroplanes covered by Part!!, Chap. 3 Vol 1 of Annex 16   Directive 2006/93/EC
   - Introduction of noise-related Restrictions   Directive 2002/30/EC
   - Management of environmental noise   Directive 2002/49/EC

6. Airport
   - Allocation of slots   Reg. (EC) No. 95/93
   - Ground handling   Directive 96/67/EC

7. Air Traffic Management
   - Framework for the creation of the Single European Sky   Reg. (EC) No. 549/2004
   - Provision of air navigation services in the SES   Reg. (EC) No. 550/2004
   - Organisation and use of the airspace in the SES   Reg. (EC) No. 551/2004
   - Interoperability of the European ATM network   Reg. (EC) No. 552/2004
   - Requirements for the provision of air navigation services   Reg. (EC) No. 2096/2005
   - Rules for the flexible use of airspace   Reg. (EC) No. 2150/2005
   - Air traffic controller licence   Directive 2006/23/EC
   - Airspace classification and access of flights   Reg. (EC) No. 730/2006
   - Automatic systems for the exchange of flight data   Reg. (EC) No. 1032/2006
   - Procedures for flight plans in the preflight phase of the SES   Reg. (EC) No. 1033/2006
   - Common charging scheme for air navigation services   Reg. (EC) No. 1794/2006
   - Establishment of a joint undertaking to develop SESAR   Reg. (EC) No. 219/2007
   - Requirement for the application of a flight message transfer protocol   Reg. (EC) No. 633/2007
   - Safety oversight in air traffic management   Reg. (EC) No. 1315/2007

80 *European Liberalisation*

8. Personnel and Social Issues
   - Mutual acceptance of personnel licences   Reg. (EC) No. 216/2008

9. Competition Rules

9A. Antitrust Practices Law
   - Implementation of the rules on competition   Reg. (EC) No. 1/2003
   - Application of Art. 85-3 in the air transport sector   Reg. (EC) No. 487/2009

9B. Economic Concentration Law
   - Control of concentration   Reg. (EC) No. 802/2004

9C. State Aids
   - Transparency of financial relations   Directive 2006/111/EC

6 Open Skies

Introduction

We have seen how the deregulation of US domestic air services destabilised the aviation industry, and not only in the US. The philosophical underpinnings of deregulation/liberalisation soon spread around the world, not least in Europe where multiple bilateral agreements were swept away to be replaced by a single, fully liberalised domestic market. However, even in Europe, the old bilateral restrictions on aviation relations with third countries remained in place, and the same was true for every other country. Initially, deregulation/liberalisation was treated essentially as a domestic issue and was, of course, far from universally pursued. International reform was slower to emerge, but when it did, it was again the US which took the lead, formulating what came to be known as *'open skies.'* The export of this policy globally has been one of the key characteristics of international aviation regulation for the past 40 years, although several significant countries are yet to be persuaded to support it fully. Indeed, as we shall see in a later chapter, there is some evidence that more recently the process may be going into reverse.

United States

The transformation of US international aviation policy, from protectionism to the promotion of a liberal open skies regime, was a gradual, evolutionary process spread over many years. While broadly heading in a more liberal direction, initially it frequently faced a strong domestic political challenge. Nevertheless, it eventually proved to be a major success. The timeline outlined below shows the main developments, from the negotiation of the Bermuda 2 agreement and the deregulation of US domestic air services to what some might regard as the greatest success of US external aviation policy, the negotiation of an open skies ASA with the EU.

DOI: 10.4324/9780429448973-6

1976	–	US International Air Transportation Policy
1977	–	Bermuda 2
1978	–	US domestic deregulation
1978	–	Carter administration policy statement
1979	–	International Air Transportation Competition Act
1990/91	–	Cities Program
1992	–	US–Netherlands ASA
1995	–	Baliles Commission Report
1995	–	Clinton administration open skies policy
2007	–	EU–US Agreement Stage 1
2010	–	EU–US Agreement Stage 2

Chapter 3 explained how the renegotiation of the UK/US Bermuda agreement was strongly criticised within the US. The feeling that the US had given away far too much to the UK was reinforced by the relatively poor performance of US airlines compared with their UK competitors on trans-Atlantic routes. In fact, the decline in the US share of the UK–US market was a continuation of a trend visible before the negotiation of Bermuda 2 (something the UK chose to ignore at the time) and was far from a reflection of the new, more restrictive ASA. The US' share, which had stood at 70% in 1971, had fallen to 61% by 1977 when Bermuda 2 was signed and hovered around the 50% level by the late-1980s; by 2007, at the time of the EU/US agreement, it had fallen to 42%.[1] From 1977, a key objective of US international aviation policy became the replacement of Bermuda 2 with an agreement granting increased access for US airlines to the UK market, and especially to Heathrow Airport. To a large extent, the same was true of the Japanese market, where the Government was reluctant to grant further market access to US carriers, feeling that the 1952 Bermuda 1-type ASA had been imposed on them in the immediate post-war period and was biased in favour of the US. London and Tokyo were seen not only as substantial markets in their own rights, but also as gateways to large hinterlands, Europe in the case of London and Asia in the case of Tokyo.

Just as the reaction to the negotiation of Bermuda 2 may have influenced the debate on the deregulation of domestic air services, deregulation itself similarly impacted the competitive position of US airlines internationally and eventually affected US external aviation policy. Traditionally, most traffic to the US flowed over New York on the East coast and Los Angeles in the West, even if destined for points behind these initial cities, as much of it was. TWA and especially Pan Am were the overwhelmingly dominant US flag carriers. That changed with deregulation. New competitors emerged, each wanting to develop international services from their own hub airports and each with far stronger domestic networks than Pan Am and, to a lesser extent, TWA. As a result, the flow of traffic changed, with reductions in the relative positions of the previously dominant gateways. US carriers were far more able to serve the large domestic hinterland market than their foreign competitors, who were prevented from operating beyond their US gateways. To at least partly counter this disadvantage and gain access to connecting feeder traffic, foreign airlines had little choice but to seek commercial arrangements with US carriers, which were often their direct or indirect competitors on North Atlantic routes. This change in the competitive balance inevitably affected international air services negotiations with the US.

The US is no different from other countries in pursuing its own national interests in negotiating ASAs. Equally, however, US mercantilism manifested itself differently from that experienced in most other countries, which tended to focus more on the interests of a single or a very small number of national carriers. In the post-deregulation world, the US market was initially characterised by a significant number of major airlines seeking international market access. It is not surprising that such airlines, in pursuing their own interests, did not always promote the same international policy. This created both a problem and an opportunity for the US Government. It was a problem because usually not all US carriers' demands could be satisfied and inevitably the policy adopted frequently attracted considerable criticism from those not favoured. It was an opportunity because the US was able to pursue policies of broader benefit to its economy than just representing the interests of individual airlines, while still protecting the overall interests of its airline sector. This was certainly a different approach to that found in most other countries at this time, although it is doubtful that in the eyes of many foreign observers it made the US any less protectionist.

Broadly, the US' initial approach to international aviation negotiations was to seek to restrict the access of foreign airlines to the US market while maximising the opportunities available for its own carriers. The International Air Transportation Policy statement, issued in 1976 under President Ford, highlighted this more traditional approach, and in particular the close association of government and industry interests. The statement recognised "the fundamental importance of maintaining a scheduled US flag system" and argued that

> air transport interests are best assured for Americans by the presence of a strong, viable, privately owned US flag international air fleet.... US carrier participation on [major international trunk routes] is essential to the maintenance of a US flag system.

Competition between US airlines was not encouraged if it threatened the viability of existing services. Restrictions on sixth freedom operations by foreign carriers were also advocated, although there was no mention of the competitive advantage enjoyed by US airlines in promoting domestic feeder services. The statement was issued just two years before domestic US air services were deregulated.

The size of the US market, combined with US negotiating power, often meant that ASAs were far from balanced, at least from the perspective of the foreign partner involved. As Lobbenberg noted, writing in 1994 but applicable particularly to an earlier period:

> US aviation policy has been designed to support the US airline industry and is no less mercantilist than the policy of the various European states. Indeed, the USA has not shied away from negotiating deals that were clearly unbalanced to the advantage of their carriers.[2]

Most countries had a single principal point of access for international air services: London in the UK, Paris in France, Tokyo in Japan, Sydney in Australia, etc. The US, on the other hand, had numerous large cities which many foreign airlines were keen to serve directly. The evolution of several domestic hub airports into international hubs usually required the US to grant at least some additional access to its market, but even this was often resisted by domestic interests. Certainly, the unilateral grant of rights to foreign airlines was rare. The potential consumer benefits of increased air service barely featured in the debate, other than occasionally as lip service.

Slowly US policy began to change. Following his success in promoting the deregulation of domestic air services, Fred Kahn, Chairman of the Civil Aeronautics Board, added his voice in support of the trading of 'opportunities' rather than 'restrictions' in bilateral ASAs. The focus on opportunities had actually first been raised in a letter sent by President Carter to the Secretary of Transportation in 1977,[3] but its repetition by Kahn served to reinforce the connection between domestic deregulation and the evolution of US external aviation policy. In 1978, the Carter administration formalised the new approach when it issued a 'Statement of International Aviation Policy' designed to 'encourage vigorous competition.' New US gateways were offered, mainly in return for additional fifth freedom rights for US carriers and more liberal tariff and capacity control.[4] In line with the recommendations of Kahn and others, the new policy undertook to

> work to achieve a system of international transportation that places its principal reliance on actual and potential competition to determine the variety, quality and price of aviation service. An essential means for carrying out our international air transport policy will be to allow greater competitive opportunities for US and foreign airlines and to provide new low-cost transportation options for travellers and shippers.[5]

There is no doubt that on paper at least, this represented a significant change of direction in US international aviation policy. Perhaps not surprisingly, therefore, it attracted considerable opposition from many incumbent airlines, who feared in particular that the policy would lead to the trading of 'hard' traffic rights for 'soft' rights of much less value to them. Consequently, and after an intense lobbying campaign by the industry, Congress passed the International Air Transportation Competition Act in 1979, still superficially leaning towards a more liberal approach, but also requiring US negotiators to seek "the strengthening of the competitive position of the United States air carriers to at least assure equality with foreign air carriers." Foreign airlines could be offered increased access to the US market "if exchanged for benefits of similar magnitude for the United States carriers or the travelling public with permanent linkage between rights granted and rights given away."[6] The changes may not have been substantial, but they were by no means insignificant and served to water down the previous approach.

While several relatively liberal bilateral agreements had been negotiated, with the Netherlands, Belgium and Israel for example, US negotiators were forced to proceed far more cautiously than many had initially hoped. If the new policy represented a partial reversal, it also reflected a recognition of the strengths of the US aviation industry in the post-deregulation era. Nevertheless, it was widely seen as a success, with the number of international routes increasing significantly. In 1980, for example, 17 US gateways had non-stop service to Europe; by 1990 that number had increased to 25, and similar growth was seen in the Asia/Pacific and Latin America markets. However, as one commentator noted: "The policy had been a success – at least as far as it went. But it didn't go far enough."[7] The problem was that for those partner countries with which the US had negotiated more liberal ASAs, US airlines had gained sufficient market access for their needs, which was far from the case for many foreign carriers. At the same time, several US cities found themselves without the international service which they believed they deserved.

As a result, and despite the opposition of many US airlines, in 1990 the US launched a new policy, the so-called 'Cities Program.' Essentially, this granted access to a US gateway not currently available under the relevant ASA, for a carrier from a country with a liberal bilateral agreement with the US, provided no US airline wanted to serve the route. The policy was expanded modestly in 1991, following further lobbying by US airports, although oddly it continued to omit all-freight services. The Cities Program in itself may have had only a modest overall impact, but it has come to be seen as a precursor to the development of the far more significant policy, open skies The promotion of this new approach around the world was to be the dominant feature of US external aviation policy over the next 20 years and beyond. At the same time, the US continued to seek increased access to London's Heathrow Airport, and to a lesser extent Tokyo's Narita Airport. On both counts, open skies and increased access to Heathrow and Narita, success was by no means guaranteed, but was eventually attained.

There is little doubt that US international aviation policy became more aggressive during this period. One particular example, outlined in Chapter 2, was the publication by the CAB of a Show Cause Order to remove antitrust immunity for IATA tariff co-ordination on routes to and from the US. The move was regarded with consternation elsewhere, and especially in Europe where the application of any form of competition policy to air transport was still anathema for most States. As Shane has noted, it was immediately denounced everywhere as "an egregious example of US unilateralism that threatened the essential framework for a seamlessly connected and convenient international aviation system."[8] The result was the formation of a united front among a majority of European countries to resist the proposal. Combined with a vigorous lobbying campaign by IATA, the US soon began to back-pedal, albeit only after lengthy negotiations with the Member States of the European Civil Aviation Conference.

The second sign of a more aggressive US approach to international aviation policy was the so-called 'encirclement strategy,' also known as the 'beachhead' or 'diversionary' policy. Again, the CAB took the lead in proposing the new approach, which was firmly aimed at those larger countries such as the UK and Japan which had proved immune to US calls for faster liberalisation. (The UK, of course, argued that it was simply reacting to the US' refusal to open up its domestic market to foreign competition, and Japan complained about the unbalance of its prevailing ASA with the US.) The plan was to persuade countries geographically adjacent to the UK and Japan to sign more liberal ASAs by offering their airlines additional access to the US market. The growth in competitive pressure would result in lower fares, so the argument went, which would divert traffic from the UK and Japan and eventually force these two States to agree to increased market access for US carriers. The policy was an almost complete failure and had no discernible impact on traffic growth or market shares. It ignored in particular the reasons why the UK and Japan were such important markets, notably the strength of the underlying demand for travel to and from the US. Neither the UK nor Japan showed any real sign of conceding to US demands as a result of being encircled by countries with more liberal ASAs with the US.

The 1990s saw US airlines incur large financial losses and strengthen their pursuit of less international liberalisation. This was one of the reasons for the establishment by the new Clinton administration of a 'Commission to Ensure a Strong Competitive Airline Industry' in 1993, the Baliles Commission. (Airline economic problems were not restricted to the US. In the same year, the European Commission similarly appointed a Comité des Sages for Air Transport, which reported in early 1994.) The Baliles report finally emerged in 1995, delaying the need for difficult political decisions, and was conveniently ambivalent with respect to international aviation policy. It argued in favour of the negotiation of liberal multilateral agreements, but also noted:

> Because of our country's geographical size and population, bilateral agreements can result in the US granting foreign carriers greater access to the immense and diverse US air travel market without corresponding competitive opportunities for US carriers... A major criterion for measuring the success of our air transportation system should be our ability to use air travel as a competitive advantage in a global economy.[9]

Despite the Commission's fence-sitting, the Clinton administration pressed ahead with the publication of a new aviation policy statement which, while building on the policy which had been emerging during President Bush's final years in office, was still far more adventurous than anything that had gone before. It included a 'Plan of Action,' the first step of which was to

> extend invitations to enter into open aviation agreements with a group of countries that share our vision of liberalization and offer important flow traffic potential for our carriers even though they may have limited Third and Fourth Freedom traffic potential.

As Wesveen has noted, the Bush/Carter initiative was a 'giant step forward' in government thinking because it fundamentally rejected the notion that international aviation markets between countries must be 'comparable' or 'equivalent' in size before the US was willing to contemplate greater opportunities for foreign airlines. (The Cities Program had, of course, already started modestly along such a path, and Fred Kahn had similarly been supportive.) The principles embodied in the new policy were common in most other trade negotiations, but had rarely been part of previous aviation bilaterals.[10]

The 1995 Policy Statement has attracted particular attention because, apart from the Cities Program, it was the first formal statement of US external aviation policy since 1978. It might be viewed as part of an evolutionary process, building on much that had gone before, but nevertheless the principles on which it was based differed substantially from those behind the 1978 statement. It marked a major change in the US aviation industry, reflecting growing traffic levels, the expansion of US carriers internationally, the development of hub airports and the evolution of alliances. The statement emphasised that economic value in ASA negotiations would be viewed "more broadly than we have in the past, in terms of both direct and indirect access ..." Nevertheless, the interests of the US industry were hardly forgotten. Noting that US carriers were more efficient than their foreign competitors and were enjoying increased profitability, the statement noted that they were "well positioned to be primary participants in all aspects of the future global marketplace." Mention was made as well of the 'strategic value' of negotiating liberal agreements with smaller countries in order to put pressure on neighbouring States to follow suit and of the intention to seek reform, "consistent with US economic and security interests," of US airline foreign investment arrangements. The so-called 'encirclement strategy' was not a success, as already noted, while domestic political opposition put a stop to any reform of the airline ownership legislation.

The agreement with The Netherlands in 1992 is widely seen as the first success of the US open skies policy, although most progress only happened from 1995. Essentially open skies, as pursued by the US, represented the full deregulation of international markets, with two principal caveats: no cabotage and no reform of airline ownership and control rules. The US State

Department calls such agreements "pro-consumer, pro-competition and pro-growth," which is fair to the extent that they represent a clear move from the producer-driven regulatory policy of the first post-Chicago decades to a more consumer-led approach. In a document issued in 1992, the Department of Transportation (DOT) described the open skies policy as "a further progression along the path toward a truly open environment for international aviation services, an environment in which all the participants – communities, travellers, shippers, and providers – will reap genuine benefits."[11] Its definition of an open skies agreement went far beyond just market access and pricing, as illustrated in Table 6.1.

Table 6.1 Key Elements of US Open Skies Policy

- Open entry on all routes
- Unrestricted capacity and frequency on all routes
- Unrestricted route and traffic rights, including no restrictions as to intermediate and beyond points, change of gauge, route flexibility, co-terminalisation, and the right to carry fifth freedom traffic
- Double disapproval pricing in third and fourth freedom markets, and price leadership in third country markets to the extent that the third and fourth freedom carriers in those markets have it
- Liberal charter arrangement
- Liberal cargo regime
- Conversion and remittance arrangement, with carriers able to convert earnings and remit in hard currency promptly and without restriction
- Open code sharing opportunities
- Self-handling provisions; pro-competitive provisions on commercial opportunities, user charges, fair competition and international rights
- Explicit commitment for non-discriminatory operation of and access for computer reservation systems.

Source: US DOT, 1992.

It would be wrong to assume that producer (and labour) interests are not still an influential factor in US aviation policy, but their influence has certainly declined, as it has in many other countries. The US open skies initiative has been a remarkable success. From the first agreement signed with the Netherlands in 1992, the US today has 130 such bilaterals (as of July 2020, see Table 6.2), although admittedly some are with countries very unlikely to ever see direct air services to the US. The Netherlands agreement offered no benefits of any real value to US airlines, other than the ability to apply for anti-trust immunity for an alliance with a competitor, since they already had full access to the Dutch market. It did, however, offer new rights of access to US gateways for Dutch carriers, and even more importantly was probably the first clear indication of consumer interests playing a key, if not exclusive, role in ASA negotiations.

Many countries, particularly smaller ones, were only too pleased to agree open skies ASAs with the US. Others, however, needed more persuading, and a useful incentive in this respect was the grant of anti-trust immunity for airline alliances. As we shall see in Chapter 8, in the absence of reform of the airline ownership and control rules, multilateral airline alliances have become

Table 6.2 US Open Sky Air Services Agreements, July 2020

Albania	Germany	Pakistan
Armenia	Ghana	Panama
Aruba	Greece	Paraguay
Australia	Grenada	Peru
Austria	Guatemala	Poland
Azerbaijan	Guinea	Portugal
Bahamas (The)	Guyana	Qatar
Bahrain	Haiti	Republic of the Congo
Bangladesh	Honduras	Romania
Barbados	Hungary	Rwanda
Belarus	Iceland	Saba
Belgium	India	Saint Kitts and Nevis
Belize	Indonesia	Saint Vincent and the Grenadines
Bonaire	Ireland	Saudi Arabia
Bosnia/Herzegovina	Israel	Senegal
Botswana	Italy	Serbia
Brazil	Jamaica	Seychelles
Brunei	Japan	Sierra Leone
Bulgaria	Jordan	Singapore
Burkina Faso	Kazakhstan	Sint Eustatius
Burundi	Kenya	Sint Maarten
Cameroon	Korea	Slovakia
Canada	Kuwait	Slovenia
Cape Verde	Laos	Spain
Chad	Latvia	Sri Lanka
Chile	Liberia	Suriname
Colombia	Lithuania	Sweden
Cook Islands	Luxembourg	Switzerland
Costa Rica	Macedonia	Taiwan
Cote d'Ivoire	Madagascar	Tanzania
Croatia	Malaysia	Thailand
Curacao	Maldives	Togo
Cyprus	Mali	Tonga
Czech Republic	Malta	Trinidad and Tobago
Denmark	Montenegro	Turkey
El Salvador	Morocco	Uganda
Equatorial Guinea	Namibia	Ukraine
Estonia	Netherlands	United Arab Emirates
Ethiopia	New Zealand	United Kingdom
Finland	Nicaragua	Uruguay
France	Nigeria	Uzbekistan
Gabon	Norway	Yemen
Gambia	Oman	Zambia
Georgia		

Cargo Only Open Skies
Vietnam

an important part of the international aviation industry. Initially, smaller bilateral alliances were pursued, especially as a way of gaining additional access to the large US domestic market in the post-deregulation era. To fully integrate pricing and scheduling, such co-operative agreements required immunity from the strict US competition laws. (Only later would this also be true in Europe and elsewhere.) Responsibility for granting US anti-trust immunity normally lies with the Department of Justice (DOJ), but not for international air services, where the DOT has the final say. The DOT also has prime responsibility, of course, for US international aviation policy, leading some to claim that there is a clear conflict of interest if an ASA and anti-trust immunity are negotiated at the same time. The argument is that immunity to collude in the provision of international air services has been 'sold' far too cheaply, in terms of its competitive impact, in return for the political objective of an open skies regime. As von den Steinen has noted: "It is beyond question ... that the single biggest factor in winning acceptance for Open Skies was the US Government's final willingness to 'immunize' alliances among carriers of different nationalities that are otherwise prevented from merging."[12]

The DOT naturally sees matters differently, insisting that due consideration is given to the pro- and anti-competitive aspects of every application. Freedom of market access in particular, it argues, is a core requirement to ensure the survival of competition. However, it is certainly the case that the DOJ has been more critical of airline alliances from a competitive perspective than the DOT has. The DOJ's Gillespie and Richards, for example, have noted that "in the North Atlantic market the effect of these immunization decisions has been to significantly reduce competition. Air fares are significantly higher in routes with fewer independent non-stop competitors."[13] A number of academic studies have come to a similar conclusion. The 2001 decision by France to sign an open skies ASA with the US would seem to lend some credence to the close connection between the award of additional market access to US carriers and the grant of anti-trust immunity for an airline alliance. Not only had France traditionally been resistant to liberalisation, whether bilaterally or regionally within Europe, but it was also particularly concerned during the early 1990s about increased services by US airlines, given that its ASA with the US was a Bermuda 1 type which provided only for *post hoc* review of capacity. In 1992, France served notice to terminate its bilateral ASA with the US, and for several years thereafter flights between the two countries operated on a purely reciprocal basis without any formal agreement. Yet in 2001, France and the US signed an open skies ASA, and shortly thereafter Air France received approval to enter into an alliance with a US competitor.

One of the principal arguments of this book is that overall a more liberal approach to the regulation of international air services is of benefit to the industry, consumers and governments. There is no shortage of studies providing evidence to support this hypothesis. (Morrison and de Wit, for example, list several.) However, it is also possible to over-simplify the potential gains. Not all stakeholders benefit to the same extent. As Morrison and de Wit note:

> Overall, in terms of its relative market size and bargaining power the US has benefitted in most of the [open skies agreements] that it has made, however this fact does not speak to the distribution of benefits across US consumers and industry participants.[14]

Similarly, while open skies ASAs often replaced what on paper were highly restrictive agreements, it does not necessarily follow that in practice those agreements were applied in a particularly restrictive manner. Bermuda 2, for example, was the subject of considerable criticism by the US Government and airlines, and there is no doubt that access in particular to Heathrow Airport was limited. Yet the bilateral evolved significantly over the years, partly with the mutual agreement of the two signatories and partly by unilateral decisions in its implementation. By the time of the EU/US negotiations, the UK had effectively agreed to open skies on all routes to the US apart from those serving Gatwick and especially Heathrow Airports. Similarly, the UK CAA regulated tariffs with a very light touch, which meant that UK trans-Atlantic leisure fares were among the lowest in Europe. This was, of course, a factor, in undermining the US Encirclement Strategy, but it also meant that while in general open skies represented a major move towards a more liberal regulatory regime, at least some of the potential consumer benefits were achieved under the superficially far more restrictive Bermuda 2 bilateral. A similar pattern of relatively liberal application of superficially restrictive ASAs was seen in the Asia/Pacific region, although not with respect to the US/Japan ASA.

Europe

We saw in Chapter 5 how, between 1983 and 1992, the EU created a fully liberalised internal aviation market. This was certainly a major achievement, driven primarily by the European Commission and a minority of Member States, with the critical support of a court decision which confirmed that aviation was subject to the competition provisions of the Treaty of Rome like most other industries. However, for the Commission, the internal market and its numerous associated Regulations and Directives were far from the end of the matter. It was determined to extend EU-wide influence to include aviation relations with third countries, an approach which failed to find support from Member States, who saw no reason to relinquish the ability to promote their own international aviation policies. The Commission argued strongly that it was a well-established principle that the creation of an internal market within the EU meant that any negotiation with a non-EU State which might affect that market should be undertaken by the Commission, not individual Member States, accompanied by an agreed EU-wide negotiating mandate. The Commission had already claimed sole 'competency' in relation to various soft aviation rights, such as computer reservation system and slot allocation rules, which were the subject of specific EU Regulations. For hard rights involving market access for airlines, however, there was a complete stand-off between the two sides.

The solution again arrived in the form of a court decision. The Commission submitted a case to the European Court of Justice (ECJ), arguing that several Member States had entered into open skies agreements with the US which were illegal under Community law. The specific point at issue was the restriction on the ownership and control of European airlines under the bilaterals. In the case of Germany, for example, the US was required to accept the designation only of a carrier that was majority owned and controlled by German citizens, in line with the criteria used in the vast majority of ASAs around the world. The acceptance of the designation by Germany of any other airline was solely at the US' discretion. The Commission argued that this was discriminatory against non-German EU carriers. In a 2002 decision, the ECJ agreed, stating that "the eight agreements in question contain elements that deprive Community air carriers of their rights under the Treaty, the nationality clauses in the agreements being a clear violation of the right of establishment enshrined in Article 43."[15] The decision represented a fundamental challenge to the bilateral system in Europe, in that if implemented, individual EU States would no longer be negotiating solely on behalf of their own national interests. Other countries' airlines could gain from any agreement reached. From the Commission's perspective, of course, this greatly strengthened the argument in favour of EU-wide negotiations.

Unfortunately, while the ECJ might have been clear on the principle involved, its detailed decision left ample room for debate, and therefore delay, about the practicalities of implementation. In the circumstances, it was probably not surprising that what eventually emerged, after lengthy negotiation between the Commission and Member States, was what has been described as "pragmatic solutions to the many difficult political and legal questions raised by [the ECJ] judgements,"[16] or what might equally be termed a 'political fix.' In 2005, EU Transport Ministers agreed to a new EU external aviation policy with three so-called 'pillars':

- The updating of all Member State bilateral agreements with non-EU countries to ensure that any EU airline was able to operate a route available under a relevant ASA without discrimination. This required the co-operation, of course, of the third countries involved, which was not always forthcoming; nor were all Member States as enthusiastic as some others in pursuing the new policy during their negotiations with third countries.
- The extension of the EU internal aviation market to neighbouring countries in Eastern Europe and North Africa.
- The Commission-led negotiation with selected third countries where a Community-wide approach could be shown to 'add value' compared to action by individual Member States.

The new policy clearly represented a compromise. The Commission certainly gained significant additional powers with respect to negotiating the extension of the internal market to neighbouring States. At the same time, however, it was forced to seek negotiating mandates from Member States for agreements with other third countries, and at the outset EU governments were highly sceptical that an EU-led initiative would achieve more than they could obtain bilaterally.

The success of the new EU external aviation policy has been mixed. For example, although a few countries, including some major ones, refused to accept the principle of a Community Carrier, a substantial number did so. Similarly, in 2006, the Commission reached an agreement on the establishment of a European Common Aviation Area (ECAA) with Albania, Bosnia and Herzegovina, Croatia, the former Yugoslav Republic of Macedonia, Montenegro, Serbia and the UN Mission in Kosovo, adding to the 28 EU Member States plus Iceland, Norway and Liechtenstein and creating an integrated aviation market of over 500 million people. Switzerland later signed a very similar agreement essentially to join the ECAA. These countries agreed to adopt EU aviation standards and to implement EU aviation legislation, with a key objective of the Commission being the improvement of aviation safety in many East European States by encouraging 'regulatory convergence.' Subsequently, these so-called 'neighbourhood' agreements were extended to other countries in Eastern Europe and North Africa.

An obvious and less contentious early candidate for the negotiation of an agreement was Russia, which continued to charge European airlines high royalties for using trans-Siberian airspace to fly to and from the Far East. Repeated bilateral negotiations between Russia and several individual EU countries had failed to make headway and Member States needed little persuasion to let the Commission have a go. Unfortunately, the Russians proved to be immovable and the negotiations failed, although not before the inexperience of some of the Commission negotiators was revealed.

EU/US

What the Commission really wanted was the opportunity to negotiate a comprehensive agreement with the US. It had offered to discuss certain soft rights, where the approval of Member States was not required, but the Americans had insisted that they were only interested in a broader arrangement including hard rights. It fell to the trade body for the European legacy airlines, the Association of European Airlines (AEA), to prepare a draft negotiating mandate. To the surprise of many, this proved to be remarkably liberal. AEA proposed to create a Trans-Atlantic Aviation Area (TAA), combining Europe and the US and accounting for almost 60% of global scheduled air transport. In broad terms, the TAA sought to replicate the EU internal market, removing all the old bilateral restrictions on, for example, route access, capacity, tariffs, etc., and including cabotage rights and reform of airline ownership and control rules. According to Lelieur, it identified four core areas for liberalisation:

- The freedom to provide services between points in the TAA, including any two points in a single country.
- Unrestricted airline ownership and the right of establishment.
- The harmonisation of standards for the evaluation of airline competitive behaviour.

- The elimination of restrictions on the use of leased aircraft and on the reservation of government-financed traffic to national carriers.[17]

It might seem odd that the European States and their national airlines were willing to agree to such a liberal negotiating mandate, which matched closely the Commission's own policy preference, given the previous resistance of several of them to regulatory reform. The explanation lies in the fact that for most Member States it made little real difference. The US had succeeded in negotiating open skies bilaterals with 15 EU countries, often accompanied by approval for alliances involving the national carriers of the European countries involved. Only the UK, Ireland, Spain, Greece and Hungary still had restrictive agreements. (The remaining EU States had no ASA with the US.) In other words, the 15 European countries with open skies deals with the US had already granted US carriers virtually free access to their markets. Given the financial situation of most US airlines at the time, there seemed to be little to fear from extending this largess to cabotage and ownership reform (Table 6.3).

Table 6.3 US Open Skies Agreements with European States (and Dates of Signature)

Netherlands	1992
Belgium	1995
Finland	1995
Denmark	1995
Norway	1995
Sweden	1995
Luxembourg	1995
Austria	1995
Czech Republic	1995
Germany	1996
Italy	1998
Portugal	1999
Malta	2000
Poland	2001
France	2001

Source: Button and Dexter[18].

The Commission was delighted to have achieved one of its key aviation policy objectives, with Vice-President and Transport Commissioner de Palacio commenting in 2003: "An aviation agreement between the EU and US would set the model for the rest of the world – these negotiations provide an opportunity to achieve fundamental reform of this sector that we should not waste." A senior US official similarly forecast that an EU/US trans-Atlantic agreement would:

> facilitate the most important reinvention of international aviation we have seen…It would take liberalization to the next level, linking two

huge markets and allowing airlines from both sides of the Atlantic unprecedented flexibility in how they build, manage, and expand their operations... And it would instantly become a new multilateral template for aviation liberalization elsewhere in the world. A US – EU agreement would be, quite simply, the most important thing we could do to enhance the contribution that air transport makes to all of our economies.[19]

Such high expectations were by no means unusual at the time, but unfortunately, the reality of the negotiations proved to be far more difficult and the outcome far less impressive than many had hoped.

The US was more than happy to enter into negotiations with the EU on a multilateral trans-Atlantic aviation agreement, but in doing so it never lost sight of a key objective: the reform of Bermuda 2, and in particular increased access to Heathrow. The UK was the largest trans-Atlantic market by some way, still accounting for almost 40% of total passengers, despite US attempts to bypass it by means of liberal ASAs with numerous Continental countries. Aviation relations between the UK and US deteriorated significantly following the Bermuda 2 agreement, as we have seen, and remained poor for many years. Under pressure especially from its own regional interests, the UK did open up many of its trans-Atlantic city-pairs, but Heathrow remained firmly closed to all but two named US carriers plus British Airways and (from 1991) Virgin Atlantic, with other US carriers forced to use Gatwick Airport. The number of US cities which could be served from Heathrow and Gatwick was also restricted. The only reason the UK had been included in the ECJ action taken by the Commission against several Member States was that it had liberalised access to all its other airports.

The UK had been gradually moving away from a protectionist approach to bilateral negotiations. It had been at the forefront of pressure to create the EU internal aviation market and had negotiated several liberal ASAs of its own around the world, although remnants of the old protectionism remained. However, the UK faced a particular conundrum during the 1980s. The Government of Margaret Thatcher was firmly committed to privatisation, including British Airways. This required BA to be as strong and dominant as possible to maximise the financial return to the Treasury, an approach which was often inconsistent with an international aviation policy designed to increase competition. This "paradoxical conflict between the goals of greater competition and maximising the returns from privatisation," as Graham described the problem,[20] created tension between the Government and its independent aviation regulator which only began to disappear when BA was an established private sector company.

This partly explains the hard line which the UK took initially in negotiations with the US. However, there were other factors involved as well. In particular, the UK argued that by preventing foreign airlines from accessing the large US domestic market, trans-Atlantic competition was being distorted. In return for increased access to London, therefore, the UK insisted on the removal of all US market entry barriers to ensure that UK airlines were not forced to operate at a permanent commercial disadvantage. (This was far from an exceptional position. For example, Daniel Kaspar, previously Director of the Bureau of International Aviation at the CAB at the time of deregulation, argued in a book in 1988: "Regulatory policies that exclude foreign airlines from domestic markets constitute a substantial barrier to liberalized trade in international air services.")[21] The key objective for the UK was to obtain rights for non-US interests to own and control US carriers.

The US saw this as just a delaying tactic designed, in particular, to protect British Airways' dominant position at Heathrow, but pressure on the US increased with the announcement that Richard Branson's Virgin Group wanted to establish a US domestic airline, to be known as Virgin America. As often with Branson, the proposal attracted considerable publicity and support, not least from consumer groups. Initially, Branson insisted that he would only launch a new airline if he had the opportunity to control it fully. However, eventually out of frustration at what he saw as US intransigence, he accepted that the new carrier would have to comply with current US rules, restricting Virgin to a minority stake. Even then, US approval was not forthcoming, with suggestions that Branson's application was being held hostage to put pressure on the UK to be more amenable in, first, its bilateral negotiations with the US and then in the EU/US negotiations. Nevertheless, and despite significant financial losses, Virgin continued to support the UK's reluctance to grant additional Heathrow access without US concessions on ownership and control.

This was the background to the Commission receiving a mandate to negotiate a TAA, quickly renamed an Open Aviation Area (OAA) at the US' insistence. In practice, from the US perspective the main initial change amounted to little more than the replacement of UK by EU negotiators, since the core issues remained essentially the same, namely access to London for the US and cabotage and airline ownership reform for Europe. From the outset, however, the US made clear that its hands were legally tied on cabotage and ownership, with very little chance of being able to persuade the US Congress to accept change. (An attempt by the US DOT in 2006/07 to at least partly reform the ownership and control rules, consistent with its 1995 Policy Statement, ran into stiff opposition and had to be withdrawn, following which the EU/US negotiations were suspended for a lengthy period.) The negotiations were certainly extensive and at times very difficult. To that extent, they continued to mirror what had taken place previously during UK/US talks. However, eventually, it became evident that if a deal was to be agreed, it would have to be on terms far closer to the US' opening position than the Commission's. In other words, what emerged was a standard US open skies model agreement plus a few additions of some, but limited, value. Since, as already explained, for most EU States this largely just duplicated what they already had, they were far less concerned than the UK, which increasingly found itself isolated. Under the EU rules for approving this type of agreement, the UK could have prevented its adoption, but politically such a position increasingly became untenable.

The EU/US OAA was signed in April 2007, with Norway and Iceland joining later. It only formally entered into force in June 2020, taking the EU Member States over a decade to ratify the so-called *'mixed'* agreement, which required the approval of each State separately; Germany was the last country to do so. Commercially this was of little relevance since the agreement had been applied administratively from the beginning, but legally it was important in ensuring the final removal of the old bilaterals. From now on, those ASAs would not automatically be reinstated if the EU/US agreement was terminated. In addition to the normal open skies provisions, the agreement included some increased market access to the US for EU airlines, such as limited participation in government contracts, as well as US acceptance of the concept of a Community Carrier, as mandated by the ECJ, so that an EU airline could fly to the US from any EU country. For the Commission, the latter concession was particularly important, both legally and politically.

The OAA was also intended to include a commitment by all the signatories to increased regulatory convergence and harmonisation of air transport standards in such areas as safety, security, infrastructure, the environment, competition regulation and state aid, and included the formation of a Joint Committee to address policy variations as well as disputes over the interpretation of the new agreement.[22] (The Commission pursued the same objective in negotiations with EU neighbouring States, arguably with more success than with the US.) The agreement committed both sides to continue to negotiate on the subjects of cabotage rights and airline ownership and control rules and stated that if no substantial progress had been made on these two issues by November 2010, either side could suspend all or some of the rights granted in the first stage. In practice, this was little more than a face-saver for the UK. Those involved knew that the chance of a major shift in US policy was remote, and this proved to be the case. Phase Two of the EU/US agreement was duly signed in April 2010, with only relatively minor further amendments.

In Europe, there had been expectations of substantial economic benefits from the creation of a trans-Atlantic Open Aviation Area. The Commission had financed a major study by the Brattle Group in 2002, which concluded that such an agreement would result in between 4.1 and 11.0 million additional trans-Atlantic passengers and, through network effects, between 17.7 and 46.7 million extra passengers on intra-EU routes. Not surprisingly, the largest increases would be found on UK routes, followed by routes to Greece, Ireland and Spain, in other words, the countries which did not previously have open skies agreements with the US.[23] Similarly, a 2007 Study by the UK Civil Aviation Authority estimated that there would be a fall in airline unit costs of some 0.5% per annum over five years following the adoption of an OAA, which suggested some 24 additional daily trans-Atlantic frequencies.[24] Other, less extensive studies had similarly identified considerable consumer benefits from a liberal air services agreement. With this background and its original strong desire to obtain a mandate to negotiate an OAA with the US, it is perhaps not surprising that the European Commission was delighted with the outcome. It claimed that

> by eliminating the restrictions of the bilateral agreements, it is expected that the price of flights between the EU and US will fall for both business travellers and leisure passengers. As a consequence, the Agreement could generate economic benefits up to 12 billion [sic] over a period of five years, and around 80,000 jobs in the EU and US.

It went on to claim that the agreement constituted "a defining moment in the aviation relations between the two regions ... and established a modern regulatory framework."

Unfortunately, such hyperbole proved to be far from reality for a number of reasons, not least the fact that the potential economic benefits identified by the Brattle study and others had been based on a regulatory model going far beyond the agreement actually reached between the EU and the US. In particular, of course, there had been no meeting of minds on the critical issues of cabotage and airline ownership and control rules. Furthermore, the agreement represented only a relatively modest step beyond the open skies arrangements which many EU Member States already had with the US. The benefits in terms of traffic growth, new routes and lower fares claimed by the Commission were never likely to emerge where changes in market access were small or even non-existent. A 'modern regulatory framework' may well have been established, but it was one far closer to the US' open skies model than the negotiating mandate initially granted to the European Commission. Of the four core areas for liberalisation identified by Lelieur in the model TAA and listed above, not one was fully met.

Of course, potentially those countries with services to the US not previously covered by an open skies ASA were significantly affected by the new agreement, and none more so than the UK. However, even here the impact was less than might superficially be assumed. This was partly because, as already noted, despite the apparent restrictions of the Bermuda 2 bilateral, in many respects the agreement had been implemented relatively liberally. As Stevens has noted:

> A balanced assessment might perhaps conclude that for all its faults Bermuda 2 provided the two governments with what turned out to be a surprisingly flexible instrument for the regulation of air services over a period of some thirty years of rapid growth and change in a dynamic industry.[25]

Tariff regulation was one example of such flexibility, with UK trans-Atlantic leisure fares remaining among the lowest in Europe. The UK had maintained its share of the Europe – US market despite more liberal ASAs negotiated by the US with several other European countries.

The new EU/US agreement did mean that access to Heathrow could no longer be restricted, and all the US long-haul scheduled passenger carriers quickly joined United and American there, often paying eye-watering prices for scarce slots at the airport. (Press reports at the time suggested that most US airlines paid between US$10m and US$40m for slot pairs, with Continental obtaining four pairs of slots for an average of US$52m.) However, every one of these new entrant carriers was already present in the London – US market. Almost all of the new Heathrow services were simply transfers from Gatwick Airport, with only a modest increase in new UK–US routes and frequencies. One early study found that taking into account the reduction in frequencies and average aircraft size at Gatwick, the annual growth in total London – US traffic in summer 2008 was less than double what would otherwise have been expected, a result unlikely to be repeated in subsequent years: "The benefits of the EU/US agreement predicted by several studies look likely to be overly optimistic."[26] Similarly, the new freedom for a European airline to operate to the US from an EU State other than its home base was of limited interest to most carriers. An attempt by Air France, for example, to serve Los Angeles from London was soon abandoned, although the rights did prove more attractive in later years for some low-cost airlines such as Norwegian International.

EU/Rest of the World

The negotiations with the US were only the beginning of the European Commission's ambitions to establish EU-wide agreements with third countries. In 2009, the US agreement was followed by one with Canada, in which again the Commission failed to extend the basic open skies principles to include cabotage rights and airline ownership reform. Nevertheless, acceptance of the Commission's role in bilateral negotiations gradually increased. In 2012, Member States agreed a new policy statement, calling for "stronger coordination, unity and solidarity at EU level and for a more robust EU external aviation policy in order to strengthen the competitiveness of the European aviation industry while supporting the interests of European consumers." It is unlikely a consensus would have been reached on such a policy statement a decade or more earlier. In 2015, the Commission tabled a new proposal, 'An Aviation Strategy for Europe,' setting out its strategic priorities, including an ambitious external aviation policy aimed at growth markets.

Officially, the EU continues to support what its Director General for Mobility and Transport has described as "a genuine Transatlantic Aviation Area," or 'open skies plus' as others have called it. In a speech in Washington DC in July 2018, he emphasised that

> the dream of the negotiators of the [EU/US Air Transport Agreement] and the spirit of the text of the Agreement … [was] to remove market

access barriers, further enhancing at the same time the access of our airlines to global capital markets, and to lead by example.

He insisted that Europe was still committed to reform of the archaic airline ownership and control rules, and made the same point in another Washington speech a year later, adding, no doubt in the light of certain policies being pursued by the new Trump administration, that "the rise of nationalism, protectionism and populism around the world is fundamentally at odds with a forward-looking and liberal regulatory agenda." At the time, the US had come under pressure from some of its airlines to refuse the designation of Norwegian International to operate trans-Atlantic flights from various European airports. The US appeared to be ignoring the provisions of the OAA Agreement in the face of allegations that Norwegian was engaging in 'flags of convenience' behaviour, an approach which created considerable disappointment and frustration in Europe.

However, all is not quite what it might at first appear to be with the EU external aviation policy. There may have been particular reasons why Member States were prepared to give the Commission such a liberal negotiating mandate with the US and Canada, but those reasons are less likely to apply to many other countries. Several EU States maintain a protectionist approach to the interests of their national airlines, including the largest and most influential economies of Germany and France (ironically now apparently joined by the Netherlands following the merger of KLM and Air France, despite the country's long history of fighting for liberal ASAs). Negotiations with Brazil broke down because of the EU's refusal to incorporate liberal fifth freedom rights, a key element in open skies ASAs. Similarly, the resistance of many EU countries to increased competition can clearly be seen in their response to the requests of the Gulf carriers for more market access, with arguments about 'uneven playing fields' and 'unfair State support' which, as we have seen, are as old as aviation's bilateral system.

The Commission has received mandates to open ASA negotiations with a number of countries, but so far the only additional success has been with Qatar and the ASEAN countries. The Qatar agreement, which has been strongly criticised by several EU legacy airlines on the grounds principally of an unlevel competitive playing field, was initialled in 2019. Even more than the US and Canada arrangements, it falls well short of the full liberalisation envisaged in the original mandate given to the Commission for negotiations with the US. In June 2021, the EU announced "the world's first bloc-to-bloc air transport agreement" with the ten members of the Association of Southeast Asian Nations. Although the agreement is described as 'comprehensive' and does indeed include open third and fourth freedom rights, fifth freedoms are limited. Significantly in the light of the campaign launched by several EU legacy carriers to restrict competition from certain countries, the agreement also includes "robust fair competition provisions and doing business issues." As we have seen, such provisions are unlikely to have much of an impact and certainly will not solve any underlying competitive problems. They are, however, a potential area for future disputes.

It is notable that the recent negotiations with Qatar, like the ASEAN agreement, did not seem to feature airline ownership and control reform. Instead, the Commission highlighted that the agreement "will set a new global benchmark by committing to strong, fair competition mechanisms, and including provisions not normally covered by bilateral air transport agreements, such as social or environmental issues." Furthermore, full access to those EU States (Belgium, Germany, France, Italy and the Netherlands) which still had restrictive ASAs with Qatar, will only be granted in stages over a five-year period. This is a very different outcome, with a partner more than willing to agree to the complete reciprocal opening up of markets, to the one sought earlier on the North Atlantic. The Qatar agreement is indicative of the growing pressure on the Commission to tone down its pursuit of open skies plus deals. At the same time, the Commission is less able to resist such pressure as a result of the withdrawal of the UK from the EU. The UK, the second largest economy in the EU, had become a consistent advocate of a liberal external aviation policy and therefore an ally of the Commission, in this respect at least.

Multilateral Approaches

Many countries around the world have joined Europe and the US in pursuing more liberal ASAs, often based on the US open skies model, although it is also the case that a number of States continue to resist such an approach. It is important to note that this trend towards a less prescriptive form of regulation has not been limited to air services. As Finger and Button comment, airline liberalisation, both domestic and international, has been firmly located in a broader movement which itself is at least partly the product of globalisation. In particular, liberalisation has been seen in network industries, of which of course air transport is a prime example:

> While such regulatory reform ... triggered fierce ideological debates, it gradually became clear that greater liberalization of both operations and infrastructure sectors allowed network industries to better adapt to the efficiency and competitiveness requirements of an increasingly integrated and global economy.[27]

An additional factor, Finger and Button suggest, was the increased pressure exerted by the growth of the aviation industry, especially in emerging countries, with which governments found increasingly difficult to cope.

ICAO has established itself as a successful multilateral regulator in the areas of the security and especially safety, but much less so when it comes to economic regulation. There has never been any real prospect of a global multilateral open skies agreement, at least not since the early discussions leading to the Chicago Convention. In principle, there is no reason why international aviation should not be included in the General Agreement on Trade in Services (GATS) framework, just as the overwhelming majority of other industries are. In practice, however, with just a few exceptions, it is specifically omitted. The Annex to the GATS allows the Treaty's application to aviation services only if they are not 'directly related to the exercise of traffic rights,' such as repair and maintenance and computer reservation services. The explanation for this restriction is to be found, of course, in the bilateral approach to the negotiation of air services agreements established in 1944. An analysis by Oum, Park and Zhang highlights two specific reasons why Chicago and the GATS are irreconcilable. First, they suggest, since the regulation of domestic air services remains essentially a national responsibility, the national treatment principle inherent in the GATS approach would effectively increase market access for airlines from States with closed domestic markets without expanding access for carriers whose domestic markets have already been deregulated. Secondly, the GATS principle of 'Most Favoured Nation' (MFN), whereby a concession made by one country to another is automatically extended to all World Trade Organisation members, would permit States unwilling to open their own markets to enjoy a 'free rider' status.[28]

There is the option under the GATS of 'conditional' MFN, whereby a State's increased market access is available only to those other countries which have taken similar measures, a type of 'club' or 'targeted' approach. This is similar to plurilateral or regional rather than multilateral agreements, and here there has been some progress in air transport. A plurilateral agreement has a particular additional potential advantage, as Kaspar notes: "A targeted approach [among a relatively small group of liberal trading partners] could mitigate the inherent lowest-common-denominator problem that plagues the GATS and simplify negotiations by limiting initial participation to those nations that shared broadly consistent interests."[29] An early attempt in this direction was launched by the Netherlands in 1980, aimed at liberalisation between a relatively small group of countries, although with some selective protectionism included. The proposal envisaged "market access on a non-discriminatory and MFN basis," but it failed to attract much support from other European States or the US, allegedly because of the relatively small size of the Netherlands as a market in its own right.[30]

In 2001, five members of the Asia-Pacific Economic Cooperation (APEC) – Brunei, Chile, New Zealand, Singapore and the US, later joined by other members – signed a joint open skies agreement which went beyond the usual US model. This Multilateral Agreement on the Liberalization of International Air Transportation, or MALIAT, removed the airline ownership requirement among signatory countries, while leaving in place the need to be controlled by citizens of the designating State and adding the concept of 'principal place of business.' The agreement specifically states that its provisions do not affect a signatory's national rules governing the ownership and control of its designated airlines, a stipulation insisted upon by the US under pressure from its labour unions fearful of foreign takeovers of US carriers (See Chapter 8). However, despite the hope at the time that MALIAT would represent a significant break away from the traditional, restrictive bilateral approach to air services negotiations, in practice its impact has been modest. As Findlay has noted, if the objective is to break the mould of international air transport regulation, MALIAT was not the answer: "The Agreement does not offer enough extra benefit to potential participants in terms of its coverage of issues (such as ownership rules, competition policy, and so on) to compensate for the greater threat in more highly integrated markets."[31] Similarly, Lelieur, while recognising that the agreement represented the first major initiative by the US to move beyond its previous open skies model, concluded that "the APEC Agreement was more symbolic than practical for many signatories."[32]

A similar development came in 2008, with agreement among ASEAN members to move towards a Single Aviation Market from 2015. Table 6.4 lists the ASEAN member countries; note that some ASEAN States had also signed the MALIAT agreement. Clearly based on the example set by the successful creation of the European internal aviation market, particularly in removing the traditional market access restrictions between signatory countries, the agreement further developed the airline ownership and control restrictions by providing for an airline to be incorporated, have its principal place of business and be substantially owned and controlled by nationals of one or more signatory States, thereby laying the groundwork for the emergence of an ASEAN Community Carrier. The agreement was acknowledged by ASEAN countries as being a key strategic goal, but implementation was sluggish with ratification delayed to 2016.[33] Even then there was a reluctance to implement the agreement in full, especially from the Philippines, Indonesia and Laos. The fact that the former two countries are the largest ASEAN States by population only served to add to the implementation problems.

Table 6.4 ASEAN Member States

Brunei	Cambodia	Indonesia
Laos	Malaysia	Myanmar
Philippines	Singapore	Thailand
Vietnam		

ASEAN success was always going to be difficult. As Forsyth, King and Rodolfo point out, despite the evident economic benefits of a regional open skies arrangement, such an approach "has not been achieved, in substantial terms, by other regional groupings, except in the case of Europe, where special circumstances prevailed." Those special circumstances, of course, refer to an overriding legal framework which effectively enabled the EU Commission, with help from the ECJ, to impose a more competitive regulatory regime, despite the reluctance of most EU Member States. The ASEAN region, on the other hand, has no such common legal framework and is characterised by considerable economic diversity.[34]

A similar situation is found in Africa. The Yamoussoukro Declaration (YD) of 1999 was again a direct attempt to replicate the EU's internal aviation market. It envisaged the gradual liberalisation of air services within Africa by means of:

- A three-phase process over a period of eight years.
- The gradual elimination of bilateral traffic rights.
- Increased co-operation between civil aviation administrations and airlines aimed at minimising operating costs.[35]

Unfortunately, the YD's rhetoric was more impressive than its achievements. Despite the apparent support from several African States, the ambitious agreement was largely a failure. Signatory countries felt free to ignore its provisions when the interests of their own airlines and economies were perceived to be at stake. A further attempt at liberalisation was made in 2015 when the African Union adopted a Declaration on the Establishment of a Single African Air Transport Market (SAATM). Two years later, 11 States signed an impressive sounding 'Solemn Declaration' undertaking to implement the agreement, although its formal launch was further delayed until the 30th Ordinary Session of the African Union in 2018. By 2020, 34 States (out of a total African Union membership of 44), representing some 80% of intra-African air traffic, had ratified it (see Table 6.5).

Table 6.5 Countries Ratifying the SAATM, 2020

Benin	Botswana	Burkino Faso
Cape Verde	Cameroon	Central African Rep.
Congo/Brazzaville	Cote D'Ivoire	Egypt
Ethiopia	Equatorial Guinea	Gabon
Gambia	Ghana	Guinea (Bissau)
Guinée	Kenya	Lesotho
Liberia	Mali	Morocco
Mozambique	Dem. Rep of Congo	Rwanda
Sénégal	Sierra Leone	South Africa
Swaziland	Tchad	Togo
Zimbabwe		

The SAATM's objectives were similar to those of the original Yamoussoukro Declaration, with perhaps an increased recognition of the need for a workable enforcement regime. In particular, it sought to:

- Abolish bilateral air services agreements for intra-African air traffic.
- Recognise the concept of a Community Carrier owned and controlled by African nationals.
- Harmonise competition laws.
- Establish a Board of Appeal and an Arbitration Tribunal.[36]

The SAATM departs from normal open skies (and EU) provisions in several respects, for example, in discriminating in favour of state-owned airlines over their private-sector competitors. Cabotage rights are also excluded. It remains to be seen whether the agreement will prove to be any more successful than previous attempts to liberalise intra-African air services, either bilaterally or on a regional basis. The omens, however, are not good, not least with the impact of the COVID pandemic. One study concluded that

> ... the low commitment from AU Member States is likely to be brought on by the treaty's lack of a proper implementation framework. This framework is necessary to harmonise existing differences between airlines as well as provide a level playing field going forward.[37]

The Yamoussoukro problem is deep-seated and essentially political. As Schlumberger has noted, there is a disconnection between the policy and legal framework on the one side and the operational realities of the sector on the other, a common problem in the regulation of international aviation, but one particularly prevalent in Africa.

> This disconnection, driven mainly by the governments of a small number of African countries who aim at protecting their weak or failing national carriers by refusing to liberalize their air transport markets irrespective of the obligations they have assumed under the Decision, has hindered full liberalization of the African air transport sector and effectively prevented African nations from taking full advantage of the positive economic benefits of air transportation.[38]

The impact of this situation is graphically revealed in Kacou and El-Houry's estimate that "one dollar spent in economy class in Africa enables passengers to travel 6.04 km. The same dollar spent in Europe propels passengers an average of 44.44 km."[39]

Notes

1 Handley Stevens: *The Life and Death of a Treaty. Bermuda 2*. Palgrave Macmillan, London, 2018.
2 Andrew Lobbenberg: 'Government relations on the North Atlantic. A case study of five European – USA relationships.' *Journal of Air Transport Management*, Vol. 1(1), 1994, pp. 47–61.
3 Personal correspondence with Jeffrey Shane. I am grateful to Mr Shane for further lengthy guidance in the preparation of this chapter.
4 Daniel M. Kasper: *Deregulation and Globalization. Liberalizing International Trade in Air Services*. American Enterprise Institute/Ballinger Publishing, Cambridge, MA, 1988.
5 Quoted in James Patrick Baldwin: *The Evolution of the Airline Industry: Regulation, Events and Influencing Factors*. Kindle Direct Publishing, Cambridge, MA, 2019.
6 Daniel M. Kasper, op cit.
7 Jeffrey N. Shane: 'Air Transport Liberalization: Ideal and Ordeal.' Second Annual Assad Kotaite Lecture, Royal Aeronautical Society Montreal Branch, 8 December 2005.

8. Ibid.
9. John G. Wensveen: *Air Transportation. A Management Perspective.* Sixth Edition, Ashgate, Aldershot, 2007.
10. Ibid.
11. US Department of Transportation: 'In the Matter of Defining "Open Skies".' Docket 48130, Washington DC, 5 August 1992.
12. Erwin von den Steinen: *National Interest and International Aviation.* Kluwer Law International, Alphen aan den Rijn, The Netherlands, 2006.
13. W. Gillespie and O. M. Richard: 'Antitrust Immunity and International Airline Alliances.' US Department of Justice, Antitrust Division, Washington DC, 2011. Quoted in William G. Morrison and Jaap de Wit: 'US open skies agreements and unlevel playing fields.' *Journal of Air Transport Management*, Vol. 74(1), 2019, pp. 30–38.
14. William G. Morrison and Jaap de Wit, op cit.
15. Yu-Chan Ghang, George Williams and Chia-Jui Hsu: 'The evolution of airline ownership and control provisions.' *Journal of Air Transport Management*, Vol. 10(3), 2004, pp. 161–172.
16. Ibid.
17. Isabele Lelieur: *Law and Policy of Substantial Ownership and Effective Control of Airlines. Prospects for Change.* Ashgate, Aldershot, 2007.
18. Kenneth Button and Jonathan Dexter: *The Implications on Economic Performance in Europe of Further Liberalization of the Transatlantic Air Market.* Center for Transportation Policy, Operations and Logistics, School of Public Policy, George Mason University, Fairfax VA, 2005.
19. Jeffrey N. Shane (2005), op cit.
20. Brian Graham: *Geography and Air Transport.* Wiley, Chichester, 1995.
21. Daniel M. Kasper, op cit.
22. Erwin von den Steinen, op cit.
23. Brattle Group: 'The Economic Impact of an EU – US Open Aviation Area, a Study for the European Commission.' Washington DC, 2002. See also Kenneth Button and Jonathan Dexter, op cit.
24. UK Civil Aviation Authority: 'Modelling and Analysis of the EU – US Aviation Agreement.' London, 2007.
25. Handley Stevens, op cit.
26. Barry Humphreys and Peter Morell: 'The potential impacts of the EU/US Open Sky Agreement: What will happen at Heathrow after spring 2008.' *Journal of Air Transport Management*, Vol. 15(2), 2009, pp. 172–177. See also Paolo Malighetti, Stefano Paleary and Renato Redondi: 'EU-US open skies agreement: What is changed in the north transatlantic skies?' *Transportation Journal*, Vol. 53(3), 2014, pp. 305–329.
27. Matthias Finger and Kenneth Button (eds.): *Air Transport Liberalization. A Critical Assessment.* Edward Elgar, Cheltenham, 2017.
28. Tae Oum, Jong-Hun Park and Anming Zhang: *Globalization and Strategic Alliances. The Case of the Airline Industry.* Pergamon, Kidlington, 2000.
29. Daniel M. Kasper, op cit.
30. Ibid.
31. Christopher Findlay: 'Plurilateral agreements on trade in air transport services: The US model.' *Journal of Air Transport Management*, Vol. 9(4), 2003, pp. 42–48.
32. Isabele Lelieur, op cit.
33. Alan Khee-Jin Tan: 'The ASEAN multilateral agreement on air services: En route to open skies.' *Journal of Air Transport Management*, Vol. 16(6), 2010, pp. 289–294.
34. Peter Forsyth, John King and Cherry Lyn Rodolfo: 'Open skies in ASEAN.' *Journal of Air Transport Management*, Vol. 12(3), 2006, pp. 143–152.

35 Anne Ngumba and Mbagara Karita: *Single African Air Transport Market. Is Africa Ready?* Deloitte, 2018.
36 Ibid.
37 Ibid.
38 Charles E. Schlumberger: 'The Implementation of the Yamoussoukro Decision.' DCL thesis, McGill University, Faculty of Law, 2009.
39 Eric Kakou and Hassan El-Houry: *Fly Africa: How Aviation Can Generate Prosperity Across the Continent.* Lioncrest Publishing, Carson City NV, 2017.

7 The Low-Cost Revolution

As we saw in Chapters 4 and 5, one of the most significant outcomes of deregulation/liberalisation in the US, Europe and elsewhere was the emergence to prominence of a new airline business model, the low-cost/no frills carrier (LCC). These new airlines transformed the industry, radically changing the products on offer, reducing fares, expanding services, challenging the incumbent carriers and forcing them to reform to meet the new competitive threat or risk extinction. By any measure, LCCs have been a major success story. According to CAPA, of the ten largest pre-COVID airlines in the world, measured in terms of seat capacity, three are LCCs – Southwest, Ryanair and easyJet. (The picture is different, of course, if output is measured in terms of, say, seat kilometres.) Perhaps just as remarkable is the fact that many of the LCCs have been highly profitable, at least by the traditional standards of the airline industry. In addition, their impact has not been restricted to the airline sector; airports have also had to adapt to the new environment, developing innovative marketing strategies to attract a very different type of airline customer, especially in Europe. The low-cost/no-frills model radically changed the whole industry, almost certainly permanently. As the aviation pioneer, Sir Freddie Laker, commented: "The twentieth century largely belonged to the traditional, high-cost airlines (with a few snipers, like me, upsetting their cosy cartel). The twenty-first century will be the preserve of the no-frills airlines."[1]

None of this would have been possible under the old, restrictive regulatory regimes which had emerged from the Chicago Convention. The need to have route authorisations, tariffs and schedules approved in advance by governments is anathema to the LCC model, with its rapidly changing prices and willingness to enter and leave routes quickly in response to changing market conditions. Equally important was the fact that with deregulation/liberalisation, governments and regulators were no longer able to protect the legacy airlines and discriminate against newcomers, at least not to the same extent. For their part, the legacy carriers' own business models for short-haul routes were soon shown to be not fit for purpose and had to be substantially amended. The financial consequences were often severe, with losses, bankruptcies and consolidation, but eventually, most of the remaining legacy

DOI: 10.4324/9780429448973-7

airlines stabilised and found a way to compete with the new entrants, at least partly by following the adage: "If you can't beat them, join them." In Europe, the same was true for the substantial IT charter sector. Today this evolution continues in most markets, with the emergence of so-called '*hybrid*' LCC models and the spread of low-cost services to long-haul routes.

Button and Ison[2] have argued that what has emerged is a classic example of Michael Porter's 'competitive advantage.' Porter suggested that there are two broad ways of making abnormal returns, or in the airline industry perhaps just remaining in business. You can either seek to differentiate your product and achieve a degree of monopoly power or compete on cost. Arguably the legacy carriers achieved the first objective, initially with their hub-and-spoke route networks, computer reservation systems and alliances. Low fares achieved by low costs were clearly the model chosen by the new LCCs. However, this distinction between market power and low costs over-simplifies what actually took place, as we shall see, with the emergence of a more complex industrial structure.

North America

No description of the growth of the LCC model can be complete without highlighting the role played by Southwest Airlines, an airline which went from niche carrier to paragon over a relatively short period. Southwest grew from a small intra-State operation in Texas to become the most significant disrupter in the US domestic airline market, and one of the Big 4 US carriers. The original idea was to exploit a loophole in pre-deregulation federal aviation rules by operating turbo-prop aircraft wholly within the State of Texas, thereby avoiding strict CAB federal oversight. Initially known as Air Southwest, it was a former CIA operative, Rollin W. King, who found himself losing money with his air taxi operation, but dreamt of flying scheduled services between the so-called Golden Triangle of Dallas, Houston and San Antonio, with distances of between 190 and 251 miles[3]. Formed in 1967, Southwest's first flight did not take place until 1971, a delay explained primarily by a wave of hostility shown by the incumbent airlines, especially Texas International, Braniff and Continental. It was to help counter these legal challenges that King brought in a local lawyer, Herb Kelleher, with two initial roles: to defend the airline in the courts and to assist in finding additional investors. He did both. By 1976, for example, Southwest had faced no less than 31 judicial and administrative proceedings seeking to restrict its operations.[4] Eventually, after the departure of King in 1981, Southwest and Kelleher became inseparable as the icons of the low-cost revolution.

Southwest's financial problems were so severe that in 1973 it had to sell one of its four recently acquired jet aircraft. However, rather than reduce services and manpower, the airline chose to maintain its schedule by significantly improving turn-round times. Thus was achieved, almost by accident, two of the key factors which were to ensure Southwest's success over the coming years:

employee loyalty and high levels of innovative efficiency. Another aspect of its business model which was to become standard for LCCs around the world was the use of a single aircraft type, again to reduce costs and increase efficiency. The airline chose the Boeing 737, an aircraft which up to then had been overshadowed by the DC-9. The 737 went on to become the most successful jet aircraft ever produced and many commentators have argued that much of that success can be ascribed to Southwest's initial decision to adopt it.[5] Today, Southwest has over 750 B737s and apart from a small number of short-term leased aircraft over the years, has never operated any other aircraft type, although it has flown several different marks of the 737.

It was actually an intra-Californian airline, Pacific Southwest Airlines (PSA), which devised many of the characteristics that came to be associated with the LCC business model. PSA had been established as long ago as 1949 and had enjoyed some success in the Californian market, but unfortunately, it was not well managed. At one point it even lobbied the Californian authorities to introduce additional regulatory protection, a move hardly consistent with an innovative new entrant challenging the incumbents. Southwest took the PSA model, improved it, made it work within Texas and was ready to take advantage of federal deregulation when it came in 1978. (The man appointed to be Southwest's Chief Executive during its early years, Lamar Muse, openly admitted that he and King "had obtained complete copies of PSA's manuals during our four-day visit to PSA's headquarters in San Diego.")[6]

The ability to both achieve and maintain lower costs is critical to the success of the LCC model. As David Bonderman, long-standing Chairman of Ryanair, noted in 2000: "Long-term success in this high growth area depends on one's ability to maintain low cost and efficient operating practices, establishing a long-term record of sustained profitability, and above all maintaining a disciplined and controlled rate of annual growth."[7] This focus on costs was unusual among airlines at the time, who were far more likely to concentrate on achieving higher yield as a route to profitability. For Southwest, low costs came first, enabling it to offer significantly lower fares and thereby overcome the market advantages enjoyed by its incumbent competitors. (Southwest always maintained that in its early years its principal competition came from car and bus travel rather than scheduled airlines.) It was notable as well that the customer experience on Southwest was significantly superior to that on most other US domestic airlines at the time, something which was not always the case when the LCC model was exported to other countries.

The key elements in the Southwest model might be summarised as follows:

- Make everything as simple as possible by removing complexity.
- Concentrate on point-to-point services with no formal hubbing or interlining.
- Operate a single aircraft type to minimise maintenance and crew costs.
- Achieve high seat factor levels, significantly above the industry norm at the time.

- Achieve high levels of aircraft utilisation, for example by turning aircraft around more quickly, often within fifteen or twenty minutes, and ignore the carriage of cargo.
- Provide only a basic catering service rather than seek to compete by offering more extensive meals.

(Perhaps a less politically correct initiative, albeit typical of the time, which did not survive, was the recruitment of what The New York Times described as "the most shapely girls in the air" as cabin crew, wearing tangerine hot pants designed by Lamar Muse's first wife.) Southwest was a unionised airline with salary levels at least comparable to those of other carriers. Nevertheless, it created what has been called an 'egalitarian culture' with a co-operative and loyal workforce, not something most of its competitors could claim. From this culture emerged a brand image which clearly resonated with its customers. The result was a success, and a profitable one. While each of the other US major airlines experienced periodic losses and occasional bankruptcies, apart from its early financial challenges Southwest has been profitable in every subsequent year up to the COVID crisis.

Herb Kelleher's role in promoting the airline's brand was certainly critical. A hard drinker and heavy smoker, probably the antithesis of the corporate airline executive, his charismatic persona fitted perfectly with the image of an upstart carrier challenging the established operators. (He was once quoted as saying: "Because I am unable to perform competently any meaningful function at Southwest, our employees let me be CEO. That is one among many reasons why I love the people of Southwest Airlines.") Despite such (false?) modesty, on his death in 2018, Kelleher was said to be worth some US$2.5 billion, a reflection of the financial success of the airline he headed for so long. Southwest itself is now one of the largest airlines in the world. A 2015 case study of the carrier highlighted the reasons for its success and concluded that:

> Southwest airlines .... is a company that has captivated the attention of the business world over the course of its forty year history as an airline displaying relentless growth coupled with a much envied employee spirit and a passionately loyal customer base. Since its inception in 1971, the company has maintained the momentum and agility of a young start-up, has nourished a unique and powerful culture, and continued to grow and fluidly adapt to the changing environment year after year.[8]

The Southwest model has been copied throughout the world, with varying degrees of success. The airline welcomed a steady stream of visitors intent on discovering the secrets of its success. Kelleher himself argued that this didn't matter as other airlines were incapable of fully understanding what really drove the Southwest phenomenon. He may well have been right with respect to the legacy carriers, but the success of several new LCCs in the US,

Europe and elsewhere showed that much of the underlying business model could indeed be copied. Although Southwest remained broadly loyal to its founding principles, changes were introduced when necessary, including a frequent flyer programme, for example, to match the legacy carriers. However, it resisted the pattern set by many other LCCs and eventually most airlines in seeking to maximise ancillary revenues, refusing to charge extra for checked bags for instance. The airline expanded throughout the US and beyond, mostly dominating each new market.

We saw in Chapter 4 that a 1993 study by the US Department of Transportation identified what was termed the '*Southwest Effect,*' whereby the entry of the airline into a new market resulted in significantly lower average fares and a disproportionate increase in traffic. Despite the emergence of other LCCs and the resurgence of the (now consolidated) legacy airlines, it appears that this effect is still present. A study in 2017, by Beckenstein and Campbell, for example, concluded that:

> The presence and magnitude of the Southwest Effect has endured through time. Even today, where new markets have frequently been affected by Southwest's fares on connecting services, the Southwest Effect still shows, on average, an additional market fare reduction of 15% and corresponding traffic increase of 28% to 30%, from the introduction of nonstop service by Southwest. A few industry writers have questioned whether the Southwest Effect still exists today, or has it been overtaken by the fares/traffic effect created by other low cost carriers? The answer is clear. The Southwest Effect is alive and well. We find no evidence that the Southwest Effect has been eroded or overtaken in significance or magnitude by other airlines.[9]

Beckenstein and Campbell estimated that in 2017, Southwest produced US$9.1 billion annually in US domestic consumer fare savings. Put another way, single average fares were US$45 lower when Southwest served a market non-stop than when it did not; the corresponding figure was a fare reduction of US$17 if Southwest provided only a connecting service.

These are impressive numbers, all the more so when the growth of other LCCs is taken into account. Many US airlines have followed in Southwest's footsteps. Not all have survived, but several have done so and gone on to be very successful in their own rights. Virgin America, for example, was established by the British Virgin Group after a long fight with the US authorities over its control by non-US interests. It was subsequently merged with Alaska Airlines, the fifth-largest US carrier by several measures. JetBlue was co-founded by David Neeleman, who had previously established and led another LCC, Morris Air, which was acquired by Southwest in 1993. He was subsequently closely involved with other LCCs in Canada (Westjet), Brazil (Azul) and the US again (Breeze). Airlines such as JetBlue and Virgin America developed a hybrid low-cost model, retaining much of the original Southwest concept but with added service elements adopted from the more traditional carriers, such as a business/first class. JetBlue also based itself initially at one of the largest US airports, New York's JFK, rather than a secondary airport frequently favoured by other LCCs, exploiting the fact that as primarily an international airport, there was significant runway under-utilisation at certain times of the day. This enabled JetBlue to negotiate code share interline arrangements with numerous foreign carriers, again a departure from the 'pure' LCC model. It subsequently entered into an alliance with American Airlines (at the time of writing subject to a challenge by the US Justice Department) and sought to take over another US LCC, Spirit. Virtually all of the second-generation LCCs also relied far more on direct sales than Southwest had originally done. Table 7.1 shows domestic market shares, in terms of seats operated, for US airlines and highlights the prominent role now played by LCCs.

At the same time, the US legacy carriers were forced to adapt, for example by reducing costs, eliminating free meals and free checked bags, and adopting many of the LCC model's operational standards. Some progress was made in reducing the efficiency gap, but it was impossible to reach the cost levels enjoyed by the LCCs. In other words, while many LCCs were moving towards the legacy carriers in terms of service provision, the latter were moving towards the LCCs with lower costs and a more basic onboard service. The second line of defence for the legacy airlines was the establishment of low-cost subsidiaries, such as Delta's Song and United's Ted (see Table 7.2). These tended to piggy-back on their parent companies' licences and often failed to overcome basic inefficiencies, not least those associated with labour agreements. None of them was a success (Continental's subsidiary, Continental Lite, was described in one study as "an unmitigated failure, as it straddled both the low fare and full fare markets")[10] and eventually they were all abandoned. Consumers frequently failed to distinguish between these dual brands (the name 'Ted' was taken from the last three letters of 'United,' so it was hardly surprising that some confusion emerged), although the approach was more successful in other countries such as Australia and even Canada. The US legacy carriers were to find that Chapter 11 bankruptcy was a far more effective way of reducing costs to compete with the LCCs.

Table 7.1 US Domestic Market Shares (Seats), 2019

American	22.4
Delta	21.2
Southwest	20.5
United	16.2
Alaska	5.6
JetBlue	3.7
Other	10.3

Source: CAPA – Centre for Aviation.

Table 7.2 LCC Subsidiaries of US Major Airlines, 2005

Parent Airline	LCC Subsidiary	Start of Operations
Delta	Song	2003
United	Ted	2004
Continental	CALite	1993
United	Shuttle	1994
Delta	Delta Express	1996
US Airways	Metrojet	1998

Source: P. Morrell, 2005.

Morrell,[11] writing in 2005, identified three possible objectives in the establishment of LCC subsidiaries of full-service carriers:

- To spin off profitable businesses.
- To see off low-cost competition in key markets.
- To establish a testbed for adapting low-cost business processes to their mainline operations.

He concluded that the majors failed on all three counts, mainly because of the inability to close the cost gap.

> …[F]ew of these offshoots in the US conformed to the Southwest model, and those that did suffered from brand confusion and union restrictions on their operations. None were ring fenced in separate subsidiary companies with their own accounts and financial and operating autonomy… The conclusion from this is that these offshoots were principally a means of targeting LCC competition in key markets, and could never be spun off as profitable businesses. [While] the gap in distribution [costs has narrowed significantly], … the gap in both labour and other costs does not appear to have narrowed much.

Luca Graf, writing at the same time, identified similar problems with the LCC subsidiaries of European legacy airlines (see below).[12]

The emergence of hybrid LCCs left a market opening for airlines offering basic service at the lowest possible fares, known as Ultra Low-Cost Carriers (ULCCs), such as Spirit, Frontier and Allegiant, which together accounted for some 11% of the US domestic market in 2019, up from 4% in 2009. The ULCC concept had in fact first appeared in Europe before spreading to the US, and many of the ULCCs launched in the US had previously operated as more traditional LCCs. Spirit, for example, turned itself into an ULCC only in 2006., and Frontier transitioned as late as 2014, in both cases after being acquired by Indigo Partners, an LCC conglomerate with airline investments in several countries. ULCC profitability has been high, at least by airline standards, with operating margins for the year ending March 2018, of 17% for

Allegiant, 16% for Frontier and 14% for Spirit, according to Airline Weekly. These results positioned the US ULCCs among the top ten most profitable airlines in the world by this measure. Whether they will be able to keep their costs so low, and whether passengers will continue to accept such basic service standards, remains to be seen.

Arguably the most significant LCC development globally since the emergence of Southwest, perhaps together with the substantial growth in average seat factors, has been the increased focus on ancillary revenue, something Southwest itself has largely resisted. Ancillary revenues consist of the charges airlines make for anything other than the basic fare, such as onboard drinks and food, bag check-in, seat assignment, etc. It can also include the sale of frequent flyer points to third parties, such as banks. The attraction of low fares accompanied by a wide variety of additional charges has proved to be irresistible for the LCCs and was soon copied by the legacy airlines. This has made comparing the impact of deregulation on air fare levels more difficult, as a traveller who previously did not check a bag and resisted the temptations of the onboard meal and drinks would almost certainly have seen more of a reduction in their fares than someone who now has to pay for these formerly 'free' products.

Cartrawler surveys the world's airlines annually to determine the importance of ancillary revenue. (Its 2020 report covered 81 carriers representing almost 70% of global air traffic.) Table 7.3 shows the increasing importance of such income over the past decade or so, growing from 4.8% of global airline revenue in 2010 to 14.4% in 2021. Table 7.4 lists the top ten airlines in terms of ancillary earnings for 2019. The dominance of US carriers is partly explained by the inclusion of frequent flyer revenue. Table 7.5 shows the split between frequent flyer and other ancillary revenue for 2018, and Table 7.6 lists the top 15 airlines solely in terms of non-FFP ancillary revenue for 2019. The domination of LCCs, and indeed ULCCs, in the latter Table is self-evident.

Table 7.3 Proportion of Total Global Airline Revenue Accounted for by Ancillary Revenue

Year	%
2010	4.8%
2011	5.6%
2012	5.4%
2013	6.0%
2014	6.7%
2015	7.8%
2016	9.1%
2017	10.6%
2018	10.7%
2019	12.2%
2020	13.6%
2021	14.4%

Source: CarTrawler/IdealWorks Co.

Table 7.4 Total Ancillary Revenue, 2019 (US$m)

American Airlines	7,413
United Airlines	6,580
Delta Air Lines	6,198
Southwest	4,498
Ryanair	3,311
Air Canada	2,550
Alaska Air Group	2,034
Lufthansa Group	1,933
IAG	1,932
Emirates	1,927

Source: CarTrawler/IdealWorks Co.

Table 7.5 Frequent Flyer and Other Ancillary Revenue, 2018

	FFP	Other
American Airlines	77%	23%
United Airlines	73%	27%
Delta Air Lines	74%	26%
Southwest	84%	16%
Ryanair	–	100%
Lufthansa Group	32%[a]	68%[a]
Air France/KLM Group	21%[a]	79%[a]
easyJet	–	100%
Spirit	3%	97%
Air Canada	39%	61%

Source: CarTrawler/IdealWorks Co.
[a] Estimated.

Table 7.6 Non-FFP Ancillary Revenue as a Proportion of Total Revenue, Top 15 Airlines, 2019

Spirit	47.0%
Allegiant	46.5%
Wizz Air	45.4%
Viva Aerobus	45.0%
Frontier	43.6%
Volaris	38.5%
Ryanair Group	34.5%
Pegasus	26.4%
Vietjet	25.2%
Jetstar Group[a]	23.9%
Jet2	23.2%
Alaska Air Group	23.2%
Azul	22.4%
Hong Kong Express	21.7%
easyJet	21.6%

Source: CarTrawler/IdealWorks Co.
[a] Estimated

Doganis undertook a so-called Cascade Study of the cost advantage enjoyed by LCCs. (See Table 7.7 – in this context a Cascade Study involves the gradual removal of cost items as operating patterns are adjusted.) It showed that potentially, LCCs' costs could be some 49% less than their legacy competitors. (Interestingly, in the late-1970s the UK Civil Aviation Authority carried out a similar exercise, with similar results, comparing the costs of scheduled and IT charter airlines.) Again, the crude figures hide some of the reality. The largest cost advantage, for example, reflecting the LCCs' higher seat density, can mostly be explained by the operation of business class among the legacy airlines; the associated higher costs are accompanied by far higher revenue and therefore cannot really be termed a disadvantage. Other cost items changed as competition developed, for example the move to larger airports by several LCCs and the reduction in free catering by the legacy carriers. Nevertheless, the comparison serves to highlight the factors which enabled the new LCCs first to establish themselves and become effective competitors to the legacy airlines.

Table 7.7 Coat Advantage of Low-Cost Carriers on Short-Haul Routes: A Cascade Study (2005)

	Cost Advantage Per seat (%)	Cumulative Cost Advantage (%)
Conventional Scheduled Airlines	100	
LCC Operating Advantages:		
- Higher seating density	16	84
- Higher aircraft utilisation	2	82
- Lower flight/cabin crew costs	3	79
- Use cheaper secondary airports	4	75
- Outsourcing maintenance/single aircraft type	2	73
LCC Product/Service Features:		
- Minimal station costs/outsourcing handling	7	66
- No free inflight catering/fewer passenger services	5	61
LCC Differences in Distribution:		
- No agents[a] or GDS commissions	6	55
- Reduced sales/reservation costs	3	52
LCC Other Advantages:		
- Smaller admin./fewer staff and offices	3	**49**

Source: Rigas Doganis: *The Airline Business*. (Second Edition), Routledge, London, 2005.
[a] Assumes 100% direct sales.

Europe

Just as LCCs emerged nationally in the US following deregulation, so European liberalisation saw an explosion of similar airlines, of which the two largest were easyJet, based in the UK, and Ryanair, based in Ireland but with much of its early growth focused also on the UK market. The likelihood of such industry disruption had barely registered during the liberalisation debate. One respected commentator, for example, noted in 1994:

> By 1996, if not earlier, the top six European airlines will control close to 85% of the intra-European market. The vast majority of routes, including the densest routes, will be duopolies. There will be no new entrants of any size because there are too many barriers to entry. For intra-European and especially intra-Community air transport we shall have a highly oligopolistic market structure. If there is going to be real competition on intra-European routes it can only come from the surviving large carriers competing more aggressively with each other on those routes on which they already operate as duopolies or from their entry onto new routes.[13]

Such a conclusion, which was shared by many, despite earlier US experience, proved to be very wide of the mark.

Far more attention was paid to what would happen to the charter sector, which as we saw in Chapter 3 had for many years provided cheap packaged tours, mostly for Northern Europeans wishing to holiday in the Mediterranean, and accounted for about half of intra-Europe air traffic. One study of the impact of European liberalisation on the charter sector published in 1995, for example, made no mention of LCCs at all.[14] By far the largest charter markets in Europe were the UK and Germany, amounting to 25.9 million and 23.7 million passengers respectively in 1998; the next largest market was Spain with 5.0 million. Some 80% of charter flights carried IT passengers.[15] The creation of the EU internal aviation market removed all regulatory distinctions between scheduled and charter air services. The question at the time was whether charters, now released from any remaining regulatory restrictions, would expand further into the scheduled carriers' markets, or would the latter use their increased freedom and still dominant positions to curtail the charter competition?

The answer was neither: both the charter and legacy airlines were soon faced with a new competitive threat, which rapidly ate into their basic markets, and both were forced to adapt radically. It was not long before commentators were highlighting the vulnerability of charters to LCC expansion. George Williams, for example, writing in 2002, noted that despite charters apparently still benefitting from a cost advantage, "it would seem inevitable that more and more consumers will begin to put together their own holiday packages, leaving charter carriers to face an overall decline in the demand for their traditional product."[16] This is exactly what happened, with both charter and scheduled airlines significantly exposed. In terms of seat capacity, by the second quarter of 2019, seven of Europe's top 15 airlines, including the largest two, were LCCs (see Table 7.8). The fastest-growing European airlines over the previous 12 months, by a significant margin, were Wizz Air, easyJet and Ryanair. In terms of capitalisation, LCCs also accounted for five of the top ten European quoted airlines in 2018 (see Table 7.9).

Table 7.8 Europe's Top 15 Airlines (Millions of Seats), 2019

Ryanair[a]	142.1
easyJet[a]	100.3
Lufthansa	71.8
Turkish	64.1
Aeroflot	47.9
SAS	40.4
Vueling	39.1
British Airways	38.9
Wizz Air[a]	37.1
Eurowings[a]	36.1
Air France	33.9
Pegasus Airlines[a]	27.2
KLM	26.8
Iberia	25.6
Alitalia	24.2

Source: CAPA – Centre for Aviation.
[a] LCC or ULCC.

Table 7.9 European Market Capitalisations, 31 March 2019

Airline	Market Capitalisation (Euro)
Ryanair[a]	13,651
IAG	12,208
Lufthansa	9,221
easyJet[a]	5,131
Wizz Air[a]	4,426
Air France/KLM	4,298
Finnair	1,028
SAS	593
Aegean[a]	591
Norwegian[a]	163

Source: HSBC.
[a] = LCC or ULCC.

EasyJet is closely associated with Stelios Haji-Ioannou, who was given a large amount of money by his multi-millionaire Greek/Cypriot father to invest in an airline. There is no doubt that Haji-Ioannou was the dominant force in the creation of easyJet, and indeed in all the subsequent companies established to exploit the *easy* brand, but in terms of the airline's longer-term success credit also has to be given to Ray Webster, an Air New Zealand manager who, like others, returned from time spent in the US enthusiastic about the Southwest LCC model. With help from consultants, he developed a business plan for an Air New Zealand LCC subsidiary operating within Australia, taking advantage of the relaxed regulatory environment agreed between the two close neighbours. Unfortunately, the plan never got off the ground because of reimposed regulatory restrictions, and Webster departed for Europe and easyJet.[17] The creation of the EU internal aviation market provided the ideal environment for a Southwest clone.

EasyJet was based at Luton, an airport closely associated at the time with packaged holidays. Its first flight took place in November 1995, some two years after the final EU liberalisation 'package' came into force, opening up the European market and reforming the old airline nationality restrictions. Despite being a British carrier, therefore, easyJet was able to operate throughout the EU, including on cabotage routes. It followed the Southwest model quite closely, but with a few exceptions, as became increasingly common among LCCs throughout the world. In particular, as we have seen, it generated significant revenues from charging for many elements of the flight product which previously had been incorporated into the ticket price. EasyJet was also the first airline in the world to insist that every passenger book directly, initially by phone and then increasingly via its website, paying by credit card and thereby saving costs by cutting out the travel agent. The airline's contact number was prominently displayed on the side of its aircraft.[18,]

EasyJet solved the problem of Switzerland not at the time being part of the EU internal aviation market by buying a small Swiss carrier, TEA, and rebranding it easyJet Switzerland. This initiative highlighted the type of problem new entrant carriers experienced before liberalisation and why regulatory reform was such a critical factor in the LCC revolution. EasyJet Switzerland soon faced objections from incumbent airlines to its proposed services, especially from Swissair. The authorities insisted that the long-standing rule requiring accommodation to be included with certain flights should be applied to easyJet's first route between Geneva and Barcelona. The LCC's response, similar to that of many charter carriers seeking to enter the trans-Atlantic market in the 1970s, was to set up a tent on a rocky hillside close to Spain's border with France, about 100 miles from Barcelona, and claim that it was available for use by its passengers. The Swiss authorities eventually relented and the tent was displayed proudly in easyJet's Luton headquarters.[19] More significantly, in the longer term, after Switzerland had joined the EU internal aviation market, Swissair was forced into bankruptcy and replaced by a new airline, Swiss, a subsidiary of Germany's Lufthansa, while easyJet went from strength to strength.

Initially, easyJet focused mainly on serving the leisure market, where greater price sensitivity succeeded in generating substantial additional demand, as Southwest had found in the US. However, increasingly it has turned its attention to business travel, a trend accompanied by greater use of primary airports rather than the secondary airports that many LCCs originally served. (EasyJet is now by far the largest operator at London Gatwick, for example, and has announced its intention to serve Heathrow if a third runway is built there. Substantially most of its services operate into slot-constrained airports.) A similar trend has been seen elsewhere in the world (see Table 7.10). EasyJet also developed products previously associated primarily with legacy carriers, such as a loyalty programme and through-ticketing. Its 'Worldwide by easyJet' product, for example, links easyJet flights with those of other airlines to facilitate transfers, providing a one-stop booking process, missed connection cover and often bag transfers. This is very different from the basic point-to-point concept, with its emphasis on removing complexity, originally associated with LCCs and still promoted by the ULCCs.

Table 7.10 LCC Penetration at Selected Airports, 2018

	Number of Passengers (m)	% of LCC Seats (February 2018)
Europe		
London Stansted	28.0	96.7
London Gatwick	46.1	62.2
Paris Orly	33.1	34.5
Copenhagen	30.3	32.9
Amsterdam	71.1	22.2
Madrid	57.9	20.6
North America		
Fort Lauderdale	36.0	72.9
New York JFK	59.3*	26.4
Toronto	47.1*	23.3
Los Angeles LAX	87.5	22.3
Asia Pacific		
Kuala Lumpur	60.0	52.5
Delhi	69.9	45.8
Singapore	65.6	31.2
Sydney	44.4	19.6
Latin America		
Mexico City	47.7	45.5
Sao Paulo Guarulhos	42.8	29.5
Buenos Aires Ezeiza	9.8	13.3
Middle East		
Riyadh	22.5**	24.6
Dubai	89.1	18.0
Kuwait	11.8***	13.8
Africa		
Johannesburg	21.2	26.6
Nairobi	6.5**	12.6

Source: CAPA -Centre for Aviation.
[a] 2017.
[b] 2015.
[c] 2016.

There is also evidence that this evolution of the original LCC concept is occurring in the holiday market. The LCCs' core product is the provision of flight seats, but it was not long in Europe before they began to offer third-party travel services such as hotels and car hire via their websites. This provided the opportunity for passengers to create their own packaged holidays. At the same time, as we have already seen, the integrated tour operators began to unbundle their products and offer more seat-only services. Now, however, we see the LCCs beginning to move into the old IT charter sector, bundling flights, hotels and ground arrangements into a single product. EasyJet established a new tour operator subsidiary, easyJet Holidays, in 2011, but with only limited success. The appointment of a new Chief Executive, Johan Lundgren, previously Deputy Chief Executive of the Tui Group, the largest integrated holiday company in Europe, has led to a fresh push. EasyJet Holidays was re-launched in 2019, ready for the 2020 summer season, and of course the COVID pandemic. Other European LCCs are following a similar path. Jet2, for example, established Jet2 Holidays early in its existence and has seen the proportion of its passengers travelling on packaged tours increase from about 2% in 2009 to some 50% today. Ryanair established Ryanair Sun in 2018, based in Poland, to work with tour operators. It was rebranded as Buzz in 2019.

The largest European LCC is Ryanair, described by Herb Kelleher as "the best imitation of Southwest Airlines that I have seen."[20] It was established in 1985, with its first flight the following year, and like Southwest began with small aircraft, in Ryanair's case a 15-seater Embraer Bandeirante. Sean Barrett points out that its licensing came about almost by accident. The Irish Government, like most of its European counterparts, had been highly protective of its national carrier, Aer Lingus. However, a decision by the Irish Supreme Court lifted an injunction preventing a US charter airline, Transamerica, from selling unapproved trans-Atlantic fares, another example of a European court decision directly affecting the airline liberalisation debate. It resulted in a change of policy on the part of the Government and a new, liberal air services agreement with the UK.[21] It also led to the Irish Government supporting British and Dutch attempts to liberalise EU aviation regulation. By 1990, Ryanair was serving 26 city-pairs, carrying some 700,000 passengers and incurring significant losses. A restructuring in 1991 created a jet operating LCC just in time to take advantage of European liberalisation, under the leadership of a charismatic, if controversial, Chief Executive, Michael O'Leary.

Ryanair followed the ULCC model closely, with point-to-point services, standardised fleet, high aircraft utilisation and seat factors, basic onboard product with significant ancillary sales, direct sales only and no frequent flyer programme. At the same time, it set itself apart from many similar airlines. Its particularly aggressive focus on low costs, and apparent indifference to customer service and loyalty, succeeded in producing very low fares and therefore high rates of growth. It concentrated on flying to secondary airports, often some distance from the cities they were supposed to serve, driving hard bargains on airport charges and exhibiting a willingness to enter and leave routes frequently and quickly in reaction to market changes. Initially, capital costs were minimised by taking advantage of cheaper second-hand aircraft during a period of economic downturn. All this created rapid growth and high profitability.

The downside was poor and less harmonious public and employee relations, arguably the antithesis of the Southwest approach despite Herb Kelleher's apparent admiration for the European ULCC. As easyJet and others moved towards a more hybrid model, Ryanair rigorously pursued the ULCC path. Unfortunately, the extreme lengths to which the airline was prepared to go to keep costs as low as possible proved to be unsustainable. Ryanair was forced to change track, partly because staff shortages and over-scheduling associated with a new pilot rostering system led to a poor level of flight reliability, and partly because of growing public and political antagonism towards its service ethos. It sought to adopt a more consumer-friendly profile, began to accept union recognition and was more willing to serve primary airports. Ryanair has also shown a willingness to absorb other European LCCs, first Buzz in the UK and then Laudamotion (renamed Lauda) in Austria, and has created a holding company structure with five subsidiaries, Lauda, Ryanair Sun in Poland (renamed Buzz), Ryanair UK, the original Ryanair based in Ireland and most recently Malta Air. Some have suggested that the new subsidiaries are designed to hide the principal brand, which has become rather toxic in certain markets.

Numerous other trans-European LCCs have emerged since liberalisation, not all of whom have survived. Among the more successful have been Jet2 based in the UK and Wizz Air based in Hungary. In addition, following the pattern set in the US, several European legacy carriers have established LCC subsidiaries to compete against the new entrants. Success has been varied, although overall certainly greater than US experience. An early example was Go, created by British Airways in 1998. It achieved some success in its own right, but was seen to be cannibalising BA's traffic. As one BA insider explained: "We were pouring money into a company that was stealing our customers and reducing our yields. It was mad."[22] Go was sold off to its management backed by a venture capital company, apparently at a profit for BA, and eventually absorbed into easyJet. With BA's incorporation into the IAG consortium, it found itself again with sister LCCs in the form of Vueling and Level, albeit operated independently and with less market duplication than was the case with Go. KLM's LCC subsidiary Buzz was similarly sold off, to Ryanair, although the Dutch airline acquired another former charter carrier, Transavia, which became the low-cost unit for the merged Air France/KLM operation. Other legacy airlines such as Lufthansa and SAS also set up low-fare subsidiaries, with varying degrees of success. Lufthansa's Germanwings never succeeded in establishing competitive cost levels, at least partly because of the use of expensive mainline crew, and was eventually closed down. Lufthansa had more success with another subsidiary, Eurowings.

Rest of the World

It is clear that as liberalisation has spread around the world, the LCC model has followed. For example, according to CAPA estimates, from virtually zero in 1998, LCCs accounted for 14% of total seat capacity within the Asia/Pacific region in 2008, 24% in 2013 and 29% in 2018, with the top four LCC city-pairs in the world now all falling within Asia/Pacific. The LCC penetration rate for capacity to/from the region was 8% pre-COVID, up from just 3% in 2008. By 2018, there were seven markets in the Asia/Pacific region where LCCs had more than 50% of domestic capacity and six markets where they had over 30% of international capacity. Of the 20 largest LCC city-pairs, in terms of passengers carried, 13 were in Asia, with none in either Europe or the US. Pre-COVID LCC growth in Asia has averaged 19% per annum since 2008, compared to just 9.4% in Europe, and LCC penetration of the Asian market had been forecast (pre-COVID) to overtake that of Europe by 2030.

What particularly stands out from the data, however, is the fact that so far, LCCs have had only a modest impact in China, reflecting continuing regulatory constraints there. In 2018, LCCs accounted for 10% of Chinese domestic capacity (admittedly up from 2% in 2008), compared with over 70% in both India and Thailand. The 14% penetration rate for international services reflects mainly the activity of non-Chinese carriers. On the other hand, some have argued that Chinese LCCs are in a 'sweet spot' and well positioned to enjoy a 'decade of vibrant growth,' with an escalation of the modest regulatory reform achieved since 2013.[23] In Australia, Qantas established a successful subsidiary, Jetstar, with significantly lower costs than its parent company, to operate both short and long-haul services. The LCC launched by the Virgin Group in 1999, Virgin Australia (originally Virgin Blue), similarly had some success, but was forced by competitive pressure to adopt a more hybrid model, serving both the business and leisure markets, and eventually faced financial problems.

In Singapore we find four airlines incorporated into a single corporate structure, Singapore Airlines and SilkAir operating as full-service carriers and Tigerair and Scoot acting as LCCs. The Japanese legacy carriers have similarly adopted a multi-brand approach, with the relatively restrictive regulatory environment limiting the expansion of independent LCCs. The five Japanese LCCs (Jetstar Japan, Peach, Vanilla Air, Spring Airlines Japan and Air Asia Japan) had a combined domestic market share by early 2019 of less than 9%; their share of international traffic to/from Japan was just 3.8%. Asia has also spawned a number of LCCs operating as cross-border joint ventures, helped by a relatively benign regulatory environment in some markets. Air Asia, for example, has participated in such ventures in several countries. Asia/Pacific is also the home of two of the first low-cost airline alliances, U-FLY and Value Alliance, to which we will return in Chapter 8. Thus, overall we see a mixed picture in the Asia/Pacific region, with a variety of operating models, but a clear trend of an increasing LCC presence, with ample opportunity for further growth in many markets (Tables 7.11 and 7.12).

Table 7.11 Largest Low-Cost Carriers in Asia (Millions of Seats), 2018

Airline	Number of Seats (million)
Indigo (India)	71.4
Lion Air (Indonesia)	51.8
Air Asia (Malaysia)	37.2
Thai Air Asia (Thailand)	25.4
Cebu Pacific Air (Philippines)	21.4
Viet JetAir (Vietnam)	21.1
SpiceJet (India)	20.1
Spring Airlines (China)	18.8
Citilink (Indonesia)	18.1
Thai Lion Air (Thailand)	13.6

Source: OAG

Table 7.12 LCC Penetration of Asian Markets, 2008 and 2018 (%)

Country	2008 Domestic	2018 Domestic	2008 International	2018 International
China	2	10	3	14
Japan	6	17	0	26
India	48	70	11	23
Indonesia	40	53	26	40
Thailand	32	72	11	32
Australia	19	26	7	15
South Korea	7	53	1	35
Malaysia	50	57	29	51
Hong Kong	–	–	3	11
Singapore	–	–	12	31

Source: OAG.

Latin America exhibits a similar picture, with rapid LCC growth challenging the legacy carriers, combined with the emergence of hybrid airlines and ULCCs. Table 7.13 shows airline market shares, in terms of the number of passengers carried, in two major Latin American countries, Mexico and Brazil, while Table 7.14 shows market penetration of LCCs (this time in terms of available seats) in five North and South American markets. LCC expansion in the Middle East and especially Africa has been relatively modest, with most activity concentrated in Saudi Arabia, the UAE and South Africa. According to CAPA, by early 2019, the 200 or so aircraft operated by LCCs in these two regions represented just 3% of the worldwide LCC fleet, far less than the 10% of the global total aircraft fleet operated by Middle East and African airlines.

One group of LCCs spans the US, Europe and Latin America. Indigo Partners was founded in 2002 by Bill Franke and David Bonderman. Franke was an early investor in Ryanair and Bonderman was Chairman of the airline for many years. Indigo was involved in the establishment of Tiger Airways in Singapore, now owned by Singapore Airlines, and the defunct Indonesian carrier Mandala Airlines. However, its current investments focus on Wizz Air (Hungary), Frontier (US), Spirit (US), Volaris (Mexico and Costa Rica) and Jet Smart (Chile). In 2017, Indigo placed an order for 430 A320 family aircraft, the largest single aircraft order ever received by Airbus, with a list value of some US$50 billion. (It is a reasonable assumption that Indigo obtained a substantial discount on the list value.) The aircraft were destined for each of the carriers in which Indigo had a stake and is indicative of the increasing influence and buying power of the LCCs. In 2021, Indigo placed a further Airbus order for 255 aircraft, bringing its total A320 family order book over its relatively short life to 1,145.

Table 7.13 Airline Domestic Market Shares (number of passengers) in Mexico and Brazil, 2019 (%)

Mexico	Aeromexico	10.0
	Volaris	31.3
	Interjet	19.7
	Viva Aerobus	20.2
Brazil	GOL	35.9
	LATAM	33.1
	Azul	27.0

Source: CAPA – Centre for Aviation.

Table 7.14 LCC Market Penetration (Number of Seats) the Americas, 2019 (%)

Puerto Rico	57.8
Mexico	58.0
Brazil	57.8
United States	28.9
Canada	26.1

Source: CAPA – Centre for Aviation.

Long-Haul LCCs

The LCC revolution was initially centred on short/medium-haul services, but inevitably attention eventually shifted to longer routes. It is important to remember, however, that such services have a long history, especially across the Atlantic. To a large extent, charter flights involving dubious club membership and subsequently superseded by Advanced Booking Charters (see Chapter 3) sought to serve the same market niche. Perhaps even more relevant was Freddie Laker's Skytrain and other similar initiatives such as People Express. All of these services had far lower costs than the incumbent airlines, provided innovative service and for a while achieved some success. Critically, however, they all eventually failed. The legacy airlines were not prepared to see their lucrative long-haul services undermined. They fought back, with the result that the new entrants were either forced out of business or saw their market shares substantially reduced. Undoubtedly part of the problem for the LCCs is the fact that the economics of long-haul air transport are very different from short-haul operations. Many of the advantages which LCCs initially enjoyed in the US, Europe and elsewhere are just not available when it comes to longer flights.

This problem was highlighted by Barkin, Hertzell and Young, writing in The McKinsey Quarterly as early as 1995. They argued that the cost advantages accrued in short-haul, high-traffic markets, such as low input costs and cheaper product and process designs, are significantly weaker on longer routes, For example, passengers are likely to demand better in-flight service, more leg room, and so forth, when they are on a longer flight and the benefit stemming from the fast turn-around of aircraft is not as important.[24] Put more simply, it is impossible to turn around a wide-bodied aircraft in the 20–30 minutes achieved by LCCs on short-haul routes, most long-haul legacy airlines were already achieving high levels of aircraft utilisation on their long-haul networks, and given the nature of such routes, there is little opportunity for the LCCs to increase operational efficiency. Similarly, product innovations such as maximising auxiliary revenue, which airlines such as Laker and People Express had previously tried, are relatively easily replicated by the legacy carriers if necessary. (We already see examples of innovative pricing by the legacy carriers on the North Atlantic in response to LCC entry, such as Virgin Atlantic's Economy Delight, Economy Classic and Economy Light fare structure offering different product features. Other airlines have followed a similar path.) The established airlines also have the benefit of carrying far more business passengers willing to pay premium fares for increased comfort and better service.

Nevertheless, in recent years numerous LCCs have sought to establish themselves as long-haul carriers. They have achieved some market penetration success, especially on the North Atlantic where the LCC share of available seats grew from virtually zero in 2013 to some 8% in 2018. Elsewhere their market share remained very modest, such as 1% between Europe and Asia/Pacific, less than 2% between Europe and sub-Sahara Africa and just over 3% between Europe and Latin America. However, the picture is rather different within the Asia/Pacific region, where route density tends to be greater than elsewhere other than the North Atlantic. If we assume that ownership of wide-body aircraft equates with the operation of long-haul services, which may not always be the case, in early 2018, according to CAPA, 22 LCCs operated 175 wide-body aircraft worldwide, with fleet penetration far higher in Southeast Asia than anywhere else (see Table 7.15). It remains to be seen how the LCCs will recover following the impact of the COVID pandemic, but the real game changer for long-haul routes may not be the threat from LCCs operating wide-body aircraft, but rather from the new technology short-haul equipment such as the Airbus A321LRX, which combines relatively small size with operating economics comparable to much larger aircraft. The LCCs are well placed to take advantage of this development, although they will certainly be challenged by the legacy carriers. We will return to this subject in Chapter 9.

Table 7.15 Number of Wide-Body Aircraft in LCC Fleets, April 2018

Southeast Asia	64
Western Europe	40
North America	29
Northeast Asia	13
Southeast Pacific	11
Eastern/Central Europe	8
Upper South America	7
North Africa	2
Middle East	1

Source: CAPA – Centre for Aviation.

Notes

1 Foreword to Simon Calder: *No Frills. The Truth Behind the Low-Cost Revolution in the Skies*. Virgin Books, London, 2002.
2 Kenneth Button and Stephen Ison: 'The economics of low-cost airlines: Introduction.' *Research in Transportation Economics*, Vol. 24(1–4), 2008, pp. 1–84.
3 Lamar Muse: *Southwest Passage. The Inside Story of Southwest Airlines' Formative Years*. Eakin Press, Austin TX, 2002.
4 Alan R. Beckenstein and Brian Campbell: 'Public Benefits and Private Success: The Southwest Effect Revisited.' Darden Business School Working Paper No. 206, August 2017.
5 Lamar Muse, op cit.
6 Ibid.
7 Quoted in Thomas C. Lawton: *Cleared for Take-Off. Structure and Strategy in the Low Fare Airline Business*. Ashgate, Aldershot, 2002.
8 Hervé Mathe, Xavier Pavie and Marwyn O'Keefe: 'ESSEC Business School Case Study.' Institute for Strategic Innovation and Services, 2015.
9 Beckenstein and Campbell, op cit.
10 Michael E. Porter: 'What is strategy.' *Harvard Business Review*, November/December 1996, pp. 61–78.
11 Peter Morrell: 'Airlines within airlines: An analysis of US network airline responses to Low-Cost Carriers.' *Journal of Air Transport Management*, Vol. 11(5), September 2005, pp. 303–312.
12 Luca Graf: 'Incompatibles of the low-cost and network carrier business models within the same airline grouping.' *Journal of Air Transport Management*, Vol. 11(5), September 2005, pp. 313–327.
13 Rigas Doganis: 'The impact of liberalization on European airline strategies and operations.' *Journal of Air Transport Management*, Vol. 1(1), March 1994, pp. 15–25.
14 Andrew Lobbenberg: 'Strategic responses of charter airlines to Single Market integration.' *Journal of Air Transport Management*, Vol 2(2), June 1995, pp. 76–91.

15 UK Civil Aviation Authority: *The Single European Aviation Market: The First Five Years.* CAP 685, London, 1998.
16 George Williams: *Airline Competition: Deregulation's Mixed Legacy.* Ashgate, Aldershot, 2002.
17 Peter Harbison: 'They just didn't get it.' Airline Leader, March/April, 2018.
18 Simon Calder, op cit.
19 Thomas C. Lawton, op cit.
20 Sean Barratt: 'Air transport liberalization: The case of Ireland.' In Matthias Finger and Kenneth Button (eds.): *Air Transport Liberalization. A Critical Assessment.* Elgar, Cheltenham, 2017, pp. 69–91.
21 Simon Calder, op cit.
22 Ibid.
23 David Wu and Sonia Luo: 'China Low-Cost Carriers.' HSBC Global Research, June 2019.
24 Thomas I. Barkin, O. Staffan Hertzell and Stephanie J. Young: 'Facing Low-Cost Competitors: Lessons from US Airlines.' The McKinsey Quarterly, No. 4, 1995. Quoted in Thomas C. Lawton, op cit.

8 Ownership and Control

We have seen how over the past 70 years the airline industry has been characterised by growing economic liberalisation, progressing at first quite tentatively and then at some speed. However, despite the widespread removal of the old regulatory fetters, often replaced by new regulations focused on consumer protection, two areas have remained firmly stuck in the past. One is cabotage services, the operation of routes within a country by airlines of another State. Hardly any countries permit such operations, other than within regional groupings such as the EU's internal aviation market. The second area where reform remains limited relates to the ownership and control of airlines. These restrictions have had, and still have, a major impact on the airline industry, to a large extent dictating its very structure and affecting its profitability. They stand out as an anachronism in a world of deregulation/liberalisation, but unfortunately one with little immediate prospect of substantial reform.

The Origins

It is often claimed that the origins of international ownership and control rules in the airline industry lie in the Chicago Convention of 1944. This is correct only to the extent that Chicago established a clear role for national jurisdiction over airspace, as we saw in Chapter 2. (National ownership restrictions, on the other hand, date back to earlier aviation regulations, such as the US Air Commerce Act of 1926.) Article 77 of the Convention even allowed for two or more contracting States to constitute "joint air transport operating organizations or international operating agencies." It was the International Air Services Transit Agreement (IASTA), also initially signed in 1944, establishing for the first time the principle of the automatic right of transit and emergency landing (the first two Freedoms of the Air), which referred specifically to airline ownership:

> Each contracting State reserves the right to withhold or revoke a certificate or permit to an air transport enterprise of another State in any case where it is not satisfied that substantial ownership and effective control are vested in nationals of a Contracting State, or in case of failure of such

air transport enterprise to comply with the laws of the State over which it operates, or to perform its obligations under this Agreement.

Two elements are worth noting in this statement. First, it refers to 'substantial ownership and effective control' without defining either 'substantial' or 'effective.' Secondly, ownership and control are required to be vested in '*a* Contracting State,' not necessarily in the State designating the airline under IASTA. Both of these shortcomings, if that is the right term, were addressed in the many bilateral air services agreements signed over the following years.

As noted in Chapter 3, the UK/US Bermuda Agreement of 1946 was the first of thousands of bilateral ASAs between States, virtually all of which included an airline ownership and control clause. Bermuda broadly followed IASTA in stipulating that one party could refuse to accept the designation of an airline under the agreement if that carrier was not majority owned and controlled by nationals of the other party. Thus, clarity was added by replacing 'substantial' with 'majority.' Bermuda was also permissive in that States had the right to refuse a designation if the ownership test was not met, but they were not required to do so. In addition, as already mentioned, States had their own definitions of what constituted a national airline, quite separate from any ASAs they may have signed. These definitions varied significantly from country to country, partly in terms of the percentage of national ownership required and partly in the interpretation of 'control,' and these different approaches continue to the present day (see Table 8.1).

Table 8.1 Foreign Ownership Limits for Airlines in Selected Countries, 2019

Australia[a]	49%
Brazil	20%
Canada	49%
Chile	100%
China	35%
European Union	49%
Japan	33%
Korea	50%
United States[b]	25%

Source: CAPA – Centre for Aviation.
[a] No limit for domestic airlines.
[b] 25% voting shares, 49% of all shares.

There were many reasons during the early post-war years for adopting airline ownership and control rules. For example, like numerous other sectors at the time, air transport was regarded as a strategic industry critical to the economic development of a country. Such protectionism was relatively short-lived for most industries, but not for aviation. A more aviation-specific reason for the rules lay in the nature of the bilateral approach to the trade of international traffic rights. In negotiating such arrangements States did not want to see third country airlines inadvertently benefit (the so-called 'free-rider' principle), for example, by establishing a subsidiary carrier in one of the two parties to an ASA able to exploit that country's route rights. There was also concern about effective safety regulation, many States being particularly keen to avoid the problems seen in the shipping industry with the creation of so-called 'flags of convenience.' As discussed further below, there are alternative ways of addressing all of these problems, but in the environment of the 1940s and 1950s, strict control over the nationality of airline owners appeared to be the best way forward. The issue is not the adoption of such rules, but finding a way to remove them as the industry has matured.

The extent of foreign ownership which individual States permit in their airlines varies considerably quantitatively and qualitatively. In addition to restrictions on overall share ownership and management control, for example, some countries also have limits on the percentage of shares that can be owned by a single investor and/or by other airlines. It is worth highlighting two examples in particular to illustrate the range of policies applied. The US' rules are among the most prohibitive in the world. Foreign interests are allowed to own just 25% of the voting shares in an airline (49% of total shares), but there are also numerous restrictions on the nationality of Board members and senior executives, designed to minimise any hint of foreign influence on the company's operation. Despite attempts by other governments to persuade the US to reform its rules and bring them more in line with those applicable in most other countries, so far the US has declined to do so.

Domestic pressure to change the rules has also arisen. In 2003, for example, the Bush Administration proposed increasing the ownership cap to 49% of voting shares. This was supported by most US airlines, as well as consumer interests and academics, but strongly opposed by the unions and failed to become law. Another attempt at reform was made in 2018, with a proposal introduced into Congress requiring foreign-owned airlines wishing to operate within the US to establish a subsidiary there employing only US citizens. This was designed to allay fears about the loss of jobs overseas but again failed to attract sufficient political support.

The UK, on the other hand, has adopted a far more flexible, some might say pragmatic approach. Prior to the creation of the EU internal aviation market, the UK focused primarily on the control of an airline, arguing that the percentage of shares owned by foreign interests was less relevant given that in certain circumstances control could still be exercised with a minority stake in a company. Airlines were accepted as being British even if wholly owned by foreign interests provided that their operational bases and management were clearly centred on the UK. (They might not, of course, be accepted as British by other countries under the relevant ASAs.) This explains why when the UK was required to accept a numerical limit on airline share ownership following EU liberalisation, the legislation specified two British exceptions to the general rule: Monarch Airlines, which was fully owned by Swiss interests, and Britannia Airways (later Thomson Airways), formally owned by a Canadian company.

Following its exit from the EU, the UK has reverted to its former, more liberal approach, and the initial post-Brexit air services agreement between the EU and UK provides for British airlines to be owned and controlled by EU or UK interests, although the arrangement is not reciprocated for EU carriers. The hope, so far unsatisfied, is to eventually negotiate a fully liberalised ownership and control arrangement. In the absence of such an agreement, some EU airlines, such as Ryanair and Wizz Air, have had to adjust their shareholder registers to ensure that they are still regarded as Community Carriers. One way of doing this, which Ryanair has adopted, is to re-register some shareholders' stakes as American Depository Receipts, a mechanism that preserves most of the ownership rights, including dividends, but without the ability to vote at General Meetings. It is one of several fudges, as we shall see, designed to avoid the worst effects of the airline ownership and control restrictions, but which also add to governance complexity and costs.

There are other examples of a less restrictive approach around the world. In Latin America, for example, Iberia Airlines was permitted to acquire a majority shareholding (85% at one point) in Aerolineas Argentinas in the early 1990s, although the Spanish carrier later withdrew. (The US took advantage of this investment to demand additional Argentinian traffic rights for US carriers.) Several Latin American countries have adopted a 'principal place of business' regime (see below), combined with complex governance structures, rather than limiting the extent of foreign share ownership. This has facilitated the merger of Chile's Lan and Brazil's TAM airlines to form the cross-border LATAM, the combination of Colombia's Avianca and El Salvador's TACA and most recently the proposed merger of Brazil's GOL with Avianca under the umbrella of the Abra Group and incorporating Viva, a low-cost carrier serving Colombia and Peru, and a 5% stake in Chile's Sky Airlines. Oddly, the Abra Group is to be incorporated in the UK. Argentina has opened its market further, with domestic and international route rights made available to foreign-owned carriers.

Australia and New Zealand have allowed 100% foreign ownership of domestic airlines, but a 49% limit still applies to carriers serving international routes from Australia. In the case of Ansett, before it went bankrupt, this necessitated the creation of a separate company, Ansett International, majority owned by an investment company under contract to the parent airline, which guaranteed to cover any losses; this was widely known as the 'Ansett Fiction' and was yet another fudge of the underlying rules. Japan raised concerns, but eventually accepted the subterfuge.[1] In India, the rules have been progressively relaxed to the extent that they are now very similar to Australia's, with some additional restrictions on ownership by other airlines. In 2018, Canada increased the foreign ownership cap from 25% to 49%, although foreign airlines are still limited to a 25% stake individually or in combination.

In the Asia/Pacific region, the members of the Association of South East Asian Nations (ASEAN) have agreed on paper to follow the EU example with respect to the ownership of airlines within the region, but so far practical progress has been very slow. Instead, common branding combined with local investors with majority stakes has been a more common model there, pursued by Air Asia and Jetstar for example. As we saw in Chapter 6, the Single African Air Transport Market (SAATM) was an initiative of the African Union in 2015, designed to expedite the full implementation of the Yamoussoukro Decision of 1999. As with the ASEAN countries, the objective is to replicate the EU internal aviation market, including the removal of airline ownership and control rules among the signatory States. SAATM countries account for some 80% of the African aviation market, but so far good intentions have not been matched by significant progress. Mention should also be made of SAS, Gulf Air and Air Afrique, each of which involved cross-border government control with shared nationality. This frequently necessitated difficult bilateral negotiations with other States. Only SAS survives in anything like its original form.

The Arguments

Given their importance as a limiting factor in the normalisation of the airline industry, it should not be a surprise that airline ownership and control rules have attracted considerable attention from commercial interests and academics. The International Chamber of Commerce, for example, noted as early as 1994 that cross-border investment is one of the most important aviation policy issues of the 1990s.[2] In her 2003 book on the subject, Isabella Lelieur listed over 60 peer-reviewed relevant articles, overwhelmingly most of which supported reform. The list is far from comprehensive, and of course there have been many more articles published since 2003. Lelieur herself, echoing the views of others, concludes that:

> ... the time has come to offer the aviation industry a new regulatory framework, similar to those of other industrial sectors that benefit from a global and liberal market.... Removal of foreign ownership restrictions should be a matter of priority for the respective national authorities worldwide, since it would play a paramount role in the future global consolidation of airlines and would be an important step towards the normalisation of the industry.[3]

Another academic analysis concluded: "If there is a single serious barrier to achieving air transport liberalisation, it is airline ownership and control restrictions."[4] A significant study in 2006 by the UK Civil Aviation Authority (CAA) came to very similar conclusions, noting that "aviation has ... emerged as a particularly conspicuous anomaly in a world of widespread trade liberalisation." The CAA research showed that restrictions on investor nationality have had a profoundly negative effect on the development of the airline industry and have provided no benefits in terms of safety or labour standards that could not be replicated by other, less onerous means:

> In conclusion, liberalisation of ownership and control is essential to the healthy development of a truly global industry, introducing freedoms

for airlines that should bring considerable benefits to the industry and its users and play a considerable role in enhancing related global economic activity.[5]

There is little doubt, therefore, that the weight of economic opinion points strongly towards reform of what has increasingly come to be seen as an archaic set of rules which have served to distort the development of the sector and prevent it from behaving like most other industries, in particular in terms of cross-border mergers and acquisitions. Aviation is one of the most international businesses, but there is not a single truly global airline. Essentially, air carriers remain nation-based, despite the steady progress, at least until recently, towards a more liberal regulatory environment. Lelieur describes this as "the fundamental contradiction ... between national ties and the international activities of airlines."[6] There is evidence that the industry's failure to consolidate has adversely affected its viability, and that in markets where significant consolidation has been possible, such as within the US, profitability has increased substantially, although this is not universally true. As we shall see below, airlines have attempted to replicate some of the benefits of cross-border mergers by forming alliances, but this has proved to be very much a second-best solution to the underlying issue. Where international mergers have been attempted, they have usually required the construction of complex and economically inefficient governance structures.

Not everyone, of course, agrees that the ownership and control rules should be reformed. As Cosmas, Belobaba and Swelbar have commented: "It is commonly acknowledged by industry experts that increased foreign ownership ... will increase competition, but they disagree on whether the resulting impacts are positive or negative."[7] A particular issue arises in the US in relation to the Civil Reserve Air Fleet (CRAF), under which US carriers agree to provide supplemental airlift to the Department of Defense during national emergencies in return for preferential access to government contracts. The CRAF has been invoked three times, most recently in 2021 for the evacuation of US citizens from Afghanistan. The arrangement, it is argued, could be jeopardised if US airlines were controlled by foreign citizens, who might be less willing to support US military engagements. However, there are alternative ways to achieve the same objective which many other countries have adopted, notably by legally requiring airlines to make aircraft and crew available to governments at times of national emergency. As Dorothy Robyn has argued, provided an airline had its principal place of business in the US, the US authorities would retain the same legal and economic leverage over a foreign-owned carrier as it has over a US-owned airline.[8] The US already has protections in place to prevent the purchase of any US company by unacceptable foreign interests.

More generally, the arguments in favour of retaining the status quo have focused primarily on concerns about labour protection, safety and what might be broadly defined as 'national interest,' to which more recently has been added a fear of the competitive threat provided by the new 'super hub' carriers in the Middle East. Such concerns have been widely debated for many years, and mostly shown to be unjustified. For example, representatives of labour, and especially the pilots, have argued strongly that liberalising the ownership and control rules will enable airlines to force down staff costs by transferring operations between countries at will. The CAA study referred to above found no evidence to support such an argument and concluded that in fact the opposite appeared to be the case. Certainly, the evidence from the creation of the European internal aviation market, with its complete removal of ownership restrictions within the EU, suggests that full liberalisation results in more flights and additional employment. It is also worth noting that in the context of the deregulation of trans-Atlantic air services, pilots' unions in both the US and Europe have highlighted the risk, if ownership restrictions are reformed, of job transfers between the Continents to take advantage of lower salaries and less restrictive employment laws. Both sets of unions cannot be correct; more likely, they are both wrong.

With respect to safety, the experience of the shipping industry, especially the emergence of 'flags of convenience' in the absence of nationality ownership restrictions for international services, has raised fears of a deterioration in aviation standards if airline regulation were to follow a similar path. However, again such an argument does not withstand detailed analysis. It goes without saying that safety should be the prime focus of any regulatory regime and every effort made to resist deterioration. There are nevertheless alternative ways of achieving this objective without resorting to the current protectionist measures, which come at such a high economic price. It seems certain that governments will want to ensure that airlines are subject to tight regulatory safety control and unable to find ways around the rules. Many commentators have argued that this objective can be achieved by replacing the current ownership and control rules, reflecting the nationality of the shareholders, with ones based on the concept of 'principal place of business' of the company itself, also known as 'nationality by establishment.' As already noted, such an approach was initially adopted by the UK Government following British withdrawal from the EU and has also found favour in some Latin American countries. Furthermore, it is far from a new concept. For example, for several decades it was successfully pursued by Hong Kong, then a British colony, reflecting the fact that the local flag carrier, Cathay Pacific, was owned and controlled by non-Hong Kong interests. There have been other, more recent, examples and there is no evidence to suggest that adopting such an approach has led to any deterioration in safety standards.

Carney and Dostaler comment that:

> Not all investors are equal. Investors differ with respect to their interests and their ability to actively intervene in management decisions to achieve this interest. In this regard, it is the identity and interest of the equity owner and not his or her nationality that ought to be the material consideration in the debate about foreign ownership in airlines.[9]

This raises an additional factor which has increased in significance in more recent years and which further reduces the effectiveness of current airline ownership rules, namely the growing influence of institutional investors as shareholders in publicly-quoted airlines. Funds such as Blackrock and Vanguard are now among the largest owners of US carriers, for example. A study by Martin, Schmalz and Tecu found that in early 2016, American Airlines' top seven shareholders, who jointly controlled 49.5% of its stock, were also among the top ten investors in Southwest Airlines and various other competitors. At the same time, each of Southwest's largest six shareholders was also among the top ten investors in American and Delta, and five of them were among the top ten holders of United shares as well.[10]

Airlines are by no means unique in this respect; institutional shareholder ownership of publicly quoted US companies increased from 37% in 1980 to 62% in 2015, and a similar pattern is found in other countries. This has raised questions about the potential for anti-competitive behaviour among institutional investors, resulting in an investigation by at least one competition authority.[11] For present purposes, however, the point is that the ultimate ownership of institutional funds is often opaque, making it difficult to identify their nationality. This, it might be argued, drives a coach and horses through any attempt to enforce national ownership of airlines. Unfortunately, that has not stopped governments from trying.

Airline Profitability

One of the key problems facing the airline industry is its inability to achieve long-term, sustainable profitability. (Chapter 10 contains a more detailed discussion of this subject.) There are, of course, some highly profitable carriers, but it is often claimed that overall, the industry has destroyed more value than it has created since the first Wright brothers' flight. Only in the most recent (pre-COVID) years has the industry come close to earning its cost of capital, aided by a benign general economic environment and the substantial improvement in performance by one region's carriers. A key element in airlines' ability to increase yields and therefore profits is control of capacity. Such control is far easier to exercise with fewer players in the market, particularly given the level of competition in the airline industry and its underlying cost structure. This is why consolidation is so important for the industry's long-term viability. The downside, of course, is that higher fares result in reduced consumer benefits. Crucially, however, it has to be asked whether the general level of air fares to which passengers have become accustomed is compatible with an economically sustainable industry.

Evidence to support such a hypothesis is provided by US experience. For most of the post-deregulation period, US major airlines as a group suffered extremely low levels of profitability, often experiencing actual losses (see Table 8.2). Almost all were forced into so-called Chapter 11 bankruptcy on more than one occasion. According to IATA, in 2008, following the global

Table 8.2 US Passenger Airlines' Profits, 1978/89 to 2010/16 (US$ billions)

1979/89	+1.8
1990/94	−11.4
1995/00	+20.6
2001/09	−65.0
2010/16	+61.7

Source: Airlines for America/Aviation Strategy.

financial crisis, the four largest US airlines at the time accounted for US$18 billion (almost 70%) of the global industry's US$26 billion losses. The reduction in the number of major US airlines to just four (see Table 8.3) eventually resulted in a dramatic change. Over a relatively short period of time, the US went from having the worst-performing carriers to the world's most profitable (see Table 8.4), a direct result of consolidation and the consequential move to a more rational market structure with greater control over capacity.

Table 8.3 US Airline Consolidation, 2015–2016

US Airways/America West	2005
Delta/Northwest	2008
United/Continental	2010
Southwest/AirTran	2011
American/US Airways	2014
Alaska/Virgin America	2016

Table 8.4 Global Airline Profitability by Region, 2018

Region	Net Post-Tax Profit (US$ bn.)	% of Revenue
	−0.3	2.1
Asia	+10.4	3.8
Middle East	+0.8	1.2
Latin America	+0.7	1.6
North America	+16.6	6.0
Europe	+7.4	3.4

Source: CAPA – Centre for Aviation.

To some extent, this simply followed the experience of other industries, but airlines certainly lagged behind the trend. The investor Warren Buffet once described himself as a "reformed aeroholic" after losing some US$300 million from an investment in US Air. It is a sign of the changed circumstances of US airlines that by the end of 2018, his company's holdings included 9.6% of Delta's shares, 8.7% of Southwest's and 8.1% of United's. In mid-2018, Doug Parker, Chief Executive of American Airlines, even went as far as to say: "I don't think we are ever going to lose money again. This is an industry that will be profitable in good and bad years. [It has been] materially and permanently transformed." This may have been an overly ambitious prediction, as the COVID epidemic was to show only too clearly, but it certainly highlights the increased optimism among US airline executives.

US carriers were able to consolidate because they were all majority owned and controlled by citizens of a single country, with access to ample capital. They did not, therefore, fall foul of the ownership restrictions contained in most bilateral ASAs. Often these rules are not enforced, but there is always the chance that they will be. Few airlines are prepared to take the risk of putting their route rights, the foundation of their networks, in significant danger. In Europe, some consolidation was also possible following the creation of the internal aviation market, particularly for airlines operating almost wholly within the Continent, such as initially the new low-cost carriers. For the legacy airlines, however, with extensive networks beyond the coverage of the EU internal market, life has been more difficult. There have been acquisitions, such as KLM by Air France, Austrian Airlines, Brussels Airlines, Swiss, etc. by Lufthansa and the formation of the International Airlines Group (IAG), but most have involved complicated governance mechanisms which have limited the full benefits of consolidation. As one commentator put it:

> There is change, but change is seen more in the airlines' ability to find ways around the rules than in government actions to abolish the rules – or even to seek significant liberalisation of the rules… Simultaneously [this] illustrates both the increasingly irrelevance of the rules and their enduring stickiness.[12]

The creation of Air France/KLM and IAG illustrates this problem. The Air France take-over of KLM took place in 2004, yet even as late as 2018, the airline's Chief Executive was forced to comment on the company's dysfunctional governance, noting that it was time for the French and Dutch arms to begin behaving like a single unit. This hardly suggests that the merger between the two airlines had been a success. A complicated governance procedure, designed to protect KLM route rights and described by CAPA as a 'legal fiction' and by HSBC as 'an artificial regulatory construction,' purported to keep control of the Dutch and French subsidiary carriers in the hands of their respective citizens. It did this, in the case of KLM, by creating a trust based in the Netherlands which holds a majority of the voting shares in the Dutch airline, but with 100% of the economic benefits accruing to the shareholders of the Air France/KLM holding company. Overall management control lies firmly in Paris (see Table 8.5). Despite concern on the part of some bilateral partners, the governance structure has not been seriously challenged, at least up to now. However, there has been internal conflict, reflecting the special political status airlines still have even in liberalised markets.

KLM has significantly outperformed Air France by most measures. For example, despite being significantly smaller (two-thirds of the revenues of

Table 8.5 Shareholdings in Air France/KLM and KLM, 2018

Air France/KLM	
French State	15.8%
Employees	9.7%
Treasury stock	1.9%
Floated shares	72.6%
KLM	
Air France/KLM	49.0%
Dutch foundations	44.0%
Dutch State	6.0%
Private	1.0%

Air France, 60% of its employees, just over half the fleet size), KLM's operating profit has exceeded that of Air France in every year but one during the past, pre-COVID decade; in 2018, it enjoyed an operating margin of almost 10%, compared with less than 2% for Air France. However, the plan by the new Chief Executive of the holding company to focus more of its strategic functions at the group level was seen by many in the Netherlands as a threat to KLM's special status and to its relative independence. As a result, in 2019, the Dutch Government announced unilaterally that it would take an additional 14% stake in Air France/KLM "to be able to exercise direct influence over future developments … to ensure that Dutch public interests are optimally assured." The move followed threats of strike action by KLM employees campaigning to ensure the maintenance of the previous level of independence, including the retention of the existing KLM Chief Executive. This is not what one might expect to happen in most other industries and highlights the particular problems experienced by airlines when seeking to consolidate. The Dutch Government was, after all, one of the principal proponents of the liberalisation of air transport and of the 'normalisation' of the airline industry. The Chief Executive of Air France/KLM acknowledged at the time that the company had experienced 'internal struggles' and that more could have been done to "optimise and do what most major groups do when they consolidate." Unfortunately, for airlines, even in apparently deregulated markets, that is easier said than done.

The ownership of IAG is even more complex than that of Air France/KLM. British Airways and Iberia merged in 2011, absorbing the Spanish LCC Vueling in 2012 and Aer Lingus in 2016. IAG is a Spanish company with its headquarters in the UK. Like Air France/KLM, it distinguishes between the economic/financial and voting rights of its subsidiary airlines, with a majority of the latter held in the hands of citizens of the relevant home country by means of trusts. According to a 2010 corporate registration document, a British company known as LDC(NCS) holds 50.1% of BA's voting rights and minimal economic rights, while IAG holds 45% of the voting rights and 90%

of the economic rights. A recent set of accounts for LDC(NCS) states that its business objective is "to enable British Airways to preserve its UK nationality for the purpose of certain international traffic rights." A similar structure exists for Iberia, with a Spanish company, Garanair, owning 50.1% of the voting shares and IAG 86% of the economic rights.

Lufthansa has adopted a different approach in acquiring ownership of several European airlines, many of them former national flag carriers. It bought Swiss in 2005, Austrian (and bmi) in 2009, and Brussels Airlines in 2017. In each case it depended on the support of the respective Government to protect the relevant traffic rights. On the whole, this has been a successful approach, but it has come under pressure. Russia, for example, has questioned Austrian's bilateral rights under the Austria/Russia ASA, following a dispute with Germany unconnected with aviation. The dispute was settled. (KLM's access to trans-Siberian traffic rights was similarly disputed when Russian carriers were experiencing problems acquiring airport slots at Schiphol Airport.) India also challenged the operating rights of Austrian and Swiss at the time of Air India's negotiations to join the Star Alliance. What all of these examples illustrate is that while generally many countries are prepared to turn a blind eye to airline ownership issues, the risk always remains that failure to comply with the letter of the rules could be used in the future to exert negotiating leverage. This certainly increases the risk associated with airline investment.

Mention should also be made of the activity of the European Commission in seeking to ensure that airline mergers which cross intra-EU borders are accepted by other countries. Following the Commission's legal challenge to the ownership and control restrictions contained in several Member States' ASAs (see Chapter 6), the EU adopted a policy of replacing these clauses wherever possible with ones recognising the concept of a *Community Carrier*. In other words, whereas previously an EU State could not automatically designate an airline not majority owned and controlled by its own citizens without the agreement of the other party to a bilateral agreement, all Member States were now required to seek an amendment to ASAs with third countries to ensure that objections would not be raised as long as a designated carrier is majority owned and controlled by EU citizens. Of course, there is no way of forcing other countries to agree to such reform, but over 150 ASAs have been changed. (China joined the list in 2019.) In addition, the Community Carrier clause is included in the so-called 'horizontal agreements' with non-EU countries, meaning that overall, a substantial number of markets are now covered. Nevertheless, several significant aviation States have refused to co-operate, including Russia, India and South Africa, with the result that there remains a traffic rights risk for many merged EU airlines.

Reform

There have been several attempts over the years to reform the airline ownership and control rules. One proposal from IATA, unanimously supported by its AGM in Shanghai in 2002, reflected a compromise which would have left individual countries free to determine the ownership structure of their own carriers while accepting the policies of other countries.[13] In other words, if one country was prepared to permit 100% foreign ownership and control of its own carriers, others would agree to allow those airlines to operate under the relevant ASAs. Building on this theme, IATA's 2008 Agenda for Freedom initiative concluded that it is:

> ….. time to acknowledge the direct link that exists between anachronistic economic regulation of the industry and the airlines' long history of suboptimal financial performance… It is time to make aviation just another normal, global business… A real breakthrough … would come from a change to ownership and control restrictions. This alone could facilitate the search for optimal cross-border structures for airlines, give them greater access to international equity markets, and allow foreign venture capital to invest in airlines.[14]

This approach received support within ICAO, and at the organisation's 37th Assembly in 2010, the US submitted a very similar proposal "to foster liberalization and facilitate airline access to international capital markets." The draft Multilateral Convention tabled precluded a State from rejecting the designation of an airline from another signatory State on the grounds of either ownership or control, although "nothing in this Convention requires a Party to permit foreign ownership or control of airlines of that Party." Multilateral reform of airline ownership and control rules remains an ICAO objective.

Unfortunately, reform has failed to gain political traction among governments, and eventually, even the airline trade body lost interest. Recently IATA has withdrawn from lobbying for reform, perhaps a reflection of the industry's more general move away from further liberalisation and towards more protectionism. The Director General of IATA, speaking in mid-2018, noted:

> There appears to be no dearth of capital available to airlines from domestic sources, which means that the airlines have not found a compelling need to campaign for a change in national law that they know will be controversial in many countries. Moreover, the advent of immunised joint ventures among airlines and global branded alliances is delivering most if not all of the consumer benefits … that cross-border mergers, if permitted, would deliver. In short, because the restrictions on foreign investment in airlines do not appear to have impeded the industry's growth or development, the issue is not on IATA's agenda.[15]

It is fair to say that far from all of IATA's members agree with the new approach and several aspects of this statement are open to challenge.

To be fully effective, reform of the airline ownership and control rules requires a multilateral approach. Agreement between two States, or even a small number of States, is not sufficient since operational risks will remain on routes to other countries. Hope for substantial reform arose with the negotiations between the EU and the US for a trans-Atlantic Open Aviation Area. As we saw in Chapter 6, the EU proposal was for a highly liberalised arrangement, going beyond the US model open skies agreement. Effectively it would have taken the EU internal aviation market and stretched it across the Atlantic, including access to cabotage rights and common ownership and control rules. Unfortunately, the US refused to play ball and the agreement eventually reached failed to address either of these issues, other than a recognition on the part of the US of the concept of an EU Community Carrier. The EU and US were the two largest aviation blocks in the world, accounting for over 50% of the global market at the time of the EU/US ASA negotiations. (The share has now (pre-COVID) fallen to less than 40% with the rapid growth of Asian air services.) Had they been able to agree on common liberal airline ownership rules, it is likely that other reform-minded countries would have joined them and a momentum may well have been created which at long last would have put an end to the archaic rules worldwide.

What was at stake in the EU/US negotiations was highlighted by a report produced by the Brattle Group for the European Commission. Following a detailed economic study, it concluded:

> The liberalisation of aviation trade and investment likely would lead to significant cross-border flows of capital as airlines engage in consolidation and deeper integration and establish new operations in markets that are opened and made more accessible by liberalisation. Cross-border investment would in turn play a major role in driving many [other] … benefits.[16]

The EU has continued to press the US to engage in further reform, but there seems to be little prospect of early success, despite Article 21 of the EU/US agreement committing both sides to continue to remove market access barriers, enhance the access of airlines to global capital markets and encourage other countries to follow. In a speech in Washington DC in July 2018, the Director General for Mobility and Transport at the European Commission noted that

> in order to enhance competition and advance investments to the European carriers, we need to re-think the ownership and control regulation more generally. It is very difficult to understand why we have these restrictions that are not present in any other industry.

However, he went on to say that he was concerned that with respect to trans-Atlantic aviation relations, "we might be moving in the opposite direction."

The European Commission also appears to have loosened its strict definition of what constitutes control of an airline. EU Regulation 1008/2008 defines effective control as:

> A relationship constituted by rights, contracts or any other means by which, either separately or jointly and having regard to the considerations of fact or law involved, confer the possibility of directly or indirectly exercising a decisive influence on an undertaking.

This is a high barrier to gaining acceptance as a Community Carrier under EU law. However, it is evident that more recently it has not been applied as strictly as before. For example, when Singapore Airlines acquired a 49% interest in Virgin Atlantic in 2000, the EU Commission went to considerable lengths to ensure that any control over the British carrier was strictly limited. When pre-Brexit, Delta bought Singapore's shares in Virgin, on the other hand, concern over control seemed to be significantly less. Some 70% of Virgin Atlantic's capacity was provided on North Atlantic routes, where it has a 50/50 Joint Venture with Delta. In other words, Delta has a 74% share of the Joint Venture, via the 50% direct stake plus its 49% stake in Virgin Atlantic. This has led some commentators to conclude that Delta has significant control of the EU airline.

The US, however, continues to apply extremely tight restrictions on both the ownership and control of airlines. We saw in an earlier chapter the problems experienced by UK's Virgin Group in seeking to establish a new carrier in the US. At one stage Virgin was even required to replace the new carrier's initial Chief Executive, a US citizen with a long and distinguished career in the aviation industry, on the grounds that he risked being too influenced by a non-US company. Compare this experience with Sir Richard Branson's launch of Virgin Galactic, a US company established to build and operate commercial spacecraft. This is a company operating on the edge of technological development which was majority owned by non-US interests, including a substantial stake in the hands of the sovereign wealth fund of Abu Dhabi. One might expect it to experience considerable problems in accessing the US market, but this has not been the case. If Virgin Galactic was an airline, it would run foul not only of the ownership and control rules, but also be prevented from operating any flights as the services to be provided are, by definition, cabotage: each one departs from and arrives back in the US without landing anywhere else!

Alliances

In the absence of reform of the ownership and control rules and the ability to engage in full-scale cross-border mergers and acquisitions, airlines were forced to seek alternative ways of achieving the same objectives. This meant pursuing various forms of co-operation with other carriers. A 2010 report produced jointly by the European Commission and the US Department of Transportation differentiated between 'tactical' and 'strategic' airline alliances. The former, it was argued, are designed to address a specific deficiency in carriers' networks and typically involve just two airlines and a limited number of routes. There have been many such airline alliances over the years. Strategic co-operation, on the other hand, can be seen in the emergence of the three branded global alliances (oneworld, Skyteam and Star) and involve deeper integration on a multilateral basis.[17] Membership of a strategic alliance is often accompanied by participation in one or more tactical alliances, frequently with members of other strategic alliances. In addition, a sub-group of a strategic alliance takes the form of joint ventures, usually involving immunity from competition law to permit collusion on tariff setting, scheduling, etc.

Diana Moss, in a paper written for the pro-market American Antitrust Institute,[18] differentiated airline alliances in a different way, ranking them in order of the growing intensity of co-operation among the participants:

- *Interlining.* This is the way in which carriers are able to offer a single fare and related transfers for a journey involving multiple flights and more than one airline. ('Intralining' involves multiple flights with the *same* airline.) It was a fundamental part of the legacy carrier business model for many decades, a product of tight regulation and IATA-negotiated tariffs. With the reduction of IATA tariff co-ordination, interlining has become less important, but it is still applied to certain fare types and more widely between members within alliances.
- *Cross-membership of frequent flyer programmes* (FFPs). FFPs were first introduced by American Airlines in 1981, and have become a powerful, ubiquitous marketing tool in the industry. As one study noted: "They are widely recognised, along with the creation of hub-and-spoke route networks and computer reservation systems, as being among the most significant and yet unexpected developments since the deregulation of US domestic air services."[19] Michael Levine suggested that when first introduced, FFPs "seemed to many observers in and outside the airline industry, and perhaps to American itself, to be a marketing 'gimmick' of only peripheral importance. It is now apparent that [they] are very important keys to competitive viability."[20] This was written in 1987, since when FFPs have become a global phenomenon and increased substantially in importance as an airline marketing tool. However, the fact that any individual carrier could serve only a relatively small proportion of global routes meant that passengers were often restricted in their ability to earn and use rewards. Consequently, co-operation agreements between carriers soon emerged, facilitating cross-participation in a number of schemes.
- *Codeshares.* This is the placing by an airline of its designator code on an air service operated by a different carrier. It is another marketing

initiative which enables an airline to appear to operate a larger network of routes than, physically, it actually does. Like FFPs, codeshares have become ubiquitous in the industry. Their origin lies in the late-1960s, when under the strict regulation applied at the time by the US Civil Aeronautics Board, a carrier (Allegheny, later known as USAir) encountered difficulties in extricating itself from certain thin loss-making routes. It developed marketing and operational alliances with smaller independent airlines, each of which carried the larger airline's designation code on the services in question. This was found to be acceptable by the CAB. However, the example was barely followed by others until the emergence of computer reservation systems. (See Chapter 5) US regulation prevented airline owners of CRSs from giving display priority to their own services, but it said nothing about allowing priority for online connections, even if the services in question only pretended to be online by means of a codeshare. (European regulation banned such an approach.) This led to a rapid escalation of code sharing, first in the US and then elsewhere, a trend reinforced as the non-CRS benefits of such marketing alliances became increasingly recognised.[21]

- *The creation of global branded airline alliances*, seeking to replicate many of the benefits of full mergers. We will focus on this below.
- Finally, *the co-ordination of pricing and scheduling with other alliance members*. This usually requires the grant of immunity from competition laws, since such activity is illegal in most jurisdictions. A further refinement is so-called 'full-metal' integration, involving revenue and profit sharing.

Each of these five stages of co-operation represents an attempt, with growing intensity, to expand an airline's reach beyond its own route network. They have resulted in a complex web of alliances, "a global network of strategic and tactical alliances, joint ventures, codeshares and other forms of co-operation that come to resemble a three-dimensional wiring diagram on steroids" as CAPA described it.[22] Rhoades[23] concludes that they reflect four key drivers for airlines:

- The need to gain entry into markets restricted by bilateral agreements.
- The desire to build a global, seamless network.
- The search for cost reduction, for example, by sharing facilities or entering into joint marketing initiatives.
- The attempt to maintain a market presence in an area whose traffic pattern and growth make it unprofitable to serve alone.

Other industries also have international alliances, of course, but for airlines, the need is greater because of the regulatory restrictions placed on their ability to achieve the same goals through cross-border mergers.

Today, when most people talk of airline alliances, they think of the three global alliances which dominate much of international air travel. Although in their present form they date only from the late-1990s, their origins can be traced back much further. An early attempt at co-operation, for example, was the formation in 1958 of Air Union, comprising KLM, Lufthansa, Air France, Alitalia and Sabena. Designed to meet growing competition from US carriers with the introduction of the new long-haul jet aircraft, the plan failed to get off the ground. The 1970s saw the creation of two consortia in Europe: KSSU, comprising KLM, SAS, Swissair and the French carrier UTA, and ATLAS, comprising Alitalia, TAP, Lufthansa, Air France and Sabena. SEAMA was similarly established in South East Asia by Cathay Pacific, Garuda and Thai International. These were technical alliances, focusing on aircraft maintenance and shared parts inventories, with the longer-term objective of common aircraft acquisition and specification. They were short-lived, mainly because of a reluctance on the part of individual carriers to cede control over their own operations. A broader association was attempted in 1994, the Alcazar Alliance, comprising KLM, SAS, Swissair and Austrian Airlines, formed primarily as a reaction to growing liberalisation. It similarly failed to survive, principally as a result of disagreement on the choice of a US partner. (One result, however, was a closer co-operation agreement between Lufthansa and SAS which became the foundation for the creation of the Star Alliance.)[24] The Global Excellence Network, which went further in having small cross-shareholdings between Delta, Swissair and Singapore Airlines, did not fare much better.

It was not until 1992, and the beginning of talks between the US and the Netherlands on a ground-breaking open skies air services agreement, that a firmer foundation for global alliances emerged. A meeting took place in Washington DC between three individuals representing KLM and Northwest Airlines. Rutger and Laer describe what happened:

> ... the two airlines' future co-operation in an Open Skies environment was broached. A considerable difference existed, at the time, between the legal systems dealing with anti-competitive behaviour in the Netherlands and the United States and it needed to be explored how co-operation between the two airlines could be enhanced, while taking these differences into account. Soon notions were discussed such as 'antitrust exemption', 'foreign ownership restrictions', ... and it became increasingly clear that something important was being developed.
>
> By 3 pm from the maternity ward of international aviation came the metaphoric triumphant cry: the concept of antitrust immunity for cross-border airline alliances had been born – and life would never be the same.[25]

Ignoring the rather ornate wording, there is certainly some truth in this statement. The alliance between KLM and Northwest began with a US$400 million investment by the Dutch carrier in 1989. (British Airways similarly invested in USAir in the early 1990s, an alliance which included several aircraft painted in BA colours but operated by USAir crew.) However, the partnership between KLM and Northwest could go no further than limited marketing arrangements. US law precluded a full merger and significantly closer co-operation short of a merger required an exemption from US competition law. (At the time the Netherlands had no such legislation applicable to international aviation.)

It was the combination of an open skies ASA and the grant of anti-trust immunity which enabled progress to be made. As explained in Chapter 6, normally US competition policy is the responsibility of the Department of Justice (DOJ), but for international aviation, it is the Department of Transportation (DOT) that is charged with oversight and the grant of any immunities. The influence of anti-trust immunity on open skies negotiations was well illustrated by the Memorandum of Consultation signed by the US and the Netherlands in 1992 (Table 8.6), which states:

> [It is the intent of the Parties] to give sympathetic consideration, in the context of the Open Skies agreement, to the concept of commercial co-operation and integration of commercial operations between airlines of the United States and the Netherlands through commercial agreements or arrangements ... and to provide fair and expeditious consideration to any such agreements or arrangements filed for approval and antitrust immunity.[26]

There was a clear message here which others were not slow to understand. As one of the participants in that Washington meeting between KLM and Northwest has noted: "... it was the competition caused by our circumvention of bilateral restrictions that was the ... driver."[27] Once the US/Netherlands open skies agreement was signed it was not long before numerous other European countries followed suit, and several of their national airlines applied for anti-trust immunity for alliance participation (see Table 8.7).

Table 8.6 Early US Open Skies Agreements

1992	– The Netherlands
1995	– Belgium, Finland, Denmark/Norway/Sweden, Switzerland and Austria
1996	– Germany
1998	– Italy
2000	– Portugal
2001	– France

Table 8.7 Alliance Global Market Shares, 2019

		Market Share[a]
Unaligned	–	46.1%
Star	–	22.1%
Skyteam	–	16.0%
oneworld	–	15.2%

Source: CAPA – Centre for Aviation.
[a] Available seat kilometres.

Three branded global airline alliances have since emerged, beginning with Star in 1997.

Star

Founded: 1997

Founding members: Air Canada, Lufthansa, SAS, Thai International and United

Members (2022): Aegean, Air Canada, Air China, Air India, Air New Zealand, All Nippon Airways, Asiana Airlines★, Austrian Airlines, Avianca, Brussels Airlines, Copa Airlines, Croatia Airlines, Egyptair, Ethiopian Airways, Eva Air, LOT Polish Airlines, Lufthansa, SAS, Shenzhen Airlines, Singapore Airlines, South African Airways, Swiss, TAP Air Portugal, Thai International, Turkish Airlines, United. (★ Asiana Airways is due to merge with Skyteam's Korean Air)

Total Revenue (2018): US$213.2 billion

Oneworld

Founded: 1999

Founding members: American Airlines, British Airways, Canadian, Cathay Pacific, Qantas

Members (2021): Alaska Airlines, American Airlines, British Airways, Cathay Pacific, Finnair, Iberia, Japan Airlines, Malaysia Airlines, Oman Air, Qantas, Qatar Airways, Royal Air Maroc, Royal Jordanian, S7 Airlines★, Sri Lankan Airlines, Fiji Airways (oneworld connect). (★S7 is currently suspended from membership.)

Total Revenue (2018) - US$142.4 billion

Skyteam

Founded: 2000

Founding members: Aeromexico, Air France, Delta Airlines, Korean Air

Members (2021): Aeroflot★, Aerolineas Argentinas, Aeromexico, Air Europa, Air France, China Airlines, China Eastern, Czech Airlines, Delta Airlines, Garuda Indonesia, Kenya Airways, KLM, Korean Air, MEA, Saudia, Tarom, Vietnam Airlines, Xiamen Airlines. (★Aeroflot is currently suspended from membership.)

Total Revenue (2018): US$152.9 billion

Mention should also be made of two alliances formed in Asia/Pacific, focused on low-cost carriers. Value Alliance was established in 2016 by eight LCCs. (It currently has seven members.) The U-Fly Alliance, also established in 2016, has grown from four to five active members. It is evident that, so far at least, such LCC co-operation has had only a limited impact.

In certain respects, global airline alliances have replaced the role previously played by IATA in coordinating airline activity. Their objective, in the words of Star, is to offer "worldwide reach, recognition and seamless service to the international passenger." In economic terms, they seek to achieve so-called economies of scope, combining different products (route networks) to increase revenue and hopefully profits. Marketing co-operation takes place in areas such as code shares, FFPs, lounges, certain joint fares, etc. It is important to note, however, that none of the global alliances has anti-trust immunity to co-ordinate fares and schedules. It is left to groups of individual members to apply for such immunity, usually for a sub-set of their routes.

Are alliances, particularly those with anti-trust immunity, pro or anti-competitive? The answer, of course, depends on which side of the fence you sit. When applying for immunity, airlines typically downplay competitive concerns and highlight the consumer benefits. In particular, they claim that by sharing various facilities (lounges, spare parts, check-in desks, etc.) they will achieve lower costs which, in turn, can be passed on to passengers in the form of lower fares. The main problem with this argument is that repeated academic studies have failed to identify significant economies of scale in airline operations. Alliances may well reduce certain unit costs by facilitating co-operation among their members (economies of density), but there is little proof that this can be translated into lower costs at the company level. In other words, the principal benefits of airline alliances seem to lie on the revenue side rather than in overall cost reduction. Whether increased revenue is reflected in higher profits or, eventually, lower fares is the problem competition authorities have wrestled with for some time.

Fundamentally, to collude in the co-ordination of prices and schedules is illegal in most jurisdictions, although in many countries this has only relatively recently been the case for international air services. Airlines must apply for exemption from the relevant competition laws to engage in such activity or face severe penalties. It is only to be expected, therefore, that applications are subject to close investigation by the authorities. Often more than one body can be involved, for example, the US DOT and the European Commission for US–EU routes and the British Competition and Markets Authority and the Australian Competition and Consumer Commission for the Kangaroo route between the UK and Australia. One attempt to obtain immunity, for an alliance between British Airways and American Airlines, took some 14 years and three separate applications before it was eventually granted.

The competition authorities seek to ensure that competitors, actual and potential, are not disadvantaged by an alliance and are able to provide sufficient competitive pressure to protect the interests of the travelling public. Barriers to market access are particularly important in this respect and the existence of an open skies air services agreement covering the routes in question is invariably a key demand, as we saw in the case of KLM/Northwest. In addition, if airport capacity is limited, the applicant carriers may be asked to provide take-off and landing slots to new entrants. Access to FFPs and special interline fares have also featured among the 'remedies' sought to compensate for any perceived reduction in competition. Initially, especially in the US, some routes were 'carved out' of the application. In other words, any overall approval was not extended to certain routes because of particular concern about domination by the applicants in those markets. However, such an approach has become less common in recent years as the problems inherent in attempts to ring-fence certain routes have become apparent. Remedies can either be accepted voluntarily by the parties or imposed by the competition authority as a condition for approval.

This is now a widely accepted process in many parts of the world. It is less common nowadays for major airlines to object to anti-trust applications by other carriers since they are likely to require similar approvals themselves. Between 1993 and 2007, for example, US airlines filed comments, almost invariably adverse, in some 45% of DOT anti-trust proceedings, while between 2007 and 2017 there was not a single objection from a legacy carrier. (There was a small number of objections from regional airlines and LCCs.)[28] Nevertheless, the process is certainly not beyond criticism, mainly because of the market power of the alliance airlines on certain routes, often associated with hub dominance. It can be very difficult for new entrants to establish themselves in such circumstances, even with the help of remedies imposed by the competition authorities. In their 2010 joint paper, the European Commission and US DOT agreed "that one of the main challenges in the airline industry is to design a remedy that can effectively address the identified negative effects of the parties' cooperation while giving consideration to the principle of proportionality."[29] In certain cases, the European Commission has even gone so far as to make it a condition of approval of a joint venture that the applicants obtain an effective competitor on a route, an initiative which has not been noticeably more successful.

There is some evidence that in Europe at least, this problem has been recognised and alternative ways considered for maintaining a competitive marketplace, although the authorities are constrained by legal requirements.[30] This may result in a more interventionist approach in the future. Certainly, the competition authorities seem to be less willing to accept the argument that alliances and joint ventures are consumer-friendly overall, and academic studies have supported this conclusion. Diana Moss found that such studies performed in the late 1990s generally showed that immunity delivered more public benefits than costs. Empirical research undertaken more recently, on the other hand, tells a different story.

> Recent studies find that even without immunity, cooperation under alliance agreements can enhance incentives to collude on price on parallel routes between a US and European hub… As for immunized non-stop service offered by alliance partners on transatlantic routes, recent studies

find that immunity may lead to less competition in all markets, ie both non-stop and one-stop routes.[31]

Cross-Border Investments

There have been numerous cross-border investments by airlines in other carriers over the years. In the early post-Second World War period, for example, the major flag carriers of Europe and the US often helped to set up airlines in newly emerging economies. Air France alone invested in Royal Air Maroc (1947), Tunis Air (1948), MEA (1949), Air Afrique (1963), Cameroon Airlines (1971), Air Gabon (1977), and others.[32] BOAC did likewise, mainly in territories under British control, with investments in Aden Airways, Hong Kong Airlines, Middle East Airlines, Cyprus Airways, Gulf Aviation, Kuwait Airways, Iraq Airways, Malaysia Airways, Borneo Airways and Fiji Airways. One commentator has described such initiatives as "one of the best examples of colonial altruism and one which has been an enduring gift from a fading Europe,"[33] although no doubt not everyone would agree. In each of these cases, the involvement was temporary. Most subsequent investments have not been a success, such as British Airways in USAir, KLM in Northwest, SAS in Continental, Singapore Airways in Virgin Atlantic and the cross-shareholding between Delta and Singapore. None of them involved a majority shareholding and control. A notable recent example, and equally as unsuccessful, has been Etihad's so-called 'Equity Alliance' involving stakes in Air Berlin, Jet Airways, Air Serbia, Air Seychelles, Etihad Regional (previously Darwin Airline), Virgin Australia, Alitalia and Aer Lingus.

Swissair had previously attempted a similar strategy of assembling minority stakes in various carriers, with the same result: substantial financial losses and a failure to achieve any real synergy. The plan was almost certainly a factor in the airline's eventual demise. Etihad has been forced to abandon its approach following losses of some US$1.9 billion in 2016, US$1.5 billion in 2017 and US$1.3 billion in 2018. Its new Chief Executive made clear that the airline does not intend to continue the strategy: "Being a shareholder, often without full control, but providing financial and human resource assistance in an environment where you cannot derive fair and reasonable benefit, simply does not work."[34] Qatar Airways has similarly invested in other airlines, with a 10% stake in Cathay Pacific, 25% in IAG, 10% in LATAM and 49% in RwandAir (an attempt to invest in American Airlines was rebuffed), and so far at least has shown no signs of changing tack, although Air Italy (formerly Meridiana), in which Qatar had a 49% stake, has been wound up. Delta assembled minority stakes in Aeromexico, GOL, Virgin Atlantic, Air France/KLM, China Eastern and most recently (2019) Korean Air, essentially as a means of binding a group of airlines together into what it described as an 'international network of carriers.' It remains to be seen whether Qatar's and Delta's strategy will be a success in the longer term and perhaps reduce the need for reform of the ownership and control rules. Past experience, however, does not give cause for much optimism.

Finally, the Chinese conglomerate Hainan Airlines Group (HNA) has also invested in numerous Chinese and overseas airlines and deserves a mention. Founded in 1993, one of China's first privately owned airlines (albeit with financial assistance from the Hainan Provincial Government), grew at a phenomenal rate. By the end of 2019, HNA had a 16% share of the Chinese domestic market, with a fleet of 220 aircraft and 340 domestic and 77 international routes. It acquired stakes in Beijing Capital Airlines, Tianjin Airlines, Urumqi Airlines, Lucky Air and China West Air, adding another 340 domestic and 46 international routes and bringing the total fleet size to 592 aircraft. From the early 2010s, it began acquiring shareholdings in overseas carriers, notably Ghana World Airways, Aigle Azur, Comair, Azul, TAP Air Portugal, Virgin Australia, Hong Kong Express and Hong Kong Airlines. Large investments were also made in airports, hotels and associated travel and tourism companies. Unfortunately, the model proved to be no more successful than other attempts to establish a global travel-related business. Losses for 2020 were estimated at US$10 billion and the Group faced liquidity problems and potential bankruptcy, necessitating attempts to sell many of those assets which, unlike Aigle Azur and Virgin Australia, had not already succumbed to insolvency.[35] A restructuring was announced in late 2021, with new investors.

Speaking more generally about strategic alliances, beyond the aviation industry, Parke noted that they are arrangements "characterised by inherent instability arising from uncertainty regarding a partner's future behaviour and the absence of a higher authority to ensure compliance."[36] This is precisely what we see with global airline alliances. They are unstable and struggle to meet all the requirements of their members. The result is that most airlines are forced to enter into tactical alliances, often with carriers which belong to separate strategic groupings. At the same time, global alliances experience transfers between their members. For example, following the consolidation of US carriers, Continental left Skyteam to join Star and US Airways left Star to join oneworld. LATAM left oneworld, of which LAN had been a member for some 18 years, to join Skyteam when Delta became a partial owner. China Southern has withdrawn from Skyteam, while Qatar has threatened to leave oneworld because of unhappiness with the behaviour of fellow alliance members, Qantas and American, in seeking to restrict its access to the Australian and US markets respectively.

It is difficult to conclude that this degree of instability and often hostility represents a long-term viable model for the future of the international airline industry. At the same time, however, the failure to reform the airline ownership and control rules multilaterally may well mean that alliances will remain a feature of the industry's landscape for the foreseeable future. As Oum, Yu and Zhang have commented:

Alliances have provided a way for carriers to mitigate the limitations of bilateral agreements, ownership restrictions, and licensing and control regulations. In effect, both airlines and governments consider international alliances to be the second best solution to achieve free trade in world aviation.[37]

'Second best,' of course, means economically less efficient, impacting airline profitability and potentially consumer benefits. The airline ownership rules are being gradually chipped away, notably in Latin America, Europe and Australia/New Zealand, but they remain an impediment to the 'normalisation' of the industry which significantly increases investment risks.

Notes

1 Information provided by John King.
2 International Chamber of Commerce: 'Foreign Investment in Airlines: An ICC View.' Policy Statement, 8 November 1994.
3 Isabelle Lelieur: *Law and Policy of Substantial Ownership and Control of Airlines. Prospects for Change*. Ashgate, Aldershot, 2003.
4 Yu-Chun Chang, George Williams and Chia-Jui Hsu: 'The evolution of airline ownership and control provisions.' *Journal of Air Transport Management*, Vol 10(3), May 2004.
5 UK Civil Aviation Authority: 'Ownership and Control Liberalisation – A Discussion Paper.' CAP 769, 2006.
6 Isabelle Lelieur, op cit.
7 Alex Cosmas, Peter Belobaba and William Swelbar: 'Framing the Discussion on Regulatory Liberalization: A Stakeholder Analysis of Open Skies, Ownership and Control.' MIT International Center for Air Transportation, White Paper, undated.
8 Dorothy Robyn: 'The unfinished business of transportation deregulation.' *TR News*, May/June 2018.
9 Michael Carney and Isabelle Dostaler: 'Airline ownership and control: A corporate governance perspective.' *Journal of Air Transport Management*, Vol. 12(2), March 2006, pp. 63–73.
10 José Azar Martin, C. Schmalz and Isabel Tecu: 'Anti-competitive effects of common ownership.' *Journal of Finance*, Vol. 73(4), May 2018, pp. 1513–1565.
11 Barry Humphreys: 'Investment Funds and Airline Ownership.' Aviation Strategy, No. 238, August 2018. See also Patrick Dennis, Kristopher Gerardi and Carola Schenone: 'Common ownership does not have anti-competitive effects in the airline industry.' *Journal of Finance*, Vol. 73(1), February 2018, pp. 2765–2798.
12 CAPA – Centre for Aviation: 'Airline Ownership and Control Rules. An Enduring Constraint on How Airline Models Evolve.' Airline Leader, May/June 2017.
13 Note that the author chaired the IATA committee in question.
14 IATA Agenda for Freedom Summit, Chairman's Summary, October 2008.
15 Interview with Alexandre de Juniac, *Hermes Magazine*, April/June 2018.
16 The Brattle Group: 'The Economic Impact of an EU – US Open Aviation Area.' Report for the European Commission, December 2002.
17 European Commission and US Department of Transportation: 'Transatlantic Airline Alliances: Competitive Issues and Regulatory approaches.' November 2010.

18 Diana L. Moss: 'Revisiting Antitrust Immunity for International Airline Alliances.' American Antitrust Institute, March 2018.
19 Barry Humphreys: 'Frequent Flyer Programmes.' Avmark Aviation Economist, August 1991.
20 Michael E. Levine: 'Airline competition in deregulated markets; Theory, firm strategy, and public policy.' *Yale Journal of Regulation*, Vol. 4, Spring 1987, pp. 393–494.
21 Barry Humphreys: 'The implications of international code sharing.' *Journal of Air Transport Management*, Vol. 1(4), June 1994, pp. 195–207.
22 CAPA – Centre for Aviation: 'Global Alliances as the Airline System Metamorphoses.' Airline Leader, September/October 2016.
23 Dawna L. Rhoades: *Evolution of International Aviation. Phoenix Rising.* Ashgate, Aldershot, 2003.
24 Sveinn Vidar Gudmundsson: 'Mergers and Alliances: The Air France – KLM Story.' Toulouse Business School, Ref. CO2/10/2014, June 2014.
25 H. S. Rutger and Jan Toe Laer: 'Kick-starting Cross-border alliances: Approval and clearance; the past, the present and the future.' *Air and Space Law*, Vol. 32(4/5), September 2007, pp. 287–325.
26 Quoted in H. S. Rutger and Jan Toe Laer, op cit.
27 Information provided by Paul Mifsud.
28 Diana L. Moss, op cit.
29 European Commission and US Department of Transportation, op cit.
30 Barry Humphreys: 'Alliances: What the Competition Authorities Are Really Looking At.' Aviation Strategy, No. 243, February 2019.
31 Diana L. Moss, op cit.
32 Michael Z. F. Li: 'Distinct features of lasting and non-lasting airline alliances.' *Journal of Air Transport Management*, Vol. 26(2), April 2000, pp. 65–73.
33 Capt. Dacre Watson: 'British overseas airways corporation 1949 – 1950 and its legacy.' *Journal of Aeronautical History*, Paper 2013/03, 2013.
34 Interview in Airlines, No. 1, 2019.
35 'HNA: Grey Rhino topples into bankruptcy.' Aviation Strategy, Issue No. 259, January/February 2021.
36 A. Parke: 'Strategic alliance structuring: A game theoretic and transaction cost examination of interfirm cooperation.' *The Academy of Management Journal*, Vol. 36(4), 1993. Quoted in Dawna L. Rhoades, op cit.
37 Tae Hoon Oum, Chunyan Yu and Anming Zhang: 'Global airline alliances: international regulatory issues.' *Journal of Air Transport Management*, Vol. 7(1), January 2001, pp. 57–62.

9 Technology and the Environment

> Technological and climate change not only share a common intellectual heritage, but also are both of fundamental importance. Technological change raised humans out of the Stone Age living standards. Climate change threatens ... to return us economically whence we came.
>
> William Nordhaus[1]

In this chapter, two separate issues are addressed, both critical to the ongoing success and viability of the aviation industry and both significantly influencing, and influenced by, prevailing regulatory regimes:

- Technology – clearly technology has had a major impact on airline development. In particular, early limitations on aircraft performance restricted operations and dictated many aspects of the emerging international regulatory regime. As technology developed, the regulatory environment and priorities changed as well. This process continues and has implications for the industry over the coming years. The focus here will be on aircraft and engine development, although other aspects of technology have also impacted air transport, and indeed continue to do so.
- Environment – the impact of aviation on the environment has increasingly become a major concern in many parts of the world, to such an extent that pressure to introduce ever more restrictive regulations may be the greatest threat to the industry's continued growth and prosperity. Addressing that problem is far from easy, but there is now almost universal acceptance that it has to be addressed. The implications of both success and failure are considerable and will undoubtedly have a major impact on the future structure of the industry and the way it is regulated.

Technology

It is self-evident that the aviation industry made substantial technical progress between that first 12-second flight by the Wright Brothers in 1903 and an aircraft such as the Boeing 787 or Airbus A350 of today capable of flying non-stop with a full load of passengers between London and Australia. In his seminal study of the geography of air transport, written in 1957, Kenneth Sealy describes such progress during the industry's first 50 years as 'phenomenal.'[2] If anything, the subsequent 60-plus years have witnessed an even more remarkable evolution, notably in increased aircraft range and size and reduced unit operating costs. In the 1920s, a typical commercial airliner had a capacity of less than ten passengers and travelled only marginally faster than an airship, with substantially less range. Gradual increases in capacity and stage length received two quantum boosts with the development of the jet engine and wide-body aircraft. It is easy to forget today the critical importance of two factors in particular in this achievement: the progress made during major wars, and especially of course the Second World War; and the domination of the US in aircraft manufacturing, a position established during World War II and only seriously challenged with the emergence of the European Airbus consortium in the 1970s. Before the launch of Airbus' first aircraft, the A300, some 90% of all commercial aircraft in Western countries were US-made, despite the many (expensive) attempts by several other States to break into the market.

Brian Graham[3] argues that during the post-war era, advances in aircraft technology can be sub-divided into various distinct periods. Initially, the industry was dominated by four-engine piston and turbo-prop airliners, relatively slow and able to fly only for modest distances. Despite the Comet aircraft first appearing in 1952, the jet age really began with the introduction of the Boeing 707, quickly followed by the DC-8, from 1958, providing faster and smoother journeys as well as greater range than their turbo-prop predecessors. Next came the wide-body era, notably with the entry into service of the Boeing 747 in 1970, capable of carrying several hundred passengers. Many expected that the next stage in aircraft development would be supersonic travel, but Concorde proved to be a short-lived false dawn. Instead, it was progress by the engine manufacturers which facilitated a marked shift in the economics of aircraft operation, as well as extending range limitations even further. Thus was born the age of the twin-engine long-range aircraft, the full implications of which are still playing out, as we shall see.

Sealy[4] notes that "in a very real sense, the aeroplane knows no barrier. It moves in the continuum of the atmosphere which is both three-dimensional and relatively uniform." From one perspective this is certainly true, but it is equally the case that from their inception aircraft have faced numerous technical barriers which have restricted their operational capability. This in turn has influenced the way in which the industry has been regulated. An example of this is the importance placed on negotiating fifth freedom traffic rights in post-war bilateral air services agreements. The limited distance aircraft could fly without needing to refuel, even long-range versions, necessitated frequent stops. The viability of multi-stop routes was usually greatly improved if additional passengers could be delivered to and picked up at intermediate points, hence the considerable effort which went into negotiating the required traffic rights for such operations. As we saw in Chapter 2, those countries with extensive overseas territories, of which the United Kingdom was a prime example, had a distinct advantage in this respect, both in terms of access to landing rights for their own airlines and in being able to demand a price for access to their colonies by carriers of other nations. The importance of fifth freedom rights in bilateral agreements only began to diminish with significant improvements in the ability of aircraft to fly longer distances non-stop.

Fifth freedom and transit (second freedom) operations also affected airport development, sometimes with ramifications which lasted long after the disappearance of the original reason for the airport's emergence. Shannon Airport in Ireland, for example, originally built to replace the flying boat terminal in the Shannon Estuary, emerged as an important staging post for trans-Atlantic services, as well as becoming, in 1947, the first airport to offer duty-free shopping. In the 1950s and 1960s, transit passengers accounted for almost 80% of the airport's total throughput. The number and proportion of such passengers diminished rapidly thereafter as aircraft range increased and airlines were able to fly non-stop across the Atlantic, before picking up again, temporarily, with increased use by Eastern European carriers from the 1970s (see Table 9.1). Attempts by the Irish Government to protect employment in the Shannon area, in particular by requiring third/fourth freedom airlines flying between Ireland and North America to operate at least some of their services from Shannon in addition to the far more popular Dublin, had a negative impact on Irish aviation and the broader economy for many years. Such political interference only came to an end when the European Commission took over responsibility from individual EU Member States for negotiating trans-Atlantic air services agreements.

Table 9.1 Shannon Airport Passenger Traffic

	Aircraft Landings	Terminal Passengers	Transit Passengers	Total Passengers	Transit as % of Total
1950	5,976	38,171	149,849	188,020	79.7
1960	8,312	103,376	312,914	416,290	75.2
1970	8,984	473,233	360,030	833,263	43.2
1980	8,982	560,614	356,760	917,374	38.9
1990	11,484	933,812	694,953	1,628,765	42.7
2000	17,561	1,915,876	492,376	2,408,252	20.4
2010	21,713	1,460,655	295,230	1,755,885	16.8
2019	21,624	1,061,058	110,517	1,717,575	9.4

Source: Shannon Airport.

Similarly, Anchorage Airport in Alaska (known as Ted Stevens Anchorage International Airport since 2000) was for many years a critical transit point between Europe and the Far East, describing itself as the 'Air Crossroads of the World'. For a time, it was reputed to have the biggest duty-free shop in the world to take advantage, like Shannon, of the large number of transit passengers who passed through the airport and had time on their hands as their aircraft were being refuelled. Airlines flying especially between Europe and the Far East began to stop in Anchorage in large numbers from the late-1950s, following the introduction of aircraft such as the DC-7C, which had sufficient range to operate these longer routings, a trend which increased with the inauguration of jet aircraft services.

The need for a refuelling stop in Anchorage was partly a reflection of the technical limitations of the aircraft used, but also partly a result of the Soviet Union's restriction on access to its airspace for foreign airlines. Increased aircraft range and the negotiation of transit rights across Siberia meant that from 1989, the importance of Anchorage as a passenger transit point rapidly diminished. The Russians demanded (and still do) substantial payments for access to their airspace for transit purposes, especially from European carriers. They had, of course, never been a signatory to the IASTA arrangement of 1944, as explained in Chapter 2, which provided for free first and second freedom access. However, the cost savings from reduced fuel and the commercial benefits from shorter travel times meant that realistically the airlines concerned had no alternative other than to pay up in order to remain competitive. Anchorage may no longer attract large numbers of transit passengers, but it remains the fourth largest airport in the world measured by cargo throughput, with airlines reluctant to use scarce and expensive trans-Siberian rights for freighter services.

The combination of improvements in technology and the geographical location of their bases also played a key role in the development of the Gulf super-hub carriers. Airlines such as Emirates, Etihad and Qatar are able to serve non-stop virtually every population centre in the world. Their hubs have become transit points for large flows of traffic, for example, between Europe and the Far East and Australasia. As we have already seen, while certainly growing the overall market, the Gulf carriers have additionally become major competitors of the legacy airlines, accused of 'stealing' traffic which 'rightfully' belongs to other airlines. Perhaps the clearest indication of their impact is seen on routes between Europe and Australia and New Zealand, where today all but one European airline which previously operated their own equipment now rely on codeshares and other forms of alliances. Allegations of unfair competition in the form of government subsidies have added to the legacy carriers' unease, to the extent that there have been demands for regulatory intervention, which continues to pose a threat to the liberalisation and normalisation of the industry.

From an airline's perspective, technology has produced three key advances in aircraft design: increases in size; increases in range; and decreases in unit operating costs. However, while manufacturers have produced larger aircraft, the average unit size actually operated by airlines has increased far more modestly. For US carriers, for example, the average aircraft size grew from 166 seats in 1995 to 179 seats in 2018, an increase of just 7.8%. Over the same period, the average stage length grew from 839 miles to 1159 miles, an increase of 38%. A similar pattern was seen in other regions. The operation of longer non-stop routes is probably most starkly visible in the development of ultra long-haul services, such as the so-called Kangaroo route between the UK and Australia. When Qantas first flew from Brisbane to London in 1935, the trip took at least 12 days using a ten-seat De Havilland 86 and involving numerous overnight stops. In March 2018, it inaugurated a non-stop service between Perth and London (14,500 kms) using a Boeing 787. A non-stop Sydney-London service (17,000 kms) is expected to follow in 2025, with 238-seat A350–1,000 aircraft.

The fact that the Perth-London route is not even the longest scheduled non-stop air service in the world (see Table 9.2) did not prevent the Chief Executive of Qantas, Alan Joyce, from describing it as "game-changing… This is the final frontier of aviation." Technically, ultra long-haul routes may well be a significant achievement, and some, such as the Kangaroo route, will probably continue to have an iconic importance. A recent academic study even went so far as to state, rather grandly, that "ultra long-haul naturally synergises with the future visions and desires of aviation."[5] However, in economic terms their impact is far less and, overall, they are unlikely to be of more than marginal importance. While the number of such routes will almost certainly increase over time, they may well remain premium products with fares undercut by indirect, sixth-freedom competitors. The underlying cost advantage of non-stop flights over these distances, if it exists at all with the aircraft used often having reduced seating capacity, not to mention the discomfort of very long flights for most passengers, may be insufficient to have a major impact on airline route networks. Above all, there are just not that many ultra-long-haul routes with sufficient passenger demand to justify non-stop service.

The clear trend in aircraft design throughout the industry's history had been for aircraft to get bigger. A particularly significant quantum leap in size came in 1970 with Pan American Airways' inauguration of Boeing 747 services, representing a capacity increase of some 150% over the Boeing 707 in normal configuration. In total, Boeing received net orders for 1,573 B747s,

Table 9.2 Longest Ultra Long-Haul Scheduled Passenger Flights, 2020

Route	Airline	Distance (kms)	Flight Time
Singapore-Newark	Singapore Airlines	16,700	18hrs 45mins
Auckland-Doha	Qatar Airways	14,534	18hrs 30mins
Perth-Heathrow	Qantas Airways	14,499	17hrs 20mins
Los Angeles-Singapore	United Airlines	14,100	17hrs 20mins
Auckland-Dubai	Emirates Airlines	14,200	17hrs 15mins
San Francisco-Singapore	United Airlines	13,593	17hrs 05mins
Los Angeles-Jeddah	Saudia Airlines	13,409	16hrs 55mins
Johannesburg-Atlanta	Delta Air Lines	13,582	16hrs 40mins
Abu Dhabi-Los Angeles	Etihad Airlines	13,502	16hrs 30mins

Source: Aerospace, May 2020.

the last few being freighters, and construction finally ended in 2022. Its numerous variants ranged in size, in a typical three-class configuration, from 276 seats (the long-range SP version) to 467 seats (the latest 747-8 version), although with all-economy seating over 600 passengers can be accommodated. The key attraction for airlines, of course, was that the more passengers who could be carried, the lower the unit per passenger costs. On the other hand, the principal challenge was to find routes of sufficient density to support a reasonable frequency of services.

For Boeing's main competitor, Airbus, the 747's dominance of the large aircraft market presented a problem. After initially threatening Boeing's very existence, eventually the 747 proved to be highly profitable, something of a cash cow, which helped to increase the company's competitiveness across the whole range of its models. Airbus' response was the A380, which replaced the 747 as the world's largest commercial aircraft. After a decade or more of development, the A380 entered service with Singapore Airlines in 2007, but only following an intense marketing battle between the two manufacturers with very different visions of how airline networks would evolve over the coming decades. Boeing sought to defend its position by arguing that the future lay in smaller twin-engine aircraft such as its new 787, so-called '*hub-bypassers*' able to serve thinner, longer routes economically. The four-engine A380, on the other hand, was promoted as at least part of the solution to growing airport congestion, an aircraft capable of carrying very large numbers of passengers (typically 500–600, although potentially some 800) between the world's major airports. In fact, both arguments proved to be correct, and wrong. Boeing's new product did not really challenge hub dominance; in 2019, over two-thirds of 787s actually served hub-to-hub routes. At the same time, the era of very large aircraft proved to be short-lived; the future lay with smaller, twin-engine planes, and Airbus was soon forced to develop a competitor to the 787 in the form of the A350.

Initially, logic and history appeared to be on Airbus' side. A growing number of airports around the world are capacity constrained, and the A380 presented the opportunity to make more efficient use of limited take-off and landing slots. Similarly, over the years airlines have repeatedly found that carrying more passengers and freight per aircraft on a route produces lower unit costs, and therefore lower fares and freight rates, a major factor in the industry's record of maintaining significant annual growth. Tretheway and Oum describe this relationship as one of the three fundamental aspects of aircraft engineering technology which are reflected in airline costs, the other two being flight distance and the proportion of capacity occupied.[6] However, there was a counter argument which at the time many chose to ignore, namely that profitability was more likely to be achieved if capacity was restricted. There are also clear commercial benefits from being able to operate higher frequencies on thick routes, and operate thinner routes generally, with smaller aircraft. As Michael Levine commented: "I'm not aware of any airline in history that went out of business from operating too little capacity."

162 *Technology and the Environment*

A similar point was made by the legendary Chief Executive of American Airlines, Bob Crandall: "There is one iron rule in this business. You can go broke if your airplanes are too big, but you cannot go broke if your airplanes are too small."

The key to the success of the smaller long-range aircraft was the ability to match the economics of the larger planes, a development made possible mainly because of technical progress by the engine manufacturers. Twin-engine aircraft such as the Boeing 787 or 777 and the Airbus A350 can not only fly very long distances non-stop with full passenger loads, but do so at lower unit costs than four-engine planes. Air France, for example, has stated that the A380 consumes 20%–25% more fuel per seat than new-generation twin-engine aircraft. Similarly, research by the consultancy Oliver Wyman found that United Airlines' 747s had an average hourly operating cost of US$17,748, using 2017 fiscal year data, compared to US$10,123 for the same carrier's 787s. In terms of cost per passenger, the 787 was marginally cheaper than the 747, despite the size disparity.[7] This represents a significant change in airline network economics. In such circumstances, provided airport capacity does not restrict the number of services that can be operated, why would an airline not add frequencies to better meet the needs of its customers? In addition, routes which previously were not sustainable at a commercial frequency could now be served profitably. The result has been a dramatic relative fall in the attractiveness of four-engine aircraft. According to OAG, wide-body four-engine aircraft flew with 104 million seats in 2019, down some 41 million since 2010. Seats in wide-body twins, on the other hand, increased from 112 million to 716 million over the same period (see Figure 9.1).

Additional factors in the demise of the A380 included its poor emissions performance, which has become increasingly important, and ironically given its claim to be the largest commercial aircraft flying, its relatively poor cargo capacity. Eventually, the changing dynamics of the industry proved to be a disaster for the aircraft. Having originally forecast a demand for almost 900 units over a twenty-year period, in fact the manufacturer received only 251 net orders, of which more than half were acquired by a single airline, Emirates. Of the 22 airlines which placed orders, just 14 actually took delivery. In early 2019, acknowledging the inevitable, Airbus announced that production would cease in 2021. Not only had orders dried up, but several customers, including carriers one might normally expect to be loyal to an Airbus product such as Air France and Lufthansa, sought ways to reduce the number of A380s in their fleets. The Chief Executive of Air France/KLM, speaking in mid-2019, described the A380 as the "poorest performer [in the AF/KL fleet] from an operational perspective…[it] does not offer us any economical advantage versus other airplanes." Even the second-hand market has proved to be difficult, with ten-year-old aircraft being dismantled for lack of buyers, which must be unique in modern times.

Airbus has undoubtedly lost money on the A380 programme, but it has hardly been a success for the airlines and leasing companies either, not to

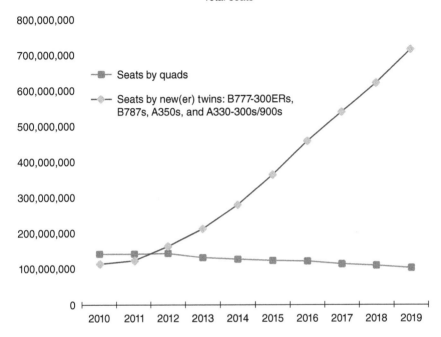

Figure 9.1 Number of Seats Flown in Four and Two-engine Aircraft, 2010–2019
Source: OAG

mention those airports which made expensive alterations to their terminals and taxiways to accommodate the new aircraft. A dismantled A380 might earn some US$40 to US$80 million from the sale of parts, compared with a list price for the aircraft in 2018 (the last year Airbus published this information) of US$446 million. (Singapore Airlines, the first airline to take delivery of the A380, reportedly paid US$250 million per unit.) It was indicative of the challenges presented by the A380 that during the 2020 Coronavirus crisis the aircraft was among the first units to be grounded, in several cases permanently.

Narrow-bodied aircraft are undergoing a similar radical shake-up. Short-haul air services have been dominated for many years by the Boeing 737 and Airbus A320 families. The efficiency of these aircraft has gradually improved, but neither has been able to operate more than a handful of long-haul routes, such as across the Atlantic, with full loads. This shortcoming is in the process of changing with the introduction of the A321LR and A321XLR. (Boeing's answer to the Airbus challenge, the 737–8ERX, has so far remained a paper aircraft.) The A321LR is capable of flights up to 4,000 nautical miles and the A321XLR up to 4,700 nm with what the manufacturer claims to be a full load. It is, however, important to look at the small print when considering manufacturers' claims for new aircraft. For example, in the case of the A321XLR, the 4,700 nautical mile range assumes slightly fewer seats than normal and short-haul baggage experience and route reserves. Changing these assumptions to typical airline rules for longer routes would reduce the maximum stage length to 4,200 nm. Configured like a current long-range aircraft, with a three-class cabin, the A321XLR will have a capacity of 150 passengers and a range of 4,600 nm, although in practice it seems likely that two class configurations will be more common.[8] In addition, the safety regulators have yet to certify Airbus' range claims, and may not do so because of the weight implications of the additional fuel tank.

Nevertheless, the A321LR and especially the A321XLR are likely to be game changers and have a major impact on the route networks of many airlines. Critical to this impact are their operating economics. The A321XLR, for example, is forecast to have the same per seat economics as, or even slightly better than, the larger and more expensive A330-800 and B787-8.[9] A sign of likely success is the fact that by mid-2022, sometime before the aircraft is scheduled to enter commercial service, Airbus had already received orders for well over 500 A320XLR units. Whereas the LR version can comfortably fly between Paris and New York, the XLR will enable routes such as Frankfurt to Chicago to be served. Other routes between, for example, Europe and the Middle East and South America and within the Asia/Pacific region will also be possible (see Table 9.3). The disruption which the new A321LR and especially the A321XLR will bring to the market will inevitably lead to higher frequencies on routes to and from hubs where airport capacity is available, and result in new services to/from and between secondary and regional airports. The legacy carriers will certainly be early participants, and several have already announced initial plans. But there is also a clear opportunity for established LCCs (as well as new entrants) currently focusing on short-haul routes to turn their attention to longer destinations. The ability to use the same basic aircraft type that is already in their fleets will be a major attraction here.

Table 9.3 Routes Forecast to be Within the Range of the A321XLR

London	–	Miami
Rome	–	New York
London	–	Delhi
Miami	–	Buenos Aires
London	–	Dubai
Dubai	–	Kuala Lumpur
Delhi	–	Tokyo
Kuala Lumpur	–	Auckland
Tokyo	–	Sydney

Source: Airbus.

There is a certain irony in this potential disruption, of course, in that Airbus, which argued so strongly, and unsuccessfully, that the future lay with ultra-large aircraft, seems to be the winner with what at present amounts to a virtual monopoly of long-haul narrow-body aircraft.

The Environment[10]

The environment is almost certainly the most important long-term issue facing the aviation industry today, one that potentially could significantly affect its ability to continue to expand and prosper. Ed Bastion, CEO of Delta Air Lines, is not alone in noting that "environmental stewardship is the existential threat to our future ability to grow."[11] Of course, aviation brings major benefits to societies and economies around the world, whether in enabling more and more people to travel for leisure and to visit friends and relatives or in oiling the wheels of global trade. At the same time, however, this comes at a price in terms of the impact on the environment. There is widespread concern about climate change and, as a result, growing opposition to the continued growth of aviation. The comment from a spokesman for the environmental lobby group Transport and Environment that "flying is the fastest way of frying the planet" is typical of the firmly held views now routinely reported in the press. The Scandinavian 'Flight Shame' campaign has had a real impact on demand for air travel in the region.

Twenty years ago, global warming was far from the focus of public attention in this context. Initially, noise was seen as the main aviation problem as jets replaced turboprops, and despite considerable technical progress, noise pollution continues to hamper airport expansion in many countries. Aircraft may be much quieter, but there are many more of them. More recently the situation has changed. Emissions are now the principal cause of concern because of their impact on global warming. The challenge is to reduce emissions while retaining the industry's social and economic benefits. A complicating element is the fact that while carbon dioxide (CO_2) is seen as the main culprit, it is not the only one. Aircraft produce other pollutants, such as vapour trails, soot particles, methane and nitrogen oxides (NO_x). However, the scientific understanding of their impact on the environment is lower than it is for CO_2 and there is far less consensus among those studying the subject. A UK report argued that

> ...the clear message is that mitigation of non-CO_2 impacts tends to raise complex questions regarding both scientific uncertainty and trade-off (with CO_2) consequences, whereas reducing CO_2 emissions has clear and long-term benefits and does not suffer from the same levels of scientific uncertainty.[12]

At the same time, others have concluded that for the two main non-CO_2 problems, contrails and NO_x, the prospects of substantial reductions are real and potentially realisable within a far shorter timescale than the options for reducing CO_2 emissions. They are, in other words, the 'low hanging fruit.'[13]

Indeed, contrails, which account for over half of the entire climate impact of aviation according to some estimates, may be a problem for only a small proportion of flights. Changing the altitude of fewer than 2% of flights, it has been argued, could potentially reduce contrail-linked climate change by 59%,[14] although not everyone would agree with this figure.

There is no doubt that aviation is a polluter, but a relatively modest one compared with several other industries, even in the transport sector (see Table 9.4). While there is debate about precise figures, most would agree that aviation CO_2 accounts for between 2% and 2.5% of global emissions and that overall, as we have seen, air transport's emissions contribution may be about 5%. This compares with 25% for food production and 10% for the clothing and fashion industry. It is also the case that aviation was a leader in setting environmental targets, although more recently it may have lagged other sectors. Nevertheless, air transport has become a prime focus of environmental lobbyists, reflecting its high level of visibility and resulting in growing pressure to reduce the number of flights and limit airport expansion. In the febrile atmosphere created by various green campaigns, combined with extensive press coverage, logical debate is often difficult. Rational argument in this context becomes far less important than the perception created by constant references to air transport's poor environmental credentials, whether true or not. A French survey, for example, showed that 90% of respondents overestimated air transport's share of global carbon emissions, and 98% underestimated aviation's record in reducing carbon emissions per passenger.[15] A recent UK survey showed similar results, with respondents considerably overestimating the impact of aviation compared with, for example, road transport.[16]

Table 9.4 Global Transport CO_2 Emissions, 2018

Road (passenger)	–	45.1%
Road (freight)	–	29.4%
Aviation	–	11.6%
Shipping	–	10.6%
Rail	–	1.0%
Other	–	2.2%

Source: IEA, Our World in Data, The Times (London) 22 July 2021.

Airbus has claimed that aircraft are roughly 80% more fuel efficient per passenger kilometre than they were fifty years ago, performance which would normally be cause for congratulations. The problem is that, pre-COVID, the industry continued to grow at a rapid rate, outstripping its environmental efficiency gains, and therefore attracted a disproportionate amount of interest from the public. The situation is compounded by the fact that at present there is no viable alternative to using fossil fuel as aviation's principal source of power. This means that the 'greening' of air transport is likely to take longer to implement than similar initiatives elsewhere, which in turn means that in the short/medium term at least, airlines will inevitably account for a growing proportion of greenhouse gases (see Tables 9.5 and 9.6). The European Aviation Safety Agency, in a 2019 report, noted that while overall the environmental impact of aviation in Europe has increased by 10% for CO_2, 12% for NO_x and 14% for noise since 2014,

> looking ahead, in the most likely traffic forecast, existing environmental impact mitigation measures are unlikely to counteract the increasing environmental impacts as the number of flights in Europe are expected to grow by 42% from 2017 to 2040. In that same timeframe, aircraft CO_2 emissions are predicted to increase by 21% and NO_x emissions by 16%.[17]

The COVID pandemic has not fundamentally changed this conclusion.

Table 9.5 Air Transport CO_2 Emissions (Million Tonnes), Assuming No Remedial Action

2005	–	332
2010	–	449
2015	–	600
2020	–	755[a]
2035	–	1,450[a]
2050	–	2700

Source: Aircraft Commerce, February/March 2017.
[a] – Projected.

Table 9.6 Proportion of Total CO_2 Emissions Generated by Aviation (Assuming No Changes to Fuel and Operating Efficiency or Use of Alternative Fuels)

2015	–	2.0%
2050	–	22.0%

Source: Aircraft Commerce, February/March 2015.

There is little doubt that there has been a step change in public recognition of the dangers of climate change and the need to do something about it. To a somewhat lesser extent, this was also true of the period leading up to the financial crisis of 2008/09, a period of relative global prosperity. Then, however, the economic downturn saw a marked reduction in the public's interest in environmental matters. The economy, and especially jobs, became the prime focus of attention and attacking the expansion of air services was seen as antigrowth. Renewed interest in the environment came with the resumption of relative prosperity after the financial crisis. One might have expected to see this interest decline again with the economic downturn caused by the COVID pandemic, but that has not happened. On the contrary, concern about global warming and its causes has increased. It would appear that there has been a fundamental global change, adding to the problems facing the aviation industry. Airlines in particular have had no choice but to react.

The core of that reaction was summarised in recent comments from two of the industry's leading representatives. The first, from the Chief Executive of London's Heathrow Airport, noted that "the answer is not to stop people flying. It has to be about decarbonising aviation," while the other came from the former Director General of IATA who argued that carbon is the enemy, not flying. In other words, the solution is not to reduce the scale of air travel, by for example taxing it more heavily to reduce demand, but rather to focus on removing aviation emissions at source to the maximum extent possible. As we shall see below, this is what the industry has increasingly committed to do, by a variety of means. Such a commitment has been impressive in many ways and is built on a record of significant technical progress already, although certainly not everyone is convinced that the targets are achievable within the prescribed timescales. However, the record of airlines in particular in responding to growing demands for action has been far less impressive. Until relatively recently most carriers and their trade bodies were slow in reacting to the threat that the environmental movement posed to the sector's continued prosperity. There appeared to be a strong preference to ignore the building pressure, or at best to engage in public relations exercises which were quickly labelled 'greenwash' by activists. At least there is now widespread acceptance that such an approach will just not work.

The reaction to the climate change crisis has not been uniform throughout the world. On the whole, its main impact so far has been in Europe, with less pressure on aviation in many other regions, although there is evidence that concern is building elsewhere. One result has been action taken by several European airlines to seek competitive advantage from their environmental credentials, often only to face strong criticism from campaigners for exaggerating their claims. Ryanair, for example, the largest airline in Europe in terms of the number of passengers carried, has maintained that it has the lowest carbon emissions of any major airline in Europe: "With the highest passenger load factor (96%) and one of the youngest fleets (average of six years), Ryanair delivers the lowest CO_2 per passenger in the EU airline industry." (May 2019 press statement) This claim was widely condemned, with the UK Advertising Standards Authority even intervening to say that it was 'misleading' and must not be repeated. This didn't stop Wizz Air stating only a few months later: "Wizz Air continues to operate at the lowest CO_2 emissions per passenger amongst all competitor airlines." The truth is that such claims rely on choosing the right statistics. Wizz Air does indeed have a lower CO_2 per revenue passenger kilometre than Ryanair, but its CO_2 per passenger is higher.

Spats like these are clearly inconsistent with an open and united industry seriously addressing the most important long-term challenge to its ability to grow. Airlines very rarely compete in terms of safety records, but the same hesitation does not appear to apply to environmental issues. One commentator, in urging a cessation of 'virtue signalling within our own tent,' went so far as to describe the approach as a 'circular firing squad.'[18] According to the European Commission, in 2019, Ryanair became the first non-coal company to join Europe's top ten carbon emitters, a select group previously the sole preserve of German and Eastern European coal-fired power stations. Greener by Design described this as a

> harbinger of what is to come, as successful airlines are unable to reduce their absolute total CO_2 in the face of rapidly rising passenger kilometres, whereas all the other occupants of the top ten will be consigned to history in the next 15 years in the face of toughening European rules.[19]

Before the war in Ukraine, Germany has set 2030 as the deadline for phasing out all coal-fired power stations and it is possible that by then all the top ten EU CO_2 producers will be airlines. None of this makes the challenge faced by aviation any easier to deal with.

One response has been a reinvigoration of the industry's campaigns to publicise the importance of air transport for the global economy, but there is clear recognition that this is far from sufficient to prevent further, damaging government intervention. Increasingly, therefore, the principal focus has shifted to ways to actually reduce the negative impact of flights on the environment. The scale of the challenge has been further highlighted by ICAO, which calculated that in 2020, air transport emissions would, in the absence of any COVID effect, be some 70% higher in total than they were in 2005 and could be a further 300% to 700% higher still by 2050 if there is no or only limited action to reduce them. Fortunately, this is unlikely to be the case. The industry as a whole, as well as individual companies, has increasingly made commitments which, while recognising that air transport will be slower than many other sectors in reaching zero emissions, nevertheless provide a clear timetable for achieving such an outcome (see Table 9.7).

Table 9.7 Top 10 European Airline CO_2 Emitters, 2018

Ryanair	–	9.9m tonnes
easyJet	–	6.3m tonnes
Lufthansa	–	4.3m tonnes
British Airways	–	3.0m tonnes
Norwegian	–	2.8m tonnes
SAS	–	2.5m tonnes
Air France	–	2.4m tonnes[a]
Eurowings	–	2.4m tonnes
Wizz Air	–	2.3m tonnes
Vueling	–	2.2m tonnes

Source: European Commission.
[a]2017.

One example of this renewed determination was the commitment by IATA, at its 2021 AGM, to achieve net-zero global aviation emissions by the middle of the current century, involving the abatement of some 1.8 gigatons of carbon in 2050 and a cumulative total of 21.2 gigatons during the period up to then. This will certainly be a significant challenge. Previously, in 2010,

IATA had outlined plans to only halve airline emissions by 2050, with carbon neutral growth from 2020. The new commitment reflects similar undertakings by an increasing number of individual airlines and States, including the US, EU and UK. As a study undertaken for the World Economic Forum concluded, there is no single 'silver bullet', overarching way to achieve this objective, "a basket of policy and regulatory measures will be necessary to incentivize investment ...."[20] IATA's Waypoint 2050 plan identifies four key ways by which success can be achieved:

- Radical new technologies, including the use of electricity or hydrogen as a power source, which in total could contribute between 12% and 34% of the emission reductions needed.
- Sustainable Aviation Fuel (SAF), which could contribute between 53% and 71% of the requirement.
- Improved operating procedures, including infrastructure reform, which could add 7%–10%.
- Finally, carbon removal will be necessary for the residual 8% of 2050 emissions.

It is evident from the size of the ranges identified that considerable uncertainty still exists as to how the industry's eventual target will be met in practice. A key question, however, is whether this will be sufficient in the face of growing opposition to more air travel. Will politicians, under pressure from vociferous campaign groups, be impatient with the industry's proposed timescale and take the initiative to reduce aviation emissions by curtailing demand for air travel? It is not surprising that various forms of aviation taxation have increasingly featured on the political agenda. Ideally, such taxation should be designed to ensure that airlines compensate for the environmental externalities generated by their services, but it is clear that they have also been used as an easy source of revenue for governments. It is notable that the 2021 proposals from the European Commission, 'Fit for 55' (referring to a 55% reduction in overall carbon emissions by 2035), in addition to SAF initiatives and reform of the EU Emissions Trading Scheme, focused on increased taxes on aviation fuel over a ten-year period. Such unwelcome (for the aviation industry at least) intervention can only be prevented, or more likely reduced, if the other initiatives supported by the industry actually deliver, and on time. At present, the best that can be said is that the jury is out.

Taxation of air services was the subject of a study carried out by the consultancy C E Delft for the European Commission in 2019.[21] The study noted that aviation was already subject to various specific taxes in many countries, but widely exempted from taxation for international travel. The Chicago Convention specifically forbids the taxation of fuel that is on board an aircraft when it lands in a signatory State, although it does not address the taxation of fuel loaded in a State. Other ICAO policies urge countries to refrain from taxing international air services and most bilateral air services agreements contain similar restrictions. Delft found that within the EU, 17 of the then 28 Member States applied VAT or other taxes to domestic air travel, and six Member States levied taxes on international aviation in the form of ticket taxes for passengers departing EU airports. The highest taxation, by some way, is levied in the UK, followed by Italy, Norway, Germany and France (see Table 9.8). (Note that in most cases taxation is significantly greater, proportionately, for domestic than for international services, mainly reflecting concern about the relative competitiveness of national carriers.) Outside the EU, 19 countries tax aviation activities according to Delft, including Australia, Canada, the US, Hong Kong, Brazil and Japan, again mostly in the form of ticket or departure taxes. Japan, Mexico, the US and Canada are among the countries which levy VAT or sales taxes for domestic travel. In some cases, fuel for domestic flights is also taxed, for example, in the US and India. Thus, there is ample precedent for taxing air services.

Table 9.8 Weighted Average Aviation Taxes per Passenger for Selected EU States, 2019 (Euros)

	Domestic Services	International Services
United Kingdom	40.04	43.83
Italy	22.82	19.59
Norway	19.98	8.77
Germany	18.12	13.69
France	15.41	9.53
Sweden	14.48	13.10
Greece	9.72	0.00
Austria	5.64	5.30
Denmark	0.00	0.00
Spain	2.57	0.00

Source: European Commission/C E Delft, Taxes in the Field of Aviation and Their Impact. Final Report, June 2019.

The Delft study found that in 2019, the weighted average aviation tax across all EU Member States and destinations amounted to €11 per ticket. If all aviation taxes were abolished, the number of passengers would increase by 4%, with a broadly equivalent increase in the number of flights, connections, jobs and value added in the aviation sector. Air transport's CO_2 emissions would also increase by 4% and the number of people affected by airport noise by 2%. The overall (net) impact on EU GDP would be plus 0.2%. On the other hand, abolishing the energy taxation exemption on aircraft fuel would result in an increase in the average ticket price of 10% and a decrease in passenger demand of 11%. There would be an 11% decrease in aviation employment, value added and CO_2 emissions and the number of people affected by airport noise would decline by 8%. The overall impact on GDP would be negligible, mainly because the higher fiscal revenues would be offset by the negative effects on employment and value added. Like any study of this kind, the Delft analysis depends on numerous assumptions, and it is fair to say that far from everyone has agreed with its conclusions. However, it does serve to give a broad indication of the likely impact of taxation (and lack of it) on air transport services.

If the way to achieve net-zero aviation emissions has been broadly mapped out, the detail is still missing. The scale of the task is enormous, and unfortunately progress so far has, at best, been limited. The tools available to achieve the overarching objective of an environmentally sustainable air transport industry by 2050 are outlined below.

Off-setting/Emission Trading

Global warming is, by definition, a global problem and the aviation industry has long lobbied for a multilateral approach to addressing it, rather than relying on action by individual or groups of countries. There has been a fear of a patchwork of overlapping, even contradictory, regulatory schemes, a problem seen in other areas of regulatory intervention in the industry. Already several countries have implemented Emission Trading Schemes (ETS) around the world. The first to do so was New Zealand, which included domestic aviation in an economy-wide scheme in 2010. It was the EU, however, which attracted most attention, and criticism. Its ETS, first introduced in 2005 for most industries, was extended to domestic and international aviation in 2012, partly because of frustration at the speed with which the rest of the world was taking action. Following strong criticism from numerous other countries, implementation of the EU scheme was put on hold for intercontinental flights pending multilateral negotiations, a reflection of the complications (and politics) of applying an ETS to air services which overfly several sovereign States.[22] (US airlines were particularly vociferous in their opposition to the EU scheme, despite the findings of one study suggesting that their profitability might actually increase under the scheme, mainly because of windfall gains from free carbon allowances.[23]) In addition to the attempt to apply ETS to extra-European air services, the EU initiative has also been widely criticised for the size of the 'free' carbon allowances permitted, which in effect, some have argued, provide a considerable subsidy to airlines. As two Dublin-based academics, Fitzgerald and Tol, noted: "European politicians would create the impression of leadership on climate policy while in fact contributing almost nothing to emissions reduction."[24]

However, while condemnation of the EU approach may have been widespread around the world, at least it helped to focus attention on the need for a more global solution. The Kyoto Protocol of 1997 had omitted reference to aviation and shipping, at least partly because of the difficulty in allocating emissions to specific countries for these international industries. Instead, responsibility was passed to ICAO and its shipping equivalent, the International Maritime Organisation. (Aviation and shipping had actually been covered in the original draft agreement, but were removed in order to increase the number of States willing to participate.) The 2015 Paris Agreement similarly does not specifically include international air transport, but it does encompass domestic flights and emissions from airports. Passing responsibility to ICAO was certainly a success for aviation lobbyists. If the objective was to delay progress for a significant period of time, the strategy appears to have worked. As one commentator recently noted, after almost a quarter of a century ICAO still has no long-term global aspirational goal for the mitigation of aviation emissions. It has spent the past 11 years "exploring the feasibility of one."[25] The OECD has made the same point.[26] It is perhaps not surprising that ICAO is occasionally known as Impossible to Conceive of Any Outcome.

ICAO launched a work programme on emission mitigation and, in 2009, a list of possible measures was produced, namely improved technology and operations, the evolution of sustainable fuels and, despite the UN organisation's poor record in dealing with politically contentious issues, market-based measures (MBMs). In 2016, the triennial ICAO Assembly set out what has been called the 'final link', a framework for a global MBM in the form of the Carbon Offsetting and Reduction Scheme for International Aviation (CORSIA), which was endorsed at the 2019 Assembly.[27] The role of CORSIA was described in an ICAO Assembly Resolution as "a complement [to the] broader basket of measures to achieve carbon-neutral growth from 2020." Originally conceived as a transient supplement, it has now become ICAO's primary emissions mitigation tool. CORSIA was certainly a breakthrough given the difficulties of reaching any multilateral agreement in aviation. It seemed to offer the prospect of avoiding a multitude of interventions by individual or groups of States. IATA was strongly supportive, despite calculating that CORSIA would cost the industry some US$40 billion by 2050. Unfortunately, despite the inclusion of the word 'reduction' in its title, CORSIA did not actually incorporate any element which would lead to less emissions.

Off-setting, as embodied in CORSIA, involves the purchase of carbon credits from sources such as large reforestation projects or solar farms to 'off-set' emissions from aircraft flights. It is an approach which numerous individual airlines and others have adopted for some time on a voluntary basis. However, the reaction of the travelling public has been less than enthusiastic. While precise figures are difficult to come by, in practice probably less than 1% of passengers on flights offering off-sets take them up, despite the relatively low charges made. (One major international airline found that while 80% of passengers consulted in a survey said that they would pay to offset their flight emissions, in practice only 0.5% did so.) It may well be that most travellers regard emissions reduction as a public good and are unwilling to contribute, preferring to rely on government action. There is also a marked absence of agreement among airlines on the cost of carbon in these schemes. The charge made by British Airways in September 2021, for example, was almost half of that charged by Ryanair on similar intra-European flights, and its long-haul charges per mile were even lower. It has been calculated that BA was pricing carbon at €8 to €10 a tonne, Ryanair closer to €18, at a time when EU and UK industrial companies were paying some €56 per tonne via the European ETS.[28] It is evident that a voluntary approach has not worked.

The fact that the industry is forced to rely on a significant element of off-setting to achieve carbon neutral growth is illustrative of its inevitable struggle to operate without oil as its principal source of fuel over the short/medium term. This is despite the acknowledged shortcomings of off-setting. Chris Lyle has commented:

> CORSIA is certainly a 'step forward' in aviation emission mitigation both in terms of its technicalities and of raising the understanding and profile of the issues worldwide. But ... [it] in effect reflects 'lowest common tolerability' amongst the 193 ICAO States ... [It] is not only complex and resource heavy, it is fragile and vulnerable.

In fact, CORSIA represents the first-ever application of ICAO Standards to an economic issue. Previously such Standards, which ICAO itself has no direct authority to implement, have applied only to safety, security and facilitation matters.[29]

The CORSIA programme faces several challenges, even ignoring the fact that the whole concept of offsetting has been questioned by some environmental campaigners. In particular, critics of CORSIA have argued that it does not go far or fast enough to deal with the underlying problem, despite attracting the support of some 200 countries by late-2019. For example, the programme is intended to run as a pilot between 2021 and 2023, then on a voluntary basis between 2024 and 2026. Only in 2027 will it become fully effective for signatory States, and even then there will be exemptions for the least developed, small island developing and landlocked developing countries. As of late 2021, just 107 States had indicated that they intended to participate in CORSIA from the outset. Although these 107 States represent almost 80% of international aviation activity, major countries such as Brazil, China, Russia and South Africa had yet to join. CORSIA inevitably looks like what it is: a weak, lowest common denominator approach. It is certainly less ambitious than the EU ETS.

Nevertheless, if a multilateral agreement is to be reached, CORSIA looks like the only show in town. It was notable that aviation featured more prominently at COP26, held in Glasgow in late 2021, than it had at previous COPs. A significant number of States launched the International Aviation Climate Ambition Coalition to pursue agreement on a long-term, net-zero target at the next ICAO General Assembly in late 2022. If aviation's emission reduction ambitions are to be taken seriously, this meeting will be crucial. Certainly, any CORSIA pricing signal will have to be significantly strengthened, despite resistance from some airlines. The final outcome of this struggle between opposing interests will determine the aviation industry's ability to progress towards net-zero emissions growth in both the short and long term.

Sustainable Fuel

A second key element in achieving air transport's emission targets is the development of SAF. The first experimental use of SAF in a commercial aircraft was in 2008, when a Virgin Atlantic 747 positioning flight flew from London to Amsterdam with the addition 500 gallons of biofuel sourced from coconut and babassu nut oils. This at least proved wrong those who had argued that SAF would freeze at high altitudes, but the mix used by Virgin was not a long-term solution because of the limited supplies of babassu nuts available and the harmful wider effects of diverting potential food for use as aircraft fuel, a recurrent theme for some forms of SAF. Nevertheless, considerable research and testing followed, using numerous other raw material sources including agricultural and forest waste, cooking oil, algae and a variety of plant-based oils. Several major airlines have been involved, and airports have also turned to biofuels to reduce their carbon footprints, which are of course far smaller than those of airlines. By the tenth anniversary of the first Virgin flight, IATA could claim that the industry was on track to carry 1 billion passengers by 2025 on aircraft partly powered by SAF, provided it received support from governments. There were 100,000 SAF flights in 2017, with (pre-COVID) 1 million expected by 2020. In the words of the IATA Director General: "The momentum for sustainable aviation fuels is now unstoppable."

The Financial Times argued that "the substitution of biofuels for traditional kerosene jet fuel represents one of the quickest ways to bring down the industry's emissions on a meaningful scale," mainly because unlike some other potential solutions, they require little change to the architecture of current aircraft. Most of today's jet turbines can take blends of up to 50% biofuels and work is underway to certify 100% SAF for newer engines.[30] However, such optimism should be put into context. IATA has calculated that by 2050, some 450 billion litres of SAF will be needed annually by the aviation industry to meet two-thirds of consumption; in 2021 total production was about 100 million litres. Put another way, in 2018 the total volume of SAF produced was sufficient to power the global aviation industry for just ten minutes.[31] In the words of the website Cranky Flyer:

> Over the last decade, there have been more experiments with alternative aviation fuels than Fast and Furious movies… It hasn't been hard to find alternative fuels that work well and produce significantly lower levels of carbon dioxide, sulphur and other emissions than traditional kerosene. But what has been hard is to find alternative fuels that are also cost effective and sustainable at scale.[32]

Biofuels are probably between two and six times more expensive than jet fuel (partly depending, of course, on the price of oil), particularly because of the small scale of production at present. At least one major airline has already introduced a fare surcharge in response to government directions to use between 0.5 and 1% SAF mix at its bases. However, the expectation is that this price gap will narrow substantially over the coming years. It is probably reasonable to assume, on current understanding, that by 2050, the average cost of SAF will be between US$760 and US$900 per tonne, well within the historical cost range of fossil fuels, although slightly higher than the historical average. Over past decades airlines have frequently absorbed a doubling of fuel prices, albeit not without complaining and increasing fares. (It should be noted, however, that if there is a large-scale move towards electric power on the part of ground transport, which seems likely, the result could be a substantial excess supply of oil, almost certainly leading to a collapse in its price. This would alter the competitive balance between SAF and fossil fuel and make SAF relatively even more expensive.) Up to 7,000 biofuel refineries may be needed, each one smaller than current fossil fuel refineries, costing between US$1,080 and US$1,450 billion and representing about 6% of the historical annual global oil and gas capital expenditure. There is no reason to believe that this is not achievable.[33] The European Commission, which has proposed minimum blending requirements of 2% in 2025, rising to 63% in 2050, has forecast that the result will be an increase in fares of 8%, although there are clearly several heroic assumptions behind this figure. IATA has set out a roadmap for achieving two-thirds SAF use by 2050 (see Table 9.9).

Table 9.9 Milestones for SAF Use

- 2025, SAF production to reach 7.9 billion litres (2% of total airline fuel use)
- 2030, SAF = 23 billion litres (5.2%)
- 2035, SAF = 91 billion litres (17%)[a]
- 2040, SAF = 229 billion litres (39%)[b]
- 2045, SAF = 346 billion litres (54%)
- 2050, SAF = 449 billion litres (65%).

Source: IATA.
[a]Plus, electric and/or hydrogen aircraft for regional air services, up to 100 seats/90-minute flights.
[b]Plus, hydrogen aircraft for short-haul air services, up to 150 seats/120-minute flights.

Thus, it is evident that in the short and medium term, SAF will remain the principal means for airlines to reduce their impact on climate change, given the timescale of other potential developments. IATA's ATAG estimates that up to the 2030–35 period, some 97% of aviation decarbonisation, other than off-setting, will come from the increased use of SAF. An alternative to SAF in the longer term is hydrogen. Attempts to use hydrogen as an aircraft fuel date back to the late-1950s, with a secret US plan to power a spy plane. The fact that this was abandoned after just two years is a testament to the size of the challenge involved. Superficially, hydrogen is an attractive fuel source. It produces zero CO_2 and some three times the energy density of kerosene, over 100 times that of lithium-ion batteries. However, it requires four times the volume for the same amount of energy as kerosene. It is, therefore, necessary to compress it as a liquid at very cold temperatures, about −253 degrees centigrade. It also produces non-CO_2 emissions which may contribute to climate change, although these probably present less of a challenge than CO_2 itself, and in its 'clean' form (current commercial hydrogen is produced from fossil fuels) requires considerable amounts of electricity. The tanks needed to contain hydrogen are both heavier than those used for kerosene and four times the size. This inevitably imposes a constraint on the range and capacity of hydrogen-fuelled aircraft.[34] Despite the considerable research currently underway to design such aircraft, especially in Europe, doubt remains as to whether anything commercially viable will emerge for several decades.

Aircraft Design

Addressing potential advances in technology, the Intergovernmental Panel on Climate Change commented:

> Aircraft designs have received substantial, ongoing technology efficiency improvements over past decades, typically offering a 20–30% reduction in energy intensity compared to older aircraft models. [Relative to 2005,] further fuel efficiency gains of 40–50% in the 2030 – 50 timeframe could come from weight reduction, aerodynamics and engine performance improvements, and aircraft system design.

If this proves to be correct, it would represent a major step towards achieving the industry's environmental objectives. Of particular note is work on applying electric propulsion to flight. The Financial Times, referring to the development of battery-powered aircraft, noted that the aviation sector "is in the throes of the greatest revolution since the development of the jet engine by Frank Whittle in 1937." That may be true in the longer term, but unfortunately, the fruits of the revolution are likely to take some time to appear. There is a danger of the reality failing to match the press hype. As another commentator, writing in the Wall Street Journal, noted: "Unlike ground activities like electricity generation or road transportation, long-haul flying doesn't have alternatives and will depend on liquid fuels for decades to come."[35] Tim Clark, President of Emirates Airlines, put it more succinctly when he said that we are in 'la la land' if we think we are going to have electric A380s flying.

Battery-powered flight is already with us, albeit on a very small scale. Early experience has focused on general aviation, but the first flight by a commercial all-electric aircraft, a modified deHavilland Canada DHC-2 Beaver seaplane, was operated from Vancouver by Harbour Air in December 2019. Much as this technology is to be admired, its modest scale is again indicative of what is yet to be achieved to solve the industry's emissions problem. Pure electric propulsion for aircraft relies on batteries and unfortunately current battery technology still has severe limitations. As Scott McCartney has noted,[36] batteries are certainly improving rapidly, with an energy density of about 200 Watt-hours per kilogram projected to increase to some 500 WH/kg by 2035. However, kerosene has an engine density of 12,000 WH/kg, 60 times greater than current batteries and 24 times the 2035 objective. What this means is that larger, long-haul battery-powered aircraft would be too heavy to get off the ground, let alone fly for several thousand miles.

The problem was aptly summed up by Tim White of Collins Aerospace in saying that "weight is not an aircraft's friend."[37] Adding to this fundamental problem is the fact that unlike kerosene, the weight of batteries on board an aircraft will be exactly the same on landing as on take-off, which creates its own challenges. It is evident that for the foreseeable future, any breakthrough in low emission, all-electric aircraft will centre on small units, initially not much larger than typical general aviation or air taxi aircraft, although with the possibility of 100/150 seater models emerging within a couple of decades. The consensus conservative forecast seems to be that 15–20 seat electric aircraft will be in operation by 2030, with 50–100 passenger units arriving by 2050. Optimistic estimates reduce this timescale by five to ten years.[38] Unfortunately, it is the larger, long-haul aircraft that produce most carbon emissions (see Table 9.10). It should be borne in mind as well that even when emission-free aircraft are readily available, it will take many years to replace the current global fleet. Aircraft in operation in the 2030s will still be flying in large numbers in the 2050s, with each replacement cycle representing an investment of some US$5 trillion at today's prices. On the other hand, modern aircraft being introduced today are significantly 'cleaner' than the models they replace. According to one estimate, if the average age of aircraft deployed in 2019 was reduced by just one year, total CO_2 produced by airlines globally would be reduced by about 40 million tonnes, or 4.5%.[39]

Table 9.10 European Flights and CO_2 Emissions, 2020

Average Flight Length	Departing Flights	CO_2 Emissions
Greater than 4,000 kms	6.2%	51.9%
1,500–4,000 kms	19.6%	23.2%
500–1,500 kms	43.6%	20.6%
0–500 kms	30.6%	4.3%

Source: Eurocontrol.

Rather than all-electric units, more rapid progress might be seen in the development of hybrid aircraft, combining jet fuel as the main power source with a switch to electric motors for propulsion during certain phases of flight. This would represent a move in the right direction, but clearly would not reduce emissions as much as all-electric aircraft would. What is evident is that replacing liquid fuel as a source of power for commercial aircraft is a major technological challenge which will take many years to produce significant results. For long-haul travel, the only alternative to kerosene for several decades is likely to be SAF. It may be that in addition to engine development, what will be needed is radical change to the traditional airframe concept, perhaps along the lines of the blended wing body, which is essentially a large flying wing with the passenger/cargo areas contained within its centre section. (The blended wing concept is not new. As long ago as the 1930s, the Junker G-38, then the largest commercial aircraft in the world, involved most of its 30 plus passengers being located in the wings, with the leading edge of each wing fitted with sloping windscreens.) As Thomas Roetger of IATA has commented:

> By applying combinations of evolutionary technologies, fuel efficiency improvements of roughly 25–30% compared to today's aircraft still appear possible. However, further significant improvements of the classic tube-and-wing configuration powered by turbofans are becoming more and more difficult to envisage after 2035 or so.[40]

Concluding Remarks

It is clear that while the threat presented by growing concern about the environmental impact of aviation has been recognised for many years, a dramatic change has occurred recently. Having adopted a strategy of delay and greenwashing, most of the industry has finally accepted that continued expansion requires a very different approach. There is at last a real focus on achieving net-zero emissions over the next 30 years, through a combination of technical improvements, alternative fuels and off-setting. Unfortunately, most of the gains are likely to come towards the end of that period, which probably means aviation will continue to attract adverse interest from campaigners and politicians in the short and medium term. In practice this is likely to result in attempts to restrict demand by increasing fares as a result of higher taxation. The signs are there for everyone to see. A key part of the European Commission's 'Fit for 55' proposal, for example, is the addition of a kerosene tax, initially for intra-EU flights. Combined with the proposed phasing out of free carbon allowances under the EU's ETS, this would, if approved by Member States, result in a significant increase in average fares. Similarly, a little commented on provision of the Treaty covering the UK's withdrawal from the EU was the removal of fuel tax exemption for flights between the UK and the EU. This was a historical first, not seen in any air services agreement since 1946. It is reasonable to assume that this was included at the EU's insistence for a reason.

The willingness of governments to encourage the aviation industry to adopt a more environmentally friendly approach by additional regulation and taxation has not always been matched by their own commitment. A glaring example is the reform of air transport management, especially in Europe. Such reform is often referred to as the lowest-hanging fruit in the decarbonisation of the industry, with the potential to reduce European CO_2 emissions by some 10%. This is, of course, almost wholly in the hands of governments, and progress has been glacial. (See Chapter 11) Airlines might justifiably question why they continue to be the focus of official disapproval for their environmental record when governments themselves choose to ignore an area where progress is readily available.

Notes

1. William Nordhaus: 'Climate change: The ultimate challenge for economics.' *American Economic Review*, Vol. 109(6), June 2019, pp. 1991–2014.
2. Kenneth R. Sealy: *The Geography of Air Transport*. Hutchinson, London, 1957.
3. Brian Graham: *Geography and Air Transport*. John Wiley & Sons, Chichester, 1995.
4. Sealy, op cit.
5. Linus Benjamin Bauer, Daniel Bloch and Rico Merkert: 'Ultra Long-Haul: An emerging business model accelerated by COVID-19.' *Journal of Air Transport Management*, Vol. 89, October 2020, pp. 1–8.
6. Michael W. Tretheway and Tae H. Oum: 'Airline Economics: Foundations for Strategy and Policy.' Centre for Transportation Studies, University of British Columbia, 1992.
7. Wall Street Journal: 'The Last 747: Airlines Drop the Jumbo Jet, Transforming International Travel.' 29 December 2018.
8. Leeham News: 'The Range of Airbus A321XLR.' 27 June 2019.
9. Ibid.
10. This section partly relies on Barry Humphreys: 'The Environment Rears its Head Again.' Airline Leader, Issue 51, 2019.
11. Delta Investors Day, 12 December 2019.
12. David S. Lee: 'The Current State of Scientific Understanding of the non-CO_2 Effects of Aviation on Climate.' Report for the UK Department for Transport, 2018.
13. John Green: 'Easy Does It for Greener Skies.' Aerospace, June 2021.
14. Beth Timmins: 'Contrails: How Tweaking Flight Plans Can Help the Climate.' BBC News (website), 27 October 2021.
15. Paul Chiambaretto, Elodie Mayenic, Hervé Chappert, Juliane Engsig, Anne-Sophie Fernandez and Frédéric Le Roy: 'Where does flyskam come from? The role of citizens' lack of knowledge of the environmental impact of air transport in explaining the development of flight shame.' *Journal of Air Transport Management*, Vol. 93, June 2021.
16. UK Institute of Mechanical Engineers: 'British Public Underestimate Heating Emissions, Overestimate Aviation – ImechE Poll.' Press Release, 26 February 2021.
17. EASA: 'Second European Aviation Environmental Report.' 2019.
18. Michael Halaby: 'The 'E' in ESG.' Jetrader, Autumn 2021.
19. Greener by Design, Annual Report, 2018/19.
20. World Economic Forum (in collaboration with McKinsey & Company): 'Clean Skies Tomorrow. Sustainable Aviation Fuels as a Pathway to Net Zero Aviation.' Insight Report, Geneva, November 2020.
21. C. E. Delft: 'Taxes in the Field of Aviation and Their Impact.' Report for the European Commission, June 2019.
22. Frank Fichert, Peter Forsyth and Hans-Martin Niemeier (eds.): 'Air transport and the challenge of climate change – how aviation climate change policies work.' *Aviation and Climate Change. Economic Perspectives on Greenhouse Gas Reduction Policies*. Routledge, London, 2020.
23. Robert Malina, Dominic McConnachie, Niven Winchester, Christopher Wollersheim, Sergei Palster and Ian A. White: 'The impact of the European Union emissions trading scheme on US aviation.' *Journal of Air Transport Management*, Vol. 19, March 2012.
24. John Fitzgerald and Richard Tol: 'Europe's airline emissions plan is a flight of fancy.' *Financial Times*, 18 January 2007. I am grateful to Cathal Guiomard of Dublin City University for drawing this article to my attention.
25. Chris Lyle: 'Code Red for Aviation.' September 2021.
26. See OECD ITF; 'Decarbonising Air Transport. Acting Now for the Future.' Paris, July 2021.

27 Chris Lyle: 'Aviation Emissions: Are We Doing Enough?' Airline Leader, Issue 51, 2019.
28 Jonathan Guthrie: 'Airline Schemes to Take Sting Out of 'flight shame' Don't Add Up.' *Financial Times*, 7 September 2021.
29 Ibid.
30 *Financial Times*, 30 March 2020.
31 Tim Johnson, Director of the Aviation Environment Federation. Aviation Week and Space Technology, 13–26 January 2020.
32 Cranky Flyer, October 2018.
33 ICF: 'Fuelling Net Zero. How the Aviation Industry Can Deploy Sufficient Sustainable Aviation Fuel to Meet Climate Ambitions.' Report for ATAG Waypoint 2050, September 2021. See also Andrew Lobbenberg and Kim Fustier: 'Sustainable Aviation Fuel. The Key to Aviation Decarbonisation.' HSBC Global Research, July 2021.
34 Peggy Hollinger: 'Hydrogen-Powered Planes: Pie in the Sky?' *Financial Times*, 14 March 2021. Also, LARA, June/July 2021.
35 Scott McCartney, Wall Street Journal, 14 February 2019.
36 Ibid.
37 Tim White: 'Op-Ed: Hybrid-Electric Propulsion Is Key to Reducing Aviation's Carbon Footprint.' *Air Transport World*, 9 April 2019.
38 Thomas Roetger: 'Now for Something Completely Different.' Airlines, No. 3, 2019.
39 CAPA – Centre for Aviation: 'Airline Sustainability Benchmarking Report 2021.' October 2021.
40 Thomas Roetger, op cit.

10 Airline Profitability

One of the most quoted comments about airline profitability is that of Sir Richard Branson, founder of Virgin Atlantic Airways: "If you want to be a millionaire, start with a billion dollars and open an airline. Soon enough you will be a millionaire." (In fact, although this quote has become closely associated with Sir Richard, he was not actually the first person to use it.)[1] Such a pessimistic view of the industry is far from unique, and for good reason. As long ago as 1969, the Edwards Report on the UK aviation industry noted:

> The structure of world civil aviation has been fashioned by many forces amongst which economic logic has played only a modest part…We have been surprised how often the evidence we have received has appeared to overlook the historical and political factors which make up the institutional basis for the air transport industry.[2]

As noted previously, since the first powered flight by the Wright brothers, airlines have destroyed more capital than they have created. This is an extraordinary state of affairs for such a high-profile industry and one that has only been possible because of its particular characteristics, not least the regulatory regimes and ownership structures under which it has existed for over a century.

The lack of long-term economic viability has been a central theme of this book. However, before looking at the evidence and reasons, it is important to emphasise that generalities and averages can often distort the full picture. Not all airlines have lost money, by any means. Some have been more than adequately profitable, even over long periods, such as Southwest in the US and Ryanair in Europe. Similarly, given that the industry is highly cyclical, there have been times when airlines overall have returned satisfactory results, just as there have been times when losses were truly breathtaking. Regional differences also played a part (see Table 10.1). Finally, there are numerous ways of measuring profitability and care needs to be taken to ensure that like is being compared with like. Figure 10.1 below illustrates this point, showing global operating profit as a percentage of revenue for the period since 2006, and suggests that airlines have more than broken even for much of this period. What this does not show, however, is a viable industry since only in the most recent years have airlines actually come close to covering their cost of capital. In other words,

DOI: 10.4324/9780429448973-10

without periodic fresh injections of finance, the industry would have withered away. That new investment came mostly from governments, as well as from private investors who often seemed strangely and unrealistically optimistic in the face of the industry's long record of economic failure (see Table 10.2).

Table 10.1 Airline Industry Profitability (EBIT[a] as a % of Revenues) by Region

	2012	2016	2019
Global	2.6	8.5	5.2
North America	3.4	13.7	9.6
Europe	0.7	6.1	4.8
Asia/Pacific	4.7	7.4	3.7
Middle East	3.0	2.2	−5.2
Latin America	1.5	5.6	2.9
Africa	−0.4	1.1	1.0

Source: IATA.
[a] Earnings Before Interest and Taxation.

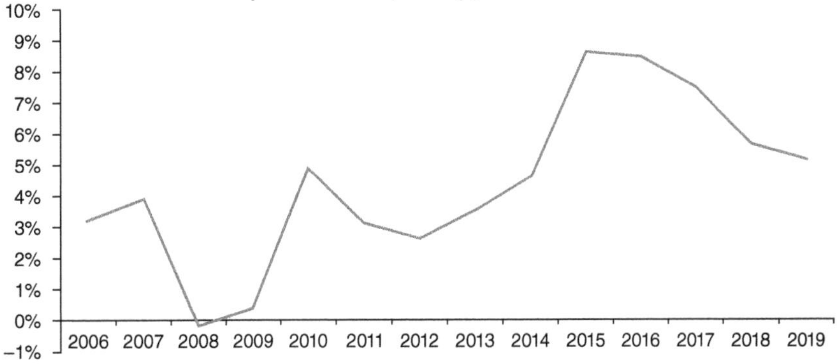

Figure 10.1 Industry-Wide Airline Operating Profit, % of Total Revenues
Source: IATA Economics

Table 10.2 Global Airline Industry Financial Performance, 2004–2019

	2004	2008	2012	2016	2019
Revenues (US$ bn)	379	570	706	709	838
Expenses (US$ bn)	376	571	687	649	795
Operating Profit (US$ bn)	3.3	−1.1	18.4	60.1	43.2
Margin (%)	0.9	−0.2	2.6	8.5	5.2
Net Profit (US$ bn)	−5.6	−26.1	9.2	34.2	26.4
Margin (%)	−1.5	−4.6	1.3	4.8	3.1
Return on capital Invested (%)	3.1	1.1	4.4	7.2	5.8

Source: IATA.

Figure 10.2 shows that for 2017 and 2018, only some 30 airlines in the world earned more than an economic profit. ('Economic' profit is defined as profit in excess of the return needed to cover the opportunity cost of the investment, or what economists call 'normal' profit.) Most of the remainder barely made an operating profit, while a significant number experienced heavy losses. It should be borne in mind that this period was relatively benign for aviation profitability, following the recovery from the financial crisis, and marked by healthy global GDP growth and comparatively low fuel costs.

Figure 10.3 shows that over the past decade (pre-COVID) the balance sheets of the top 30 airlines (measured by net debt adjusted for operational leases/EBITDAR) have improved substantially, both in absolute terms and relative to the rest of the industry. No carrier, however, has what IATA has defined as an 'investment grade' balance sheet, although the top 30 came close between 2015 and 2019. These top 30 IATA airlines accounted for about 45% of global revenue passenger kilometres and 55% of the sector's operating profits; IATA has some 290 members in 120 countries, representing 82% of the world's air traffic. Table 10.3[3] lists the top ten value-creating airlines, in terms of cumulative profit, between 2012 and 2019. The 122 carriers covered in the survey incurred an economic loss on average of some US$17 billion each year. (In 2020, the impact of the COVID pandemic meant that they lost US$168 billion.) The dominance of US and European carriers in Table 10.3 is particularly notable. Only one of the ten airlines listed is not based in North America or Europe. We saw in an earlier chapter how consolidation had transformed US airlines from heavy loss-makers to the most profitable carriers in the world. European airlines also experienced better results, while apart from a small number of Asian carriers, the rest of the world continued to see a relatively poor financial performance.

The historical lack of long-term viability among airlines is quite different from the experiences of the rest of the aviation industry. In a paper written for the OECD in 2013, Mike Tretheway and Kate Markhvida[4] divided the aviation supply chain for airlines into Upstream and Downstream segments.

Upstream:

- aircraft manufacturers
- leasing firms and other sources of financial capital
    - aviation infrastructure
    - airports
    - air navigation service providers (ANSPs)
    - aviation communication, such as air-to-air

- other suppliers
    - caterers
    - fuelling firms

- insurance providers
- ground services
- etc.

Downstream:

- distribution of airline product – passengers
    - global distribution systems (GDSs)
    - travel agents
    - travel integrators (tour operators)

Table 10.3 Top 10 Value-Creating Airlines (in cumulative profit), 2012–2019 (US$ bn)

Airline	Country	Cumulative Profit
Delta	US	14.5
Southwest	US	6.6
Ryanair	Ireland	5.8
United	US	5.7
British Airways	UK	5.7
American	US	4.7
Japan Airlines	Japan	4.2
Alaska	US	2.9
easyJet	UK	2.4
Air Canada	Canada	1.6

Source: McKinsey & Company.

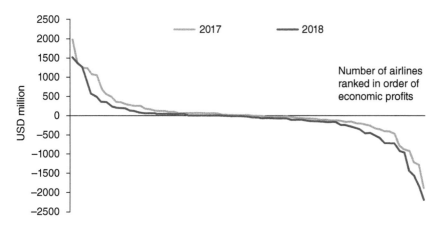

Figure 10.2 Airline Industry Ranked by Economic Profits
Source: McKinsey & Company for IATA

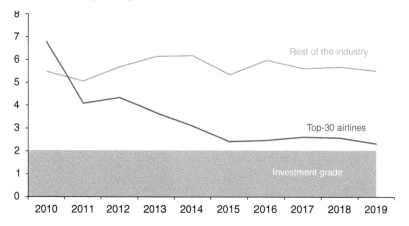

Figure 10.3 Airline Net Debt Adjusted for Operating Leases/EBITDAR
Source: IATA

- distribution of the airline product – cargo
  - freight forwarders
  - cargo integrators, such as FedEx and UPS.

Any examination of the financial performance of these various segments quickly reveals that persistently over many years the core centre, the airlines themselves, has been significantly, often substantially, less profitable than the remainder of the industry. Figure 10.4, from an annual study carried out by McKinsey and Company for IATA, illustrates this apparent contradiction. In 2018, airlines accounted for US$746 bn of capital investment in the air transport value chain, followed by airports (17%), manufacturers (3%), ground operations (2%) and the remaining segments (an average of 1%). Yet airlines produced a return on capital of just 5.9% between 2010 and 2018, compared to no less than 22.3% for GDSs. Airports recorded the second lowest return (6.5%), although their performance is distorted by the poor profitability of small/medium-sized units, as we shall see in Chapter 12. This is far from a recent phenomenon. As long ago as 1923, it was noted that "the only people who make profits out of aviation are the petrol people."[5]

There are several possible explanations for the variation in the financial health of the aviation value chain, but one factor is certainly the relative market power of the different segments, something the airlines themselves have not been slow to highlight. Given this experience, one might expect airlines to move into the other, more profitable segments of the industry, and this is precisely what has happened, with several waves of investment into, for example, GDSs, hotels, car rental companies, etc. However, repeatedly the frequent need to raise capital as a result of reduced (often cyclical) profitability, and occasionally other reasons, has resulted in subsequent divestiture.

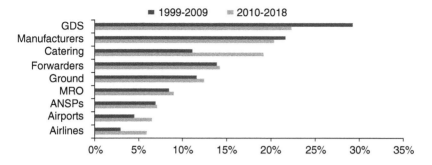

Figure 10.4 Return on Capital Across the Air Transport Supply Chain
Source: McKinsey & Company for IATA

The result has been the preservation of a disintegrated industrial structure. Tretheway and Markhvida[6] suggest that the solution to the airlines' underlying problem "may partly lie with rebalancing the value chain, injecting competition in segments which are earning economic (above cost of capital) profits or removing regulatory impediments to air carriers reaping some benefits from other parts of the value chain." So far, success in achieving such a solution has been only limited, as Figure 10.4 illustrates.

Warren Buffet, in his 2007 annual letter to Berkshire Hathaway shareholders, highlighted the investor conundrum when he said that airline "investors have poured money into a bottomless pit, attracted by growth when they should have been repelled by it." Similarly, the Australian newspaper, The Daily Telegraph, described the industry in 2002 as 'extraordinary':

> It has eaten up capital over the past century like almost no other business because people seem to keep coming back to it and putting fresh money in. You've got huge fixed costs, you've got strong labour unions and you've got commodity pricing. That is not a great recipe for success.

Alfred Kahn, commonly viewed as the father of US airline deregulation, put it more briefly: "There does seem to be something about airplanes that drives otherwise rational investors out of their minds." Such comments, and it is not difficult to find many more similar ones, raise two obvious questions: why have airlines traditionally been such poor investments; and why, given this record, do governments and private investors continue to provide finance? An earlier chapter addressed why most governments have traditionally had a very close relationship with their national airlines and the reasons why they might choose to support them financially. But it is far more difficult to explain why the sector has proved to be so attractive to private investors in the face of clear evidence that, overall, the chances of financial success are not good. This has been true for as long as airlines have operated. The first regular scheduled air service in the US, for example, operated by the nautical sounding Airboat Line, flew from Tampa Bay to St Petersburg in Florida on 1 January 1914. Just four months later the same carrier established another record when it ran into financial difficulties and became the first US airline to declare insolvency and close down. As Dawna Rhoades has succinctly commented: "The airline industry is no stranger to bankruptcy,"[7] yet capital continues to pour in.

As a generalisation, it should be easier to earn profits under a monopolistic/oligopolistic regulatory regime, whether such monopoly power is overt or covert. This should be especially true where regulation is producer rather than consumer focused. In fact, the opposite seems to be the case for airlines. As we have seen, recent years have been characterised by increased average profitability, especially among those carriers which have experienced deregulation or liberalisation in North America and Europe, albeit that this has been accompanied by more marked fluctuations in profits. For a long time after the end of the Second World War, airlines were tightly regulated throughout the world, effectively required to act as cartels. International competition in particular was strictly controlled, with tariffs, frequencies and capacity all normally subject to agreement between superficially competing carriers. Government approvals for any resultant arrangements were usually little more than rubber stamps. Yet rather than super profits, most airlines made economic losses and overall the industry failed to earn an adequate return. However, this is not the full picture. Returns (or more accurately 'rents' as economists call them) were in fact made, quite sizable ones, but they were not returned to the companies' owners. Instead, they flowed to other stakeholders in the form of inefficiency and higher labour costs. This was as true of government-controlled carriers in most parts of the world as it was of privately owned ones in the US.

There are many reasons why airline profitability may always be problematical, including:

- the industry's susceptibility to external events, such as terrorism and pandemics;
- high price sensitivity on the part of most passengers, with a perishable product;
- high cyclicality;
- long order periods for new aircraft which tend to exacerbate the underlying economic cycle;
- fluctuating prices for one of its two principal cost items, oil;
- high public profile with a strong tendency for political interference;
- relatively low market entry and high market exit barriers.

A key question advanced by certain economists is whether the economics of the industry are such that it will never be able to make adequate long-term, sustainable returns, no matter what regulatory regime it operates under, and if this is the case, whether the reasons lie in the policies adopted by the airlines themselves. Conventional economics would suggest that the problem of excessively low returns for airlines should eventually correct itself. In simple terms, if investors and lenders do not think it is worth funding companies, they can stop doing so until capacity decreases sufficiently to raise prices, normalise profits and warrant resumption of investment.[8] The problem is that such an outcome clearly has not emerged in the airline sector. The explanation lies partly in the particular characteristics of the industry outlined above, combined with what often appears to be an illogical enthusiasm for airline investment on the part of entrepreneurs and even financial institutions. However, another factor may also be relevant, namely: are the underlying economics of providing air services such that it is at best very difficult, and at worst impossible, for the airline industry as a whole to earn an economic return in the longer term? In other words, airlines may be subject to a form of destructive competition which inevitably leads to capital erosion. Several economists have argued that this could indeed be the case. The theory is known as the '*empty core.*'

Airlines are not the only companies subject to possible destructive competition. As Alfred Kahn noted in his seminal study of the economics of regulation, such a problem usually arises when companies have significant fixed and sunk costs that represent a high proportion of total costs and experience sustained and recurrent periods of excess capacity. (Kahn did not actually anticipate that this would be a problem in a deregulated airline sector.)[9] The economic arguments surrounding the empty core theory can be complex, but Timothy Smith, writing in Fortune Magazine in 1995, did his best to simplify matters.[10] He starts by suggesting that

> the next time an invisible hand yanks you off an overbooked flight and shreds your travel schedule, and you find yourself wondering whether the airline industry will ever grow up and behave like an adult, it may help to bear in mind the following simple rules:
>
> (1) To understand what keeps airlines aloft, it is instructive to think about sex.
> (2) To understand why air travel is so frequently wretched, it is instructive to think about bananas.

Smith argues that the airline business is so fundamentally sexy that people cannot resist investing in it, for reasons beyond normal investment criteria. "Jet fuel gets in your veins" as the phenomenon is often described. At the same time, just like bananas, the airline product is highly perishable; once an aircraft has taken off, any seats left empty have zero value. Finally, most passengers are very cost sensitive, often willing to accept inconvenience and discomfort for a lower price. (Nevertheless, it is wrong to describe air travel as a commodity, as the press and even some economists often do. Such talk simply misunderstands the characteristics of a commodity.)

It is the combination of these factors which, in Smith's words, produces "endless fare wars that in most businesses would quickly thin out the players but that in airlines ... have helped produce a record of chaos and wreckage..." Rather than being the result of "bad policy, bad management and bad luck," the argument goes, the industry's woes actually stem from the very nature of the business and therefore are unlikely to be susceptible to normal policy/managerial solutions. "The airlines ... are a highly visible example of a competitive market that is, essentially, absurd, ... an economic machine programmed for self-destruction or something close to it." Airline management is constantly attracted to undercutting their rivals to fill perishable seats, despite the fact that history has repeatedly shown that any price advantage will almost inevitably be very brief and soon result in lower yields and profits for everyone. This raises questions about the benefits of deregulation/liberalisation and whether government regulation or even acceptance of cartels is the only long-term solution to the industry's financial problems. The alternative, as Smith notes, may be for airlines to

> stumble along indefinitely, propelled by an urge more powerful than return on investment. That will mean more bankruptcies, more new entrants, more ferocious cost cutting, high-risk-uncertain-reward investments, rock bottom fares as far as the eye can see ... one of the world's toughest ways to make a dollar will just stay tough.

Button[11] points out that a fear of destructive competition was the *raison d'être* for much of the initial regulation of air transport. The concern was that excess supply could at times lead to price wars among incumbents, as well as inadequate supply and high prices in subsequent upturns in demand. "The market failure that results in these circumstances was deemed in need of remedial government intervention. Removal of these regulations, if the argument is valid, would leave the sector prone to market swings." Today these arguments are still active, relevant not only to the deregulation/liberalisation debate but also to whether airline alliances of different kinds should be granted immunity from general competition rules. Button acknowledges that no firm conclusions can be drawn on whether the airline industry is indeed subject to an empty core problem, but concludes that

> the nature of the airline market, ... coupled with recent experiences of how that market operates [the paper was published in 2003], suggest that there is prima facie evidence that in the absence of coalitions there may be intrinsic problems associated with empty cores.... Rigorous testing is not possible but the characteristics of the market for airline services and the reaction of airlines in the face of weaker restrictions over the period of deregulation is largely consistent with the absence of a core.

Clearly, the implications of an empty core problem, if it exists in aviation, are highly significant to any debate about economic regulation. As Telser notes, an empty core "raises important policy problems because then competition needs appropriate rules to make it serve consumers."[12] The challenge is to establish whether the theory is applicable in practice, and so far that has proved to be impossible. It might be argued that more recent developments, such as the emergence of sustainably profitable low-cost carriers and integrator cargo airlines and increased profitability among legacy North American and, to some extent, European airlines following consolidation, indicate that the industry's instability has been more a reflection of unhelpful government regulation rather than an inherent tendency towards destructive competition, but the evidence is by no means conclusive. It has also been suggested that the emergence of significant ancillary revenues, initially with the low-cost carriers and then spreading to legacy airlines, has altered the sector's underlying economics. It may be that there are just too many external factors affecting airline viability to ever come to a sound conclusion about the long-term viability of the airline industry, at least until it is treated like any other business, if that ever happens.

Notes

1 The quote was inserted into a speech for Sir Richard Branson written by the author, but had been used previously by others.
2 'British Air Transport in the Seventies. Report of the Committee of Inquiry into Civil Air Transport. (The Edwards Report).' HMSO, London, 1969.
3 McKinsey & Company: 'Taking Stock of the Pandemic's Impact on Global Aviation.' March 2022.
4 Michael Tretheway and Kate Markhvida: 'Airports in the Aviation Value Chain: Financing, Returns, Risk and Investment.' OECD Discussion Paper No. 2013–15, May 2013. See also Michael Tretheway and Kate Markhvida: 'The aviation value chain: Economic returns and policy issues.' *Journal of Air Transport Management*, Vol. 41, October 2014, pp. 3–16.
5 Quoted in E. Birkhead: 'The financial failure of British air transport companies, 1919–24.' In P. L. Lyth (ed.): *Air Transport*. Scolar Press, Aldershot, 1996, pp. 13–26.
6 Tretheway and Markhvida (2014), op cit.
7 Dawna L. Rhoades: *Evolution of International Aviation. Phoenix Rising*. Ashgate, Aldershot, 2003.
8 Bijan Vasigh, Ken Fleming and Thomas Tacker: *Introduction to Air Transport Economics. From Theory to Applications*. Ashgate, Aldershot, 2008.
9 A. P. Kahn: *The Economics of Regulation*. Wiley and Sons, New York, 1988. Quoted in Rhoades, op cit.
10 Timothy K. Smith: 'Why air travel doesn't work.' *Fortune Magazine*, 3 April 1995. Quoted in Kenneth Button: 'Does the theory of the 'core' explain why airlines fail to cover their long-run costs of capital.' *Journal of Air Transport Management*, Vol. 9(1), January 2003, pp. 5–14.
11 Kenneth Button, op cit.
12 L.G.Telser: 'Industry total cost functions and the status of the core.' *Journal of Industrial Economics*, Vol. 39(3), 1991, pp. 225–240. Quoted in Kenneth Button: 'Liberalising European aviation. Is there an empty core problem?' *Journal of Transport Economics and Policy*, Vol. 30(3), 1996, pp. 275–291.

11 Air Traffic Management

The main focus of this book has been on the regulation of airlines. However, regulation has also been an important factor in the evolution of other parts of the aviation industry, not least air traffic management (ATM) and airports. In this chapter, we will consider how the ATM industry has developed and been regulated. In the next chapter, we will consider airports.

Early Development

ATM or air traffic control (ATC) is an integral part of the aviation industry, one of the three elements, along with airlines and airports, which together form what has been described as "the complex and dynamic socio-technical aviation system,"[1] although it is probably the least familiar to the general public. It is, of course, almost wholly a product of the growth of air transport over the years. Initially, with very few aircraft in the air, there was no need for other than the most rudimentary of guidance, what one commentator has described as "the use of flags, lights, and bonfires to locate and identify airports and runways, and to communicate with pilots."[2] As the number of aircraft in the air increased, such an approach became unsustainable. A US newspaper graphically noted as early as 1924: "Time is at hand to bring some order out of the chaos of laissez-faire in the air, where constantly increasing number of ... flyers ... disport without let or hindrance."[3] Gradually a more sophisticated system evolved, frequently as a result of lessons learned from headline-grabbing crashes, as has so often been the case in the evolution of a safer aviation industry.

The modern commercial airway was an American invention, conceived in the 1920s by the US Air Mail Service with the assistance of the army. The cross-country routes to be followed were often initially indicated by nothing more than large arrows placed on the ground; in other countries, such as the UK, railway stations frequently had their names prominently displayed on roofs to guide pilots to their destinations. Radio beacons were soon introduced as a more reliable method of assistance as more generally radiotelegraphy (Morse code) was replaced by radio telephony (speech transmission). It is widely accepted that the first ATC tower, really little more than a hut 4.5 metres tall with an observation room on top, was commissioned in 1920 at

DOI: 10.4324/9780429448973-11

Croydon Aerodrome in the UK. (Croydon had recently become the principal airport serving London. Among its other claims to fame in the early 1920s were the opening of the world's first airport terminal and the introduction of what was to become the internationally recognised emergency call sign, 'Mayday, Mayday, Mayday.')

However, it was government regulation as much as technical advances which was to prove critical to ATC development as the industry prepared for its post-World War II expansion. As with so much else, this came with the Chicago Convention of 1944 and the subsequent creation of ICAO. Chicago put in place a set of rules for ATC, just as it did for much of the rest of the aviation industry, which have essentially survived to the present day. The key Article in the Convention in this respect is 28, which partly reads:

> Each contracting State undertakes, so far as it may find practicable, to .... provide, in its territory, airports, radio services, meteorological services and other navigation services to facilitate international air navigation, in accordance with the standards and practices recommended or established from time to time, pursuant to this Convention....

Thus was created a legal responsibility for each country to provide an ATC service for international flights, a responsibility which applies even where a State delegates management of its airspace to another State or body. Article 15 of the Convention also provides for any charges for ATC services to be levied on a non-discriminatory basis. Detailed implementation of the Chicago requirements fell to ICAO through its Standard Rules and Procedures (SARPS), following which, as Margaret Arblaster has pointed out, "a network of worldwide and regional air navigation routes and the procedures applicable to them have been established and resulted in an ATM system that is relatively homogeneous throughout the world."[4]

ATC Provision

Modern ATC consists of three types of services:[5]

- Airspace management, which oversees the provision of airspace between different users, such as civil, military, gliders and increasingly drones. It is worth noting that the military still occupies vast areas of airspace in many countries which often adversely affects civil ATC efficiency.
- Air traffic services, which control the flow of aircraft to maintain safe flight, essentially separating air traffic within a given sector.
- Air traffic flow management, balancing the overall capacity of the airspace and airports against the demands of aircraft wishing to fly.

It is also important to distinguish between two separate elements in the provision of ATC services. The bulk of ATC (some 70%–80% in most cases) consists of the en-route control of aircraft between two points. Nowadays such control usually takes place away from other aviation activity, in large centres overseeing extensive geographical areas. By any normal definition, en-route ATC is a natural monopoly, although occasionally the possibility exists for some competitive pressures at the margin. For example, a country offering particularly low ATC charges may attract some aircraft which otherwise would fly more directly over a higher charging (or more strike-prone) airspace. Geographically adjacent countries could, in theory, provide services beyond their own immediate jurisdiction, and licences to provide services could be time-limited and open to bids from rival companies, although the technical complexity of such a handover would be considerable. The principal barrier to any such increased competition, however, is the political environment within which virtually all air navigation service providers (ANSPs) operate. National sovereignty considerations, a natural conservatism based on an ultra-safety mindset and the lack of political incentives to change, all contribute to the maintenance of the status quo. Some have argued that competition will come with technological advances, as the need for ground-based infrastructure diminishes and satellites make radars redundant, but at best such developments are some way off.

The control of aircraft during the landing and take-off phases of flight and while on the ground is a different matter. This is undertaken mostly from the towers that are such a characteristic of even modestly sized airports. There is no technical reason why en-route and airport control have to be provided by the same organisation, as long as an efficient interface exists between the two. Thus, while realistically only one organisation can provide tower ATC at an airport at a given time, it is relatively easy to seek competing bids for such services and thereby create a contestable market. This has important implications for regulation and explains why, in those cases where en-route ATC is subject to some form of sectoral economic regulation, tower services are often excluded. A 2018 White Paper published by the ATM Policy Institute argued that liberalisation of such services would result in benefits for airports, airlines and the travelling public in the form of lower prices, better customer focus and new and innovative service offerings.[6] There has been at least modest progress towards a more competitive market around the world, although there is ample room for further liberalisation. A sign of increased competitive pressure is that where countries have liberalised their markets for tower services, there has often been a move away from a network approach to pricing, involving common charges for similar services at different locations (a clear indication of monopoly provision almost inevitably involving an element of cross-subsidy) to a location-specific approach with unique prices at each airport.[7]

We have seen how, since the Second World War, the environment in which airlines have operated has gradually progressed from one of tight government control to a far more competitive regulatory framework. Other sectors of the aviation industry have similarly experienced increased competition, to a greater or lesser extent. En-route ATC is the exception. It is the last bastion of an almost wholly protectionist approach to service provision in the air transport industry. Typically, around the world, ANSPs are government owned and highly unionised. They face no direct competition for en-route services, have a cost pass-through pricing model, and are organised essentially along national borders, resulting in a fragmented industrial structure. This is hardly a prescription for an efficient industry. At the same time, it has to be accepted that there are sound reasons why governments will always play a key role in overseeing ATC services, particularly:

- They have an obligation under the Chicago Convention to ensure that such services are provided.
- They have the right to recover charges from users, also under international treaties.
- ATC always has a security aspect which requires wide-ranging reserve powers as well as close co-ordination with the military.[8]

It is not surprising that ANSPs are the subject of frequent and extensive criticism from their airline customers, mostly for inefficiency, high charges and excessive delays. As early as the late 1980s, the trade body for the major European airlines, AEA, highlighted such concerns in a study of the economic and operational penalties inherent in the prevailing ATC structure. It proposed the development of a consolidated user-owned system, but even modest progress towards such an outcome had to wait over a decade.[9] Like the airline sector before deregulation, excessive economic rents were seen less in high levels of profitability and more in generous salaries and overmanning. There is perhaps something of a contradiction between the image of the typical ANSP at the forefront of technology and what many would see as the archaic regulatory regime within which it operates, although it is fair to point out that not everyone agrees that ATC technology has developed as fast as it might have.

The conservative nature of the ATC industry is illustrated by the way in which most en-route charges are calculated, namely a combination of distance flown and the maximum weight of the aircraft. (Some ANSPs also charge a fixed rate per annum, for example, for general aviation aircraft.) These principles were established by ICAO in the late-1940s. Some 20 years ago, ICAO revised its recommended policy to incorporate the option of demand-based pricing, but such an approach has not been widely adopted. No matter how justified the original charging principles may have been in the immediate post-Second World War period, they clearly fail to reflect the reality of airline operations today. The marginal costs of controlling an aircraft are essentially dependent on the number of interventions from the controller. They have nothing to do with the weight of the aircraft and little with the distance travelled. Thus, a small aircraft flying through congested airspace will be expensive to handle but usually pay a relatively low ATC charge, while a large aircraft taking off from an airport and heading straight off along established airways on an intercontinental flight will be cheap to handle but pay far higher charges. Such an approach makes no economic sense at all and potentially risks giving the wrong investment signals. It greatly increases the chance of cross-subsidy, itself a contradiction of ICAO principles. None of this is a revelation, of course. It has been known and criticised for a very long time, but little has changed, a reflection of the challenges involved in seeking to reform the ATC industry.

Nevertheless, recent decades have witnessed three significant changes in the regulatory environment in which ATC operates. Initially, ATC was almost universally regarded as a public service, with expenditure absorbed by the State. It operated, in the words of one commentator, in "an isolated world with no apparent financial worries."[10] The increase in traffic and in the costs of service provision, possibly combined with a realisation that airlines were a useful source of revenue for government ANSP owners, led to the gradual 'commercialisation' (sometimes called 'corporatisation') of the industry. (There are various definitions of commercialisation, but a common one refers to "the general process of moving away from a state (governmental) organisation and structuring this organisation in such a way that would allow it to operate more like a business.")[11] Today most ANSPs charge airlines (and airports in the case of tower control) and seek to recover the full costs of their services, although there are a few exceptions, notably the US as we shall see. Commercialisation is quite different from privatisation, of course, and overwhelmingly ANSPs have remained fully State owned, albeit increasingly independent of the core civil service.

The second significant regulatory change which has emerged is the separation of safety oversight from operational activities. The major exception in this respect is again the US. Finally, we have seen the emergence of economic regulation of ATC charges, particularly in Europe. Partly this has reflected the privatisation of ANSPs in a limited number of markets and partly the acceptance that State-owned monopolies require additional incentives to reduce costs and improve efficiency.

En-route accounts for the bulk of ATC services. Apart from a few exceptions, the service is nation based, with a separate ANSP for each State. For a geographically large country such as the US or China, this is of little relevance, but in Europe and elsewhere it has created a highly fragmented market which makes no economic sense. The principal explanation, as we have seen, lay originally in the desire of governments to retain control over their own airspace, and this remains a powerful factor, although other influences have increasingly played a part. Nation state borders mean little for a flight plan and strong arguments exist in favour of cross-border consolidation of ANSPs. Unfortunately, it is difficult for governments to justify the transfer of highly paid jobs to another country, especially when the provision of the service in question does not impose a financial burden on national exchequers, at least until the recent COVID pandemic. Strong opposition from vested interests is inevitable and political ideology tends to point towards national protectionism rather than international reform. Pressure to change has been most visible in Europe, in particular from the EU Commission following the creation of the internal aviation market. However, as discussed below, success has been very limited.

As already noted, there is no need in principle for tower and en-route ATC to be provided by the same organisation, and as a result, a number of countries have sought to introduce an element of competition for what are known as Terminal Air Navigation Services or TANS. Often this has involved promoting competitive bids for second-level airports, while the State-owned ANSP retains a monopoly for the major centres. The US, Spain and Germany are examples of such an approach. The United Kingdom, on the other hand, has introduced a contestable market for all TANS, overseen by a regulator to ensure fair competition. While the national ANSP, NATS (which has itself won TANS contracts in Spain), serves 13 UK airports, including all of the larger ones, some airports provide their own ATC and other companies have entered the market, in one case winning the contract for the country's second largest airport before losing it back to NATS a few years later. A study by Copenhagen Economics for a Swedish private sector provider of air traffic services concluded that increased competition for terminal navigation services resulted in a 27% reduction in charges in Sweden, 37% in Norway and 47% in Spain.[12]

It is probably fair to say that globally, progress towards a more competitive tower market has not been as fast as some would have preferred, but it has nevertheless been heading in the right direction. Further progress is likely to be helped by the development of remote towers, whereby ATC service at several airports, mostly smaller ones at present, can be provided from a single source some distance from the airports themselves. The Swedish ANSP, LFV, in partnership with Saab, opened the first such tower at Sundsvall in 2015, controlling three airports. Others are rapidly following. Not only does this innovation cut costs, it also offers the prospect of additional new entrants competing with the established ANSPs. For the full benefits of such a development to be achieved, however, requires more governments to open up their markets to competition.

There are five different types of ATM organisation:

- State-owned, commercially financed by charges levied on users and overseen by a separate safety regulator (a model common in Europe, for example).
- State-owned but not wholly commercially financed and responsible for its own safety regulation (e.g., the US FAA).
- Outsourced to other ATC providers (common in some smaller countries and the Middle East).
- Partly privatised, as in the UK and Italy.
- A hybrid, not-for-profit model at present found only in Canada.

Below we consider in more detail three of these models – the FAA, NATS and NavCanada – together with pan-European developments.

The US Federal Aviation Administration

Among ANSPs, the US FAA is often presented as an example of what other parts of the world, and especially Europe, could achieve through consolidation. Apart from some towers at smaller airports, it provides ATC services throughout the US, covering a large geographical area with dense traffic flows. It handles many more flights than its European equivalents with far fewer staff. At the same time, however, the governance of the FAA has attracted considerable criticism, with periodic financial crises as funding approval has been delayed or withheld. As part of the Department of Transportation (DOT), it has found itself subject to the vagaries of the Congressional budget approval process, adversely affecting its long-term investment programme. In addition, unlike the ANSPs in some 60 other countries following ICAO recommendations, the FAA remains both operator and regulator of ATC services, an approach which it would certainly not find acceptable if applied to the oversight of airlines, for which it also has responsibility. Originally all FAA funding came from the State, but in 1970, the Airport and Airway Trust Fund (AATF) created dedicated fuel and passenger ticket taxes for this purpose. Gradually, funding requirements exceeded the amount raised by taxes, so that since 1990, the AATF has covered only some 75% of the agency's budget.[13] The result is that the FAA continues to find itself at the mercy of political intervention.

Vasigh, Fleming and Tacker note that as traffic grew and technology advanced, it became increasingly evident that the US ATC system was outdated and in urgent need of modernisation. By the end of the 1990s, the whole system began to be overwhelmed. Since then, a number of studies and investigative committees have concluded that the US model for ATC provision is inherently flawed, but attempts to change it have repeatedly failed as a result of politics and bureaucracy.

> The fact that ATC funding flows from an unpredictable revenue stream subject to the federal budget process is a commonly raised issue… The lack of both mission focus and clear accountability, because authority is shared by Congress and FAA management in a confusing bureaucracy, is at the root of the criticism.[14]

A major 2005 study of ANSPs in Australia, Canada, Germany, New Zealand and the United Kingdom by the US Government Accountability Office found that commercialisation had not resulted in any reduction in safety standards and that all five systems had improved the provision of new technology and reduced operating costs, in stark contrast to US experience. One commentator was led to conclude in 2008: "… in the case of ATC perhaps the United States has reached a stage where the problems are so severe that the political log-jam blocking reform may soon be broken."[15] Unfortunately, that proved to be hopelessly optimistic.

Radical change has been attempted several times, the latest under the Trump administration, but so far all have failed.[16] Support has come from numerous quarters, including DOT Secretaries, FAA Administrators and perhaps most surprisingly, the trade union representing air traffic controllers. The Chairman of the Senate Sub-Committee on Aviation and Space noted in early 2019 that reform was backed by unionised workers and free-market advocates, "and there are not many policy areas where you can see that kind of intersection." Most airlines have similarly lobbied in favour of reform, despite the likelihood of having to pay direct user fees in future, although one major carrier opposed a 2016 initiative apparently on the grounds that it would lose competitive advantage, having invested heavily to optimise the use of the present system despite its acknowledged shortcomings.

There has been other opposition to change, principally from influential general aviation interests, who fear they will be faced with substantial user charges in future; at present they pay nothing other than a modest fuel tax. It has been estimated that at present general aviation contributes up to 9% of US ATC costs, while a more appropriate contribution might be about 11%.[17] Union support for a model based on the Canadian approach has also generated opposition from some conservative lobbyists and politicians who fear that commercialisation of ATC will result in a union-run organisation, which has certainly not been the case in Canada. Overall, however, and with a few exceptions, Republican Congressmen have tended to support reform, despite the position of the unions, and Democrats opposed it, despite the views of the unions. To say that the whole debate has lacked logic and clarity is something of an understatement. It has become highly politicised, perhaps not surprising in a country where President Reagan, in frustration at a strike by FAA staff, once sacked the majority of air traffic controllers, brought in the military and introduced legislation banning further industrial action. The situation today remains deadlocked.

Nav Canada

For several decades Canadian ATC was organised in a similar way to that in the US. It was mostly financed by a ticket tax supplemented by government subsidy (accounting for about 25% of total expenditure), fully owned by the State and combining both operational and regulatory functions. Like the US also, increased air traffic following the deregulation of domestic air services in the mid-1980s, combined with a reluctance on the part of the Government to provide sufficient investment, resulted in growing flight delays and complaints from airline customers. Pressure to do 'something' built up and a number of reforms were considered. To some extent the aviation industry took matters into its own hands, concluding that:

- The status quo was not an option and marginal reform would not be sufficient. A fundamental paradigm shift was needed.

- ATC is essentially a commercial business which should be operated and guided by commercial rather than government principles.
- Safety is all-important and of genuine public and political concern, but in terms of ANSP ownership it is a red herring. There is no reason why an ANSP cannot operate safely with independent regulatory oversight, just as airlines do.
- Throughout the 1980s and early 1990s, the Canadian Government was grappling with its own financial issues. It was increasingly less able to finance ATC.[18]

On the basis of such arguments, the option chosen by the Government was both radical and unique: the first privatisation of a major ANSP in the world. However, this was not a Thatcher-type privatisation. The key was consensus-building among the various stakeholders, not least the airlines, unions and even general aviation interests, to create a not-for-profit, non-governmental organisation.[19]

Nav Canada was established in 1995 and became operational in October 1996. Its original 6,000 employees (closer to 5,000 by 2020) had responsibility for a very large geographical area, stretching from the Pacific west coast of Canada to the east coast of Newfoundland and on to the centre of the Atlantic, over 18m square kilometres, today handling (pre-COVID) 3.4m flights each year. The Government received some C$1.8 bn, financed by publicly traded debt. By law, Nav Canada is not allowed to set its charges "at a level exceeding what is required to meet the cost of providing civil air navigation services." From March 1999, the previous ticket tax was replaced by direct charges on airlines, following ICAO principles, with general aviation operators paying a fixed annual fee. The ANSP describes itself as "a unique consensus among the company's four founding groups: commercial air carriers, the Government of Canada, business and general aviation, and our employees, represented by their unions." These four distinct interest groups make up the Board of Directors, with a governance structure designed to minimise the opportunity for any single stakeholder to exert excessive influence (see Table 11.1). The Board is complemented by an Advisory Committee of 20 aviation professionals. Safety regulation remained with the central government.

Table 11.1 Nav Canada Board of Directors

Number of Directors	Appointed by
4	Commercial carriers
1	Business and general aviation
3	Government
2	Employee unions
4	Independent elected by the Board
President and Chief Executive Officer	Board

Source: NAV CANADA.

There was concern that Nav Canada would have considerable monopoly power which could be abused, perhaps in the form of gold plating investments or paying excessive salaries. Consideration was therefore given to the imposition of economic regulation along the lines of that already applied to privatised utilities. However, the conclusion reached was that given the structure of the company, its legally binding not-for-profit status and the fact that customers would be well organised via trade associations, this would be unnecessary. Instead, a system of self-regulation was adopted.[20] Despite the occasional criticism, privatisation has been widely regarded as a success. In the words of Rui Neiva, writing in 2017, it has been

> the poster child of commercialization – and with good reason.... Twenty years later, safety has improved significantly, the system is in a strong financial position, user fees are practically at the same nominal level as they were when first introduced ...., labour is strongly involved in the success of the company, and some of the more modern ANS technologies are not only implemented but also developed by Nav Canada.[21]

One interesting innovation was the introduction of a 'rate stabilisation fund' to reduce the likelihood of large increases in charges in the event of a reduction in traffic. However, the fund was capped at a relatively low level and therefore unable to cope with the size of the downturn caused by the COVID pandemic.

It is inevitable in the circumstances that Nav Canada's record has been compared to that of the FAA in the US. Writing in Forbes.com in February 2016, Dan Reed concluded that

> by removing the air traffic control function from the clutches of government budget restraints and politically-driven appropriators, Nav Canada has been able to rapidly upgrade its technologies and practices and implement these with considerable success. Meanwhile, the FAA has become the laughingstock of the global air transportation management world for its chronic false starts, missed deadlines, and misunderstandings of what's actually needed or possible.

Harsh words, but ones many would agree with.

The UK's NATS[22]

The second major country to break out of the rigid ownership structure which has dominated ATC provision for so long was the United Kingdom. There was no unified system for controlling air traffic in the UK before the early 1960s, but growing safety concerns led to the creation of National Air Traffic Control Services (NATS – the 'Control' was soon dropped from the title) in 1962. Initially, it was a part of the civil service. However, the

Edwards Committee, which as we saw in a previous chapter reviewed the whole structure of UK civil aviation in the late-1960s, recommended that it should become a part (and later a full subsidiary) of the new Civil Aviation Authority (CAA) as a semi-independent commercialised company. This took place in 1972, when the CAA was created. NATS was seen as a joint civil/military organisation and for many years the Chief Executive role alternated between civil and military appointments. Gradually the military influence waned, but the company remained fully State owned and essentially run as a public-sector operation. It was expected to break even after paying the Government a return on its capital, financed by charges levied on its customers. Its performance record was far from good, with poor project management, low productivity, high charges and frequent flight delays, although it was probably no worse in this respect than many other ANSPs around Europe and beyond. Like other European ANSPs as well, NATS encountered considerable criticism from its airline customers.

Privatisation of NATS was first considered in 1994, in line with the then Conservative Government's ideological commitment to the sale of State assets (and the need to raise funds for the Exchequer), but no progress had been made by the time of the 1997 General Election. There was considerable opposition to the proposal from the left of the political spectrum, with the Labour Party loudly declaring that "our skies are not for sale." It was somewhat surprising, therefore, that when elected with a landslide majority in 1997, the Blair Labour Government soon announced that it would go ahead with the privatisation of NATS by means of a so-called Public–Private Partnership (PPP). A complex governance structure was created, partly designed to mitigate political opposition, especially from the trade unions. The Government retained 49% of the shares, 5% were given free of charge to employees and 46% were offered for sale to a single private-sector company. What was unusual was that the private investor was to be NATS' 'Strategic Partner,' effectively with control over the company despite owning only a minority of the shares. The Government retained certain powers, but for all intents and purposes, NATS was placed firmly in the private sector and expected to behave as such.

There were three serious potential investors in NATS. The successful highest bidder, and certainly politically the least contentious, consisted of a consortium of seven UK airlines known as The Airline Group (AG). (This was not the first time that airlines had acquired an interest in an ANSP. Aerothai in Thailand, for example, was purchased by the Government in 1963 from private-sector interests. Subsequently, almost 10% of the shares were acquired by several airlines, but the State retained over 90% of the company. In addition, as already noted, a proposal for airline control of ATC services throughout Europe had previously been tabled, but failed to attract sufficient political support.) The UK Government received some £700m, plus the repayment of £300m of public debt. The AG, however, provided only £50m in equity, financing the remainder of the investment by debt. This was certainly controversial, if perhaps not totally surprising given the normal state of airlines' bank balances. As one commentator noted: "In the simplest terms, the Consortium bought their share of NATS, 46%, for £50m by reducing the value of the company. It would not be unreasonable to see this as a form of leveraged buyout."[23]

The fact that the seven carriers were prepared to put aside their intense competitive instincts (the consortium included both British Airways and Virgin Atlantic, for example) to co-operate in this way was indicative of how critical ATC was for their operations and how concerned they had become about NATS' performance. They were also worried that an independent private sector investor might seek to drive down costs too quickly, resulting in industrial action which would have a highly negative impact on airline operations. The consortium committed not only to an investment, but also to an ongoing role as NATS' strategic partner. Especially during the early years, a significant airline managerial input was involved, although this declined later. Clearly, airlines have an interest in keeping ATC charges as low as possible (on average they account for about 5% of their total costs). However, far more important for them is the efficiency of the operations, particularly the minimisation of flight delays, which impose considerable costs on their networks. The AG bid was promoted as being 'not for commercial return.' This was never intended to be the same as 'not for profit,' although some found it politically convenient to interpret it as such, but as an indication that the primary focus of the investment was very much on improving NATS' operational efficiency rather than maximising a direct financial return. Since most of NATS' output would be regulated, following the RPI-X model already applied by the CAA to the UK's major airports, the expectation was that profits, if they were achieved at all, would be modest. In fact, the airlines were proved wrong. NATS was to emerge as an attractive investment, probably far more profitable for the consortium than flying aeroplanes.

As NATS' en-route services were regulated, there was never any real chance that the airline investors in the AG would be able to abuse their role to achieve a competitive advantage over other carriers, even if they had wanted to. However, to avoid any suspicion, IATA was invited to take a seat on the NATS Board, which it held for many years. The PPP was completed early in 2001, just a few months before the aviation industry experienced the impact of the 9/11 disaster. The dramatic reduction in air traffic, especially across the Atlantic (44% of NATS' revenue came from trans-Atlantic flights), put considerable pressure on the company's finances. The problem was exacerbated by the high gearing of the AG investment. It proved necessary to undertake a major refinancing, which some certainly saw as a sign that privatisation had failed. The Government provided additional finance and kept its 49% stake, a new investor, BAA (now Heathrow Airport), took a 4% stake, the employees retained their 5% and the AG's shareholding was reduced from 46% to 42%. The £65m invested by BAA for a 4% stake, which was matched by the Government, contrasts with the AG equity investment of £50m for 46% a few months earlier. The airline consortium's strategic partnership role and accompanying governance powers, however, remained largely unaffected. A few years later four of the seven original airline investors decided to sell most of their shares in AG to a pension fund, which acquired 49% of the company, while one of the remaining carriers went into bankruptcy with its stake acquired by the Government's Pension Protection Fund. These changes did not affect AG's 42% shareholding in NATS. It may perhaps be regarded as a sign of the improved financial standing of NATS that pension funds were interested in investing in it. None had been so in 2001. In addition, by 2019 the company was sufficiently robust financially to withstand the impact of the COVID pandemic, which had not been the case following the 9/11 disaster.

Like Nav Canada, the privatisation of NATS has been largely seen as a success. The fear that safety would be impaired has proved to be unfounded; like most other ANSPs, NATS' safety record has improved over the past 20 years. Project management of major investments has been transformed. As already noted, the company has earned an attractive rate of return, with a gearing ratio declining from 112% in 2001/02 to 63% by 2004/05; by 2018/19 it was down to 26%. For the airlines, of particular importance was the considerable reduction in average flight delays, from some 109 seconds in 2001/02 to almost 21 seconds in 2004/05 and 12.5 seconds in 2018/19. NATS remains a relatively high-cost ANSP, partly a reflection of the complexity of UK airspace. Nevertheless, charges have been brought down, especially over more recent years when the regulator appears to have adopted a more robust approach. This was also the period when EU regulation started to have an impact. (Between 2001 and 2012, NATS was subject solely to regulation by the UK CAA. After 2012, it was also subject to the EU Single European Sky performance scheme (see below). From the beginning of 2021, regulatory responsibility reverted solely to the CAA following the UK's exit from the EU.) Unlike Nav Canada, however, NATS' charges have had to bear the significant costs of the CAA/EU regulatory regime and dividend payments to shareholders. Finally, the airline/NATS Strategic Partnership has not evolved into a co-operative partnership between stakeholders as seen in Canada. Had it done so, there may not have been the need for economic regulation. Instead, customers of NATS' en-route services have had to rely initially on the CAA, later supported by EU intervention, to maintain a downward pressure on charges.

Europe

There were hopes among those seeking to reform the ATC industry that the radical policies adopted by Canada and the UK, given their apparent success, would be copied elsewhere. This has proved not to be the case. In some parts of the world, such as the Asia/Pacific region, there have been moves towards increased co-operation. For example, for many years Australia, Fiji and New Zealand have jointly run the upper airspace over the Pacific islands, and there are other similar examples around the world. In the Middle East, on the other hand, airspace fragmentation has been reinforced by regional conflicts, despite evidence of the substantial benefits of increased consolidation. IATA has called for "co-operation, visionary planning and strong political will" in ATC provision, but overall there are few signs of such an approach emerging. At the national level, there is a marked absence of political desire for radical reform, for all the reasons already noted, and overwhelmingly most ANSPs around the world remain firmly in government ownership, run according to public-sector ethos. This is certainly the case in Europe.

The only major European ANSP to see its ownership structure significantly changed, other than NATS, was that of Italy. Until 1979, Italian ATC was provided by the military. It subsequently came under the authority of Azienda Autonoma di Assistenza al Volo per il Traffico Aero Generale (AAAVTAG), which in 1996 became the linguistically slightly shorter Ente Nazionale di Assistenza al Volo (ENAV), a so-called 'Public Body.' In 2001, ENAV was transformed into a public limited company, "in the context of the wider process of liberalisation and privatisation of the air transport market," in its own words. Finally, in 2006, it was listed on the Italian stock exchange, although the Ministry of Economy and Finance retained just over half of the shares as well as a 'golden share.' It is therefore the only publicly listed ANSP in the world. (Some ANSPs have issued quoted bonds, but not shares.) Like Nav Canada and NATS, the partial privatisation of ENAV, which seems to have been driven mainly by government budgetary factors, has been successful by several measures. It has, for example, become increasingly profitable, with earnings growing from €66m in 2015 to €118m in 2019. It also claims to have the lowest level of average flight delays among the larger European ANSPs, despite a relatively high level of strikes, although not all of its customers might agree. Consolidation has progressed, with a focus on just two major centres and the conversion of the other two into remote tower centres. It is the fifth largest ANSP in Europe in terms of traffic handled (see Table 11.2).

Table 11.2 Largest ANSPs in Europe, 2019.[a]

Country	Number of Service Units
France	21,782
Germany	15,180
United Kingdom	12,594
Spain	11,488
Italy	10,046

Source: ENAV. [a]Measured by en-route service units.

As already noted, Europe has a highly fragmented airspace, a reflection of its political divisions which have survived the creation of the EU. The fundamental problem of this 'balkanisation' of the skies[24] is, in the words of one commentator, that historical national patterns of behaviour have served to create and entrench a system of local national monopolies in which "particularistic civil and military constituencies have been protected and feed off each other's inefficiencies."[25] For airspace purposes, Europe is usually considered as being larger than just the EU, an approach established early with the creation in 1963 of at least a measure of trans-European ATM in the form of Eurocontrol. The original Eurocontrol Convention foresaw the complete 'Europeanisation' of airspace above a certain flight level, a radical approach which was effectively sabotaged by national interests. Instead, a far more limited multilateral control area covering only the Benelux countries and part of Germany was adopted, with Eurocontrol essentially being restricted to a coordinating/supervisory role for the rest of Europe.[26] This remains the situation today. In 2018, there were 37 separate European ANSPs with 62 centres and some 55,000 staff. Table 11.3 compares the area covered by Eurocontrol with that of the FAA in the US. Of particular note is the fact that the FAA handled 1.32 flights per employee per day compared with 0.52 in Europe. Table 11.2 lists the top five European ANSPs in terms of service units, essentially the number of flights handled adjusted for size. Table 11.4 shows the top ten ANSPs in terms of revenue earned, which produces a slightly different ordering. (Note that the table includes only Eurocontrol revenue and omits other earnings such as NATS' significant Oceanic activity.)

Table 11.3 Comparison of the FAA and Eurocontrol, 2018

	FAA[a]	Eurocontrol
Area covered (square kilometres)	10.4	11.5
Service providers	1	37
En-route facilities	20	62
Airports with ATC services	517	406
Average number of daily flights	41,874	28,475
Total staff	31,647	55,130

Source: Skyway (Eurocontrol). [a]Continental US area.

Table 11.4 Top Ten European ANSPs by Revenue, 2019

ANSP	Revenue (€m)
France	1317.2
Germany	961.4
Italy	774.1
United Kingdom	736.6
Continental Spain	699.5
Turkey	397.3
Austria	225.9
Poland	201.9
Sweden	191.5
Netherlands	190.6

Source: Eurocontrol.

The liberalisation of air services in most of Europe, with the creation of the EU internal aviation market and the continued rapid growth in traffic, increased the pressure on ANSPs. The result was a decline in service standards and higher flight delays. The failure of European ANSPs to provide what their customers regarded as an acceptable level of service inevitably led to an increase in the number of complaints. The ANSPs were saved not so much by the actions of the ATC providers themselves or their government owners, but mainly by the economic downturn which followed the 9/11 disaster in 2001. The number of flights fell significantly, especially across the Atlantic, and took some years to recover fully. In the meantime, the pressure on the ATS system was reduced. However, eventually demand returned and with it more flight delays. Again, ANSPs were saved by an extraneous development, this time in the form of the financial crisis of 2008/09. Yet again demand fell and flight delays were reduced before the European economies recovered and the old problems with ATC service provision re-emerged.

Unfortunately, delays have again increased almost every year since, at least up to the COVID outbreak. It is evident that the modernisation of the European ATC system failed to make sufficient progress during times of reduced demand to enable most ANSPs to cope with the recoveries. 2020 initially brought more complaints from airlines about delays, only for the arrival of the COVID pandemic to see a dramatic fall in demand for flights in European airspace, a decline which lasted for some time. The situation was exacerbated by the sheer size of the collapse in demand, reducing ANSPs' ability to finance and maintain ATC investment programmes. These periodic downturns highlighted an underlying pricing problem with commercialised ANSPs. As monopolies with high fixed costs, any sudden significant reduction in demand drives such companies to seek to raise charges, often substantially, on top of increased borrowing, to remain profitable. Their airline customers, on the other hand, operating in a more competitive market, invariably seek to stimulate demand by reducing fares, capacity and costs.[27] This generated further conflict between ATC providers and users. (Nav Canada's stabilisation fund was designed to address this problem.)

European ATC problems in the late-1990s were highlighted in the 2000 report 'Single European Sky. Report of the high level group.' (As we shall see, official reports into European ANSPs are almost invariably 'high level' or produced by 'wise men/persons.') In the Foreword to the report, the EU Transport Commissioner noted the "general dissatisfaction with the fragmentation and lack of efficiency in the organisation of air traffic control services." The report identified four principal deficiencies:

- Vast differences between European States in the organisation of airspace, leading to inconsistency and confusion and making airspace design more difficult, ultimately reducing the effectiveness of air transport.
- A multiplicity of national ATC centres designed to meet national requirements.

- Use of a large amount of airspace by the military, including some high civil traffic density areas.
- Investment decisions often taken on the basis of national industrial interests, resulting in limited technical or operational compatibility with other ANSPs.

These problems were not new and had previously led to the creation of the Central European ATM System (CEATS). This had sought to build on experience gained from the Maastricht Upper Area Control Centre, which, as already mentioned, has for many years controlled flights above Belgium, Luxembourg, the Netherlands and North Western Germany. Consolidation was the main focus, with the single ANSP covering the whole of US airspace presented as the ideal model. Similar attempts to create Europe-wide coordinated infrastructure, to reinforce political integration, were seen in the electricity ('copper-plate Europe') and railway ('Single European Railway Area') industries. As Paul Ravenhill has noted, the theory was straightforward; the problem was political,[28] a conclusion which has been a recurrent theme in attempts to reform ATC in Europe and elsewhere. Co-ordination and consolidation across numerous States proved to be unachievable. CEATS failed and was eventually cancelled.

The 2000 high-level report recommended the creation of a Single European Sky (SES) initiative combined with a collaborative, public-private partnership to develop a new ATM system for the whole of Europe, incorporating the latest technology. This was to be known as the Single European Sky ATM Research (SESAR) project, introduced in 2004, with three distinct phases planned:

2004–2008	–	Definition
2008–2013	–	Development
2014–2020	–	Deployment

Despite the name, the focus of the SES was in fact not on consolidation as this might normally be understood. Instead, a package of reform legislation was proposed, with the EU as rule maker, a role for EASA in safety regulation, a role for Eurocontrol in achieving a pan-European dimension, separation between regulator and service provider and the involvement of both industry and social partners in decision-making.[29] This was a typical EU response to a problem which was clearly at least as much political as operational, and it achieved some success. However, many of the underlying problems still remained and it soon became evident that the 2004 framework required reinforcement to make further progress, which came in the form of SES-II in 2008. (It is worth noting that at broadly the same time a similar major development was underway in the US, known as the New Generation Air Transportation System or NextGen, launched in 2003. Like SESAR in

Europe, NextGen's implementation has been problematic, with delays and cost increases as well as the Congressional budget problems which have affected the whole of the FAA.)

The launch of SESAR also saw the creation of a performance scheme with a far stronger role for the EU as regulator.[30] Each Member State is now required to prepare a national ATC performance plan to meet four key objectives: safety, environment, capacity and economic efficiency. ANSPs have to produce their own performance plans covering five-year periods which are subject to approval by their national regulatory authority and then by the Commission, with the objective of gradually reducing costs and charges over the longer term, similar to the PRI-X approach applied in the UK for some time. Of course, this being the EU, it is impossible to remove the political dimension to such regulation, and the whole process has not been without its critics. There has been some success, particularly in reducing charges, but many would argue that more could have been achieved. Table 11.5 lists the ten most expensive European ANSPs in 2015 (the start of the second EU regulatory period, RP2) and 2019 (the end of RP2). As can be seen, most reduced their charges significantly, although care should be taken in interpreting the figures, for example, because of exchange rate fluctuations. (This is likely to affect the UK and Switzerland in particular.) The variation in the level of charges between ANSPs can be partly explained by differences in the complexity of their respective airspaces and in their underlying cost structures (for example, in how pension contributions are treated.)

Table 11.5 Relative European ATC En-route Charges, 2015 and 2019 (€)

2015		2019	
Switzerland	98.64	Switzerland	94.33
United Kingdom	92.56	Italy	78.10
Germany	90.26	Austria	67.88
Italy	78.91	Belgium/Luxembourg	67.69
Austria	75.45	Germany	63.77
Spain	71.80	Spain	61.33
Belgium/Luxembourg	70.79	France	60.95
France	70.11	Slovenia	59.65
Slovenia	68.47	Moldova	58.97

Source: Eurocontrol.

Attention was increasingly directed towards relative cost levels and environmental factors. At the same time, the ATC industry itself began to form cross-border regional alliances, such as the Borealis Alliance (a group of nine ANSPs), which achieved at least some success and certainly more than the previous government-imposed initiative of Functional Airspace Blocks (FABS). FABS were an attempt to force groups of EU Member States into alliances as a stepping stone towards broader consolidation. However, despite pressure from the European Commission, the project largely ran out of steam, with little enthusiasm among Member States or ANSPs. Frustration at the speed of progress with the SES project was the main reason for the Commission's SES-II initiative, based essentially on four inter-related pillars: safety, technology, airports and human factors. In 2012 came SES II+, launched by the then Transport Commissioner with a speech aptly entitled "10 years and still not delivering." She pointed out that ATC targets, especially in relation to costs and delays, had not been achieved despite all the efforts at reform, with ATC inefficiency wasting €5bn annually.

> In short, while the EC has been quite successful in liberalising air transport, and somewhat successful at regulating access to airports, it is currently in gridlock when it comes to realising the Single European Sky, which is a centrepiece in overall air transport liberalisation and performance.... The main bottleneck appears to be at the institutional level, where progress appears increasingly unlikely. The main reason seems to be that member states are not willing to give up national control over their airspace and especially over their ANSPs. In other words, the SES project has so far ended in (an institutional) gridlock.[31]

The EU Commission was the principal supporter of the economic regulation of European airspace. The ANSPs themselves, along with their government owners, have been far less enthusiastic. (The same was true, of course, of the legacy airlines and their governments during the debate leading to the creation of the internal aviation market.) This may explain why the Performance Review Board (PRB) has not been as successful as many had hoped, often suffering from a lack of political will at Member State level to implement its decisions fully. As one study concluded, there may have been substantial technological progress, but technology alone is not sufficient to achieve an efficient European ATM system: "The rules and institutions will have to evolve to accommodate or simply to allow these technologies to be deployed."[32] A 2020 Eurocontrol study suggested that as a result of inefficiency in the ATM network, intra-European flights are using on average between 8.6% and 11.2% more fuel than necessary. At a time of such increased concern about the environmental impact of air transport, it is surprising, to put it mildly, that governments have been so reluctant to adopt more radical ATM reform.

2019 brought another report on European ATC, this time by a so-called 'wise persons' group. This report outlined a vision for the industry up to 2035, emphasising the need for a customer-focused SES, "a safe, seamless, scalable and resilient aviation network delivered through digital ATM services for all airspace users (civil and military) and passengers." These are certainly fine words and were followed in 2020 by further proposals from the Commission, including the adoption of a single ATC charge for the whole of EU upper air space. However, given the history of European ATM reform, it is perhaps not surprising that an element of scepticism remains. Neither the wise persons report nor the subsequent Commission proposals recommended the closure of a single ATC centre, despite the evidence that Europe is considerably over-supplied with such centres. This did not prevent the emergence of opposition to even the modest reform proposed, especially from the controllers' unions, who argued that air safety and data security would be jeopardised. Other commentators, on the other hand, perhaps with more justification, pointed out that the proposed reforms were little different from what had been suggested before, which had of course repeatedly failed to achieve their principal objectives. Eurocontrol's 2018 report[33] had acknowledged that the problem seemed to be getting worse and predicted that with a (pre-COVID) forecast 53% increase in flights between 2016 and 2040, the network risked being saturated in the absence of urgent and radical action; some 1.5m flights would be unable to operate (see Table 11.6). In 2021, IATA reinforced this message by warning that the whole reform process risked collapse in the absence of political support. Nevertheless, opposition to radical reform among most States remains strong and the likelihood of achieving an efficient, coordinated European airspace remains as distant as ever. It is a theme common in many parts of the world.

Table 11.6 Eurocontrol Forecasts, 2040

	2016	2040
Number of passengers delayed	50,000	470,000
Average total delay per flight (minutes)	12	20
Average en-route flight delay (minutes)	1.2	6.2

Notes

1 Matthias Finger, Marc Baumgarten and Engin Zeki: 'The need to evolve air traffic management: Europe as a laboratory.' In Matthias Finger and Kenneth Button (eds.): *Air Transport Liberalization. A Critical Assessment*. Edward Elgar, Cheltenham, 2017, pp. 339–358.
2 Bijan Vasigh, Ken Fleming and Thomas Tacker: *Introduction to Air Transport Economics. From Theory to Applications*. Ashgate, Aldershot, 2008.
3 Buffalo Courier quoted in Nick A. Komons: *Bonfires to Beacons. Federal Civil Aviation Policy under the Air Commerce Act 1926 – 1938*. US Department of Transportation, Washington DC, 1978.
4 Margaret Arblaster: *Air Traffic Management. Economics, regulation and governance*. Elsevier, Amsterdam, 2018.
5 Matthias Finger, Marc Baumgarten and Engin Zeki, op cit.
6 ATM Policy Institute: 'White Paper on TANS Liberalisation.' September 2017.
7 Margaret Arblaster, op cit.
8 Mike Goodliffe: 'The new UK model for air traffic services – a public private partnership under economic regulation.' *Journal of Air Transport Management*, Vol. 8(1), January 2002, pp. 13–18.
9 AEA: 'Towards a Single System for Air Traffic Control in Europe.' Brussels, 1989. Quoted in Richard Golaszewski: 'Reforming air traffic control: An assessment from the American perspective.' *Journal of Air Transport Management*, Vol. 8(1), January 2002, pp. 3–18.

10 H. Dumez and A. Jeunemaître: 'Institutional Evolution of Air Traffic Management: Integrating the Perspectives on Industrial Organization, Economics and Law.' Institutionalism, February 2007. Quoted in Margaret Arblaster, op cit.
11 IATA: 'Paper Presented to ICAO 2000 Conference on the Economics of Airports and Air Navigation Services.' Montreal, 2000.
12 Sofia Nyström, Claus Kastberg Nielson and David Nordström: *Reducing Costs of Air Traffic Control. How Competition Can and Cannot Contribute to Reducing Costs of Air Traffic Control*. Copenhagen Economics, Copenhagen, 2019.
13 Rui Neiva: 'Canada and USA: A Tale of two ANSPs.' In Finger and Button, pp. 359–378, op cit.
14 Bijan Vasigh, Ken Fleming and Thomas Tacker, op cit.
15 Ibid.
16 Barry Humphreys: 'Air Traffic Control: Chances of Reform?' Aviation Strategy, June 2016, and 'Air Traffic Control: Chances of Reform in the United States?' Aviation Strategy, September 2016.
17 I am grateful to the late Mike Tretheway for this information.
18 Nav Canada: 'The Test of Time. How Nav Canada Really Works.' Ottawa, undated.
19 Glen McDougall: 'The privatisation of the Canadian Air navigation system.' In Kenneth Button, Julianne Lammersen-Baum and Roger Stough (eds.): *Defining Aerospace Policy. Essays in Honor of Francis T. Hoban*. Ashgate, Aldershot, 2004.
20 Ibid.
21 Rui Neiva, op cit.
22 Note: the author was involved in the privatisation of NATS and for several years was a Non-Executive Director of the company.
23 Max Steuer: 'The partially private UK system for air traffic control.' *Journal of Air Transport Management*, Vol. 16(1), January 2010, pp. 26–35.
24 Richard Golaszewski, op cit.
25 Erwin von den Steinen: *National Interest and International Aviation*. Kluwer Law International, Alphen aan den Rijn, The Netherlands, 2006.
26 Ibid.
27 Kenneth Button and Glen McDougall: 'Institutional and structure changes in air navigation service-providing organizations.' *Journal of Air Transport Management*, Vol. 12(5), 2006, pp. 236–252.
28 Paul Ravenhill: 'Good Tidings.' Air Traffic Management, Issue 2, 2019.
29 Ibid.
30 Ibid.
31 Matthias Finger, Marc Baumgartner and Engin Zeki, op cit.
32 Mathias Finger, Teodora Serafimova and Engin Zeki: 'The Single European Sky (SES), a European infrastructure in the making.' *Network Industries Quarterly*, Vol. 23(2), 2021.
33 Eurocontrol: 'European Aviation in 2040: Challenges of Growth.' Brussels, 2018.

12 Airports

Introduction

Airports are a key element in the overall structure of the aviation industry. Like air traffic management, most airports started out as a public service, built and owned by either central or local government. Indeed, many of today's airports around the world were initially constructed for military purposes, especially during the Second World War, and handed over for civil use at the cessation of hostilities or shortly thereafter. Beginning in the 1980s, a process of privatisation emerged, first in the United Kingdom, which gradually spread throughout the world, although so far it is by no means ubiquitous. Privatisation inevitably generated a debate about regulation, and in many respects, it has not been possible to separate the two concepts. It is a debate which has often raged fiercely in several countries and is far from settled.

Economists do not recognise airports as natural monopolies, which actually occur quite rarely. (A natural monopoly is usually defined as a single supplier which can provide a service or good more cheaply than a group of competing suppliers.) Airports do, however, have monopoly power, to a greater or lesser extent, limiting effective competition. This raises several key questions:

- How much monopoly power does each airport possess?
- At what point does market failure justify regulatory intervention?
- When is it safe to leave well alone?
- If intervention is thought to be necessary, what form should it take?

Fundamentally, these are the issues which continue to generate controversy among stakeholders and academics. When airports were primarily State-owned, it was usually assumed that any market power would not be exploited against the public interest. (There were nevertheless examples of State-owned airports favouring a particular airline customer, often the State-owned flag carrier.) Privatisation undermined that, perhaps convenient, assumption.

This chapter will initially consider the changing ownership structure of the global airport sector, focusing in particular on the transition from government-owned to privatised airports in many areas of the world. It will then look at the related subject of regulation, especially the different approaches adopted in various jurisdictions. Finally, it will outline the current structure and economic characteristics of the sector, including relative size and profitability and different business models.

Ownership

The UK Government's ideological commitment to privatisation in the 1980s has already been noted. It was not a surprise, therefore, that in 1987, the UK became the first country to privatise a major airport, in fact a whole network of airports. The sale of the State-owned British Airports Authority, renamed BAA plc, was still a radical departure from the previously accepted paradigm and arguably acted as a catalyst for change in the airport sector around the world, just as the deregulation of US domestic air services did for airlines.[1] The British Airports Authority had been created in 1966 as a public utility-type organisation to control all UK State-owned airports (apart from a few small aerodromes in the Scottish Highlands and Islands), run independently of government but responsible to Parliament. It consisted of seven airports, of which the largest by some way was London Heathrow. The others were Gatwick, Stansted, Southampton, Glasgow, Edinburgh and Aberdeen. Shares in BAA, which were oversubscribed some ten times at the time of privatisation, were quoted on the London Stock Exchange. However, in 2004 the company's Articles of Association were amended to remove the 15% limit on the proportion of equity which could be owned by a single shareholder, and in 2006 a consortium led by the Spanish company Ferrovial acquired the airport group. Further ownership changes took place subsequently and the current shareholdings are shown in Table 12.1, which highlights the attractiveness of airport investment to organisations such as sovereign wealth and pension funds.

Table 12.1 Ownership of Heathrow Airport, 2020

Ferrovial	–	25.00%
Qatar Holdings	–	20.00%
Caisse de dépôt et placement du Québec	–	12.62%
Singapore Investment Corporation	–	11.20%
Alinda Capital	–	11.18%
China Investment Corp	–	10.00%
Universities Superannuation Scheme	–	10.00%

Source: Heathrow Airport Annual Report.

It is understandable why airports, like ANSPs, should have been publicly owned. Many were developed from previous military facilities, as noted above, and therefore already under government control. During the 1950s and 1960s, levels of airline traffic were low, resulting in a struggle for airports to be profitable. Finally, airports were seen as generators of local and national growth, justifying official financial support. However, aviation's growth not only transformed the finances of many airports, but also required substantial investment in facilities, such as terminals and additional runways, which governments often struggled to provide. Increasingly as well, the bureaucracy of being part of the public service was seen as an impediment to future expansion. Anne Graham[2] lists a number of potential factors behind airport privatisation:

- To improve efficiency and/or financial performance.
- To provide new airport investment funds and/or access to capital markets.
- To bring financial gains to the government and/or remove the financial burden of operating the airport.
- To lessen government influence on airport operations.
- To improve airport service quality.
- To enhance airport management effectiveness.
- To allow diversification into new non-aeronautical areas.

Many of these factors lay behind the decision of the UK Government to privatise BAA, but of particular note was the desire to maximise the financial gain for the Government, which essentially drove the decision to privatise all seven BAA airports as a single block, despite significant opposition. The decision effectively removed any prospect of introducing more competition into the sector, for example, between Glasgow and Edinburgh in Scotland and London's Heathrow and Gatwick. Also relevant was the fact that the new regulatory regime, which is discussed further below, was based on the combined assets of all the BAA airports, enabled BAA to leverage Heathrow's market power to compensate, for example, for Stansted's poor profitability.[3] This led to some misplaced investment decisions, the results of which can still be seen today. The policy was abandoned in 2003.

With BAA's attention increasingly focused on the development of its most profitable asset, Heathrow, arguably at the expense of its other airports, criticism of its dominant position in the market increased over the years. Eventually, a review by the Competition Commission concluded that BAA's performance had fallen well short of an acceptable standard and that three of its constituent airports should be divested. In fact, BAA sold off all of its airports apart from Heathrow and renamed itself Heathrow plc. The second largest UK airport, Gatwick, was sold for £1.5bn to Global Infrastructure Partners, which also bought Edinburgh Airport; ten years later Vinci paid £2.9bn for a 50% stake in Gatwick. The other, non-BAA regional airports were principally owned by local authorities. Gradually most of these were also divested to private shareholders, either with full privatisation or on long-term leases. The major exception was Manchester, the UK's third largest airport, where a consortium of local authorities retained a stake of over 64% and which itself now owns two other UK airports.

There is a widespread view that the creation of a privatised BAA consisting of seven of the country's largest airports was a mistake, one that took many years to correct. The promotion of a competitive market would almost certainly have produced a more economically efficient outcome, and other countries have learned from this error. However, whether privatisation itself was beneficial is more difficult to determine, partly because of the close interrelationship of ownership and regulation. There was certainly extensive criticism of BAA's performance, including accusations of excessive profitability, poor service quality, lack of investment (or the wrong type of investment) and unwarranted levels of employee remuneration. However, many of these accusations, if they are indeed valid, can be ascribed to the regulatory regime put in place by the Government rather than reflecting privatisation *per se*. We will return to this point below.

Since 1987, there has been a clear global trend away from direct public ownership, financing and management of airports towards a greater role for the private sector, aided by the attractiveness of airports to investors. As one study commented:

> Airports are a uniquely appealing class of assets for investors. While they typically offer strong growth fundamentals, diverse income streams, asset resilience and cash distributions, they also provide the potential to realise significant capital gains upon disposal.[4]

It is evident, however, that no single model of privatisation has prevailed, for reasons highlighted in a 2018 study produced by Deloitte for IATA:[5]

> Airport privatization programs may stem from a variety of strategic objectives, …[which] need to be balanced against the need for government influence…. given the strategic national significance of airport assets, their critical macro-economic role, and the need to protect consumer interests.

Graham makes a similar point: "Arguably it is now more appropriate to consider a continuous spectrum of airport ownership and operating models, with government owned at one end, privately-owned and operated at the other, and government-owned with private sector participation in the middle."[6]

Graham notes that following the sale of BAA, the first significant wave of airport privatisation occurred between 1996 and 2001, mostly in Europe, Australia, New Zealand, Malaysia, South Africa and some South and Central American countries. The trend was interrupted by the impact of the 9/11 disaster, but resumed from 2004. Again, a slowdown followed the financial crisis of 2008/09, although a few governments, especially in Southern Europe, implemented privatisations as a means of raising funds. With the economic recovery came a resurgence of interest in several countries, including France, Japan and Brazil. According to the Airports Council International (ACI), the global trade body for airports, of the top 100 busiest airports in 2017, measured in terms of passenger throughput, 51% had some type of private sector participation. However, this figure drops to 31% for the top 500 airports, indicating that smaller airports are more likely to remain under government control, probably a reflection of their greater reliance on public financial support. Table 12.2 below shows the regional distribution of private sector involvement.

Table 12.2 Proportion of Airports with Private Sector Participation, 2017

Region	Number of Airports	By Passenger Volume
Europe	43%	75%
Asia Pacific	26%	45%
Latin America/ Caribbean	25%	60%
Africa	3%	11%
North America	2%	1%
Middle East	1%	13%

Source: Airports Council International: 'Policy Brief: Creating fertile grounds for private investment in airports.' Montreal, 2018.

In Europe, most major airports have undergone changes in governance, with some wholly privatised along the lines of the UK's BAA (such as Brussels and Copenhagen), but the majority subject to only a partial sale of equity with governments retaining a minority stake (such as Aeroports de Paris and Frankfurt, Dusseldorf and Hamburg Airports). In many other parts of the world, however, a different model has predominated, with Australia, Asia and Latin America mostly adopting a public–private partnership approach. Most major Australian airports, for example, were privatised under 50-year leases, with 49-year renewal options. A similar long-term lease model has been adopted in Argentina, Chile, Colombia, Mexico, Peru, India, Japan, Malaysia and the Philippines.[7]

Table 12.3 lists the ten largest investor-owned airports/airport groups in 2019, measured in terms of passenger throughput. All are either fully or partially in private ownership. Notable also is the role played by companies which own more than one airport, often in several different countries. This is despite restrictions on foreign ownership imposed by some States, such as China, where airports and air traffic control are treated as part of the defence and security sector. (This has not, of course, prevented Chinese companies from investing in airports in other countries, often as part of the country's so-called 'belt and road' foreign infrastructure development programme.) The Annex to this Chapter provides one example of a multi-airport company, Vinci of France, whose operations cover 45 airports around the world with a variety of ownership and concession structures and a total annual passenger throughput of some 255 million in 2019. It is worth mentioning as well that there have been a few examples of governments taking airports back into public ownership, such as Cardiff and Prestwick in the UK, usually smaller locations which otherwise risked being closed because of financial losses.

Table 12.3 Largest Investor-Owned Airports (by Revenue), 2019

Airport Company	Based in (Country)	Main Airport	Revenue (US$m)	Privatisation Status
Aeroport de Paris	France	Paris Charles de Gaulle	5264	Partial
Aena Aeropuertos	Spain	Madrid	4977	Partial
Fraport	Germany	Frankfurt	4150	Partial
Heathrow Airport	United Kingdom	London Heathrow	4083	Full
Vinci Airports	France	London Gatwick/ Lisbon	2947	Full
Airports of Thailand	Thailand	Bangkok	2024	Partial
New Kansai Int. Airport	Japan	Kansai Tokyo	1980	Full
Beijing Capital	China	Beijing	1565	Partial
Malaysia Airport Holdings	Malaysia	Kuala Lumpur	1259	Partial
Flughafen Zürich	Switzerland	Zurich	1218	Partial

Source: The Reason Foundation: 'Annual Privatization Report 2021.' Washington DC.

Despite a long history of private ownership of utilities and transport companies, including airlines of course, the US has not so far joined the global trend in airport privatisation. Robert Poole of the Reason Foundation[8] suggests that there are three principal reasons for this:

- US public sector airports have access to tax-exempt revenue bonds, not usually found in other countries and not generally available to investor-owned companies in the US. Such bonds are really a form of subsidy for publicly owned airports.
- All passenger airports receive federal grants under the Airport Improvement Program on condition that they agree to a number of 'grant assurances,' including that they will not make a profit from airport operations or transfer any airport revenues to the public body which owns them.
- The traditional US airport business model features long-term leases that give 'anchor-tenant' airlines considerable control over terminals, gates and potential expansion.

There is little doubt that US airports could attract investors relatively easily. Their municipal owners are sitting on property worth many billions of dollars which, as Joseph Guinto pointed out in The Atlantic journal,[9] could raise sufficient funds to shore up their shaken balance sheets and invest in badly needed city infrastructure. Instead, owners are forced to re-invest any profits in the airport.

Nevertheless, the US has not been totally immune to the global privatisation trend. There has been extensive private investment in the development of, as distinct from the ownership of, individual airports, and it is common for airlines to have long-term leases on gates and even in some cases to own their own terminals. In 1996, the Airport Privatization Pilot Program established a number of exceptions to the Airport Improvement Program, enabling the sale or long-term lease of up to ten airports. Restrictions were placed on the type of airport to be included in the Program, for example only a single large hub was permitted. Luis Muñoz Marin International Airport in San Juan, Puerto Rico, became the first airport to be privatised in 2013, with a 40-year lease agreement. However, so far further progress has been very limited. Attempts to sell Chicago's Midway Airport have failed twice. Similarly, in 2000, Stewart Airport near New York was leased to a UK company, which failed to turn it into a viable operation. Stewart was subsequently acquired by the Port Authority of New York and New Jersey, which owns the major New York airports. In 2018, the Government proposed a significant expansion of the Pilot Program, including the removal of the ten airports and single major hub limits. It remains to be seen whether this will be sufficient to stimulate further privatisation.

Gillen[10] has identified seven possible airport ownership/governance structures which have emerged since the first privatisation:

- Government owned/operated.
- Government owned, privately operated.
- Major airports which have public–private partnerships in the form of management contracts.
- Independent not-for-profit corporations.
- Fully private for-profit via an Initial Public Offering with stock widely held.
- Fully private for-profit via a trade sale with share ownership tightly held.
- Partially private for-profit with private controlling interest.
- Partially private for-profit with government controlling interest.

The extent of airport ownership varies substantially around the world. Table 12.4 illustrates the impact of privatisation by geographical region, measured in terms of passenger throughput, with the proportion of public ownership varying from 99% in North America to 25% in Europe.

Table 12.4 Proportion of Passenger Traffic Handled at Privately and Government-Owned Airports, 2018

Region	Privately-Owned	Government-Owned
Africa	11%	89%
Asia/Pacific	47%	53%
Europe	75%	25%
Latin America/Caribbean	66%	34%
Middle East	18%	82%
North America	1%	99%
World Average	43%	57%

Source: Airports Council International.

One of the expectations of those promoting airport privatisation was that the move away from central or local government control would result in efficiency gains and improved customer service. Some studies have shown that this has indeed been the case, but equally, others have found the evidence less persuasive. For example, a study by Oum, Yan and Yu [11] concluded that "airports owned and/or controlled by majority private firms, autonomous public corporations or independent authorities are more efficient than those owned and/or controlled by government branch (city/state), multiple level governments, or US port authorities." On the other hand, Oum, Adler and Yu,[12] despite sharing two common authors with the previous study, found that airports which are fully government owned are more efficient than airports with a minority of private sector investment and almost as efficient as airports with a majority of private ownership. However, they also concluded that airports with a majority of private ownership have significantly higher profit margins than other airports, despite the fact that they charge lower aeronautical tariffs, a reflection, according to the authors of the study, of the former having diversified their businesses more into commercial and other non-aeronautical activities.

Gong, Cullinane and Firth[13], writing in 2012, conclude that "there is not yet enough empirical evidence to enable a reliable assessment of the extent of success or failure of airport and seaport privatization programs." Anne Graham[14] made a similar point more recently, concluding that

> if successfulness is measured in simple operating efficiency terms, [this study] ... has not provided evidence for the superiority of private management over public management. However, arguably it is now the need for investment capital or additional government income that are more important drivers of privatisation than efficiency.

One commentator summed up much of the research by pointing out that publicly owned airports appeared to be the cheapest, all other variables considered, but privately-owned ones are more efficient. "The worst of all worlds is the partially privatised airport, which is the least cheap and the least efficient."[15] Unfortunately, this is the model which has proved to be the most popular option with politicians, representing as it does a middle way between the extremes of full government ownership and full privatisation.

The reaction of the airline customers of airports to privatisation has similarly varied. Initially, the trend was largely welcomed, but increasingly doubts have been expressed. IATA in particular has adopted a highly critical approach. For example, speaking in 2018, the organisation's Director General commented that:

> We have yet to see an airport privatisation that has, in the long term, delivered on the promised benefits of greater efficiency for airlines and a better experience for our customers. Our members are very frustrated

with the state of privatised airports. By all means, invite private sector expertise to bring commercial discipline and a customer service focus to airport management. But our view is that the ownership is best left in public hands.

This is a distinctly different view from the one IATA and most of its major members were expressing during the early stages of airport privatisation. The problem with this debate is that it has become inextricably associated with the argument about regulation. It seems likely that most of the dissatisfaction expressed by airline customers about privatisation is in fact more a reflection of dissatisfaction with the regulation of those airports with significant market power, which account for a disproportionate number of airport privatisations. To a large extent, the success and failure of privatisation and regulation go hand in hand.

Regulation

With the privatisation of BAA plc in the UK in 1984, inevitably the question arose of regulatory control over airport prices and service standards. ICAO has long recommended that airport charges should be non-discriminatory, cost-related and transparent, although the Chicago Convention itself (Article 15) focuses more on discrimination against foreign airlines than on absolute cost levels and efficiency in relation to airports. The key to whether or not an airport requires economic regulation is the extent to which it is able to exploit market power, a concept which is clearly open to debate. The UK initially concluded that three BAA airports (Heathrow, Gatwick and Stansted, all serving the London conurbation) lacked sufficient competitive pressures to restrict excessive pricing. Manchester Airport, owned at the time wholly by a consortium of local authorities, was also added to the list, despite there being no change to its ownership structure. Although applicable in principle to publicly as well as privately-owned airports, in practice the widely held assumption was that governments would act in the wider public interest and therefore would not require regulatory oversight. Private owners, on the other hand, could be expected to prioritise the interests of their shareholders and hence, in the absence of a competitive market, to maximise profits at the expense of users.

The regulatory model adopted by the UK, *RPI-X*, was already well established in the country at the time of BAA's privatisation, having been applied to several privatised utility companies. According to Toms,[16] airlines initially opposed such an approach, preferring a more straightforward Rate of Return or Cost-Plus regime. A key argument in favour of price cap regulation is that it is less vulnerable to so-called cost-plus inefficiency and over-capitalisation, since the regulated firm has the incentive to minimise all its costs. However, in practice, the outcome depends to a large extent on how regulation is actually applied. Regulated companies are also subject to greater risks and may, therefore, incur a higher cost of capital.[17]

Nevertheless, the RPI-X/price cap model was the one implemented and became widely accepted in many countries, albeit with variations. A key feature is that a fair rate of return on the capital base is estimated *ex ante*, on the basis of the regulator's perception of efficiency savings and input prices over the control period, thereby providing incentives for cost reductions which will benefit users during the next regulatory review period.[18] In theory, there is no limit on the regulated firm's profitability, provided it maintains the price levels set by the regulator and exceeds the forecast efficiency savings. In practice, however, the outcome has been less clear-cut. Concern about profits substantially in excess of the cost of capital has meant that in the UK especially, and not just in relation to airports, more attention has been directed at the rate of return considerations.[19] An additional problem stems from the Regulated Asset Base (RAB) being a key element in the calculation of the price cap. There is a clear incentive for the airport to maximise the size of the RAB, for example by over-investment or 'gold plating,' which in theory should be controlled by the regulator but in practice inevitably leads to a fierce debate between stakeholders. Finally, as with any regulatory regime, there will always be a temptation for the regulated firm to 'gameplay' the system, whose effectiveness will depend to a significant extent therefore on the competence of individual regulators.

An airport has two principal sources of revenue, aeronautical (generated from airline-related activities such as landing fees, passenger charges, aircraft parking charges, etc.) and commercial (such as retail income, car parks, etc.). Table 12.5 illustrates the global split between these two sources. On average, in 2019, an airport earned US$13.69 per passenger handled, of which US$9.95 was accounted for by aeronautical revenues and US$7.08 by commercial income. Non-aeronautical revenue has actually been falling as a proportion of total income for the past few years, especially in Europe and to a lesser extent in North America, possibly a reflection of changing consumer habits with the growth of online shopping. At the same time, however, privatisation has usually had a positive effect on income from retail concessions in particular. How these different sources of revenue are treated has important implications for airport regulation.

Table 12.5 Sources of Airport Revenues, 2019

Aeronautical	–	55.8%
Non-Aeronautical	–	39.9%
Non-Operating Revenue	–	4.3%

Source: Airports Council International.

Under a so-called 'single till' approach, all revenues are taken into account when setting an airport price cap. Under a 'dual till' approach, on the other hand, the two streams of revenue are considered separately and only the aeronautical charges are included in the regulatory review. Airlines invariably favour the single till model, which usually produces lower airport charges.

They argue that it makes no economic sense to separate the two streams of income as there would be no commercial revenues in the absence of an airport. Airports, of course, tend to lobby strongly for the dual till approach, noting in particular that commercial activity is usually subject to greater competitive pressures than charges for the use of runways and terminals. It is also possible to have a hybrid till model, such as that adopted for Zurich Airport, where in early 2019, 30% of the profits from commercial activities were used essentially to cross-subsidise the aeronautical charges. Such an approach provides a less predictable outcome since there is no 'correct' level of cross-subsidy, which can therefore be subject to political intervention.

It may be that the choice between single and dual till is more of a philosophical issue than an economic one, but some economists have entered the fray. David Starkie[20], for example, has argued against the single till model on the basis that in the longer term it introduces distorted investment incentives, requiring the regulator to make difficult judgements regarding the cost of capital not only for the air transport sector, but also for retailing and property. In the shorter term, it is argued, this can result in distorted pricing signals at congested airports. A study by Bilotkach, Clougherty, Mueller and Zhang[21], on the other hand, concluded that aeronautical charges are lower at airports when a single-till regulation is employed and are lower when airports are privatised and when ex-post price regulation is applied. The UK Competition Authority also backed the single till approach, over-ruling the airport regulator. The Authority noted in particular that a switch to a dual till could lead to higher air fares at both congested and non-congested airports.[22]

It is probably fair to say that as the pioneer of airport regulation, the UK's experience has been mixed. The RPI-X model itself has survived, despite some criticism, with the consensus view seeming to be that it is probably the least inappropriate approach, although the extent of its coverage among UK airports has diminished. Of more concern has been the role of the regulator, the Civil Aviation Authority. In an editorial in March 2009, at the time of the financial crisis, the London Times noted that "the banks need better regulators, not just better regulation," and that has also been the core of the criticism of airport regulation in the UK. There is inevitably an element of judgement in the application of any regulatory regime. It must follow, therefore, that outcomes can change when regulators change. The initial criticism of the CAA focused on allegations that it was far too lenient in controlling BAA's alleged excesses. In the words of one airline: "For over a decade the CAA's Economic Regulation Group has applied a philosophy of minimum regulation in the face of growing evidence that it was failing to control the activities of the monopoly service provider."[23] Comparing UK airport regulation to the acknowledged shortcomings of banking oversight prior to the 2008/09 financial crisis, it was alleged that BAA had been allowed to earn excessive economic rents, seen in high profits and salaries, as well as failing to operate efficiently and provide an acceptable passenger experience.

Such criticism from airline customers might not be totally surprising, but similar arguments were also advanced by others, including the UK Competition Commission following an investigation which eventually resulted in BAA being forced to divest two of its three London airports. The Financial Times[24] highlighted how a so-called 'stable' regulatory framework had allowed Heathrow to operate with almost no equity capital. In 2017, for example, Heathrow's borrowings at £13.4bn were only just short of its RAB. With equity of £703m, "investors have been pulling out more in dividends than Heathrow has been earning. Last year they received a payout of £847m even though post-tax profits were just $516m." Heathrow's airline customers might argue that the problem with the regulatory framework was not so much that it was stable, but that it was benign. Airline criticism reached an apex at IATA's 2008 AGM, when the UK CAA was given a special award as the worst regulator in the world, a proposal which resulted in an ovation among the delegates.

The regulation of UK airports by the CAA has evolved significantly since 1986. Three attempts were made to extend price control to smaller regional airports, but all were rejected.[25] Instead, regulation eventually went in the opposite direction, with the de-designation of Manchester in 2009, followed in 2014 by Stansted and the application of so-called 'lighter touch' regulation to Gatwick, leaving only Heathrow still covered by the full RPI-X regime. With runway utilisation levels of almost 100% and demand for take-off and landing slots far exceeding the supply, even the owners of Heathrow could not seriously claim that it does not possess significant market power. Lighter touch regulation of Gatwick, an approach also adopted by several other countries as we shall see below, involved a series of commitments covering, *inter alia*, the maximum level of airport charges the airport could levy during the review period, a system of rebates applicable if Gatwick missed certain quality targets and a minimum level of investment to be undertaken. The key was a reduced role for the regulator and a larger one for contractual agreements between the airport and its airline customers.

The CAA carried out a review of the new approach in 2016,[26] noting that no airline had argued for a return to the previous regulatory regime and concluding that a lighter touch regime is potentially superior to a rigid RPI-X approach. "It allows the airport and airlines to develop price and service propositions that are tailored to their interests and consumer interests, rather than being subject to a single set of overarching price and service settings." To a significant extent, of course, it also reduces the role played by the regulator's judgement. It may be relevant that a new Civil Aviation Act in 2012, while introducing only modest changes to the airport regulatory regime, fundamentally altered the structure and objectives of the CAA, leading to a more interventionist approach to regulation where it is fully applied. The result has been a marked reduction in airline complaints, at least pre-COVID, and inevitably an increase in criticism from Heathrow Airport. It is evident from UK experience that the underlying regulatory regime is only part of the issue; the latitude granted to regulators in applying the regime is at least as important.

In its 2018 report prepared for IATA, Deloitte[27] listed five different airport regulatory regimes:

- Incentive-based (price cap).
- Rate of return.
- Consultation and appeals process.
- Regulation by contract.
- Price monitoring (light touch regulation).

Several countries have followed the UK's lead and amended their approach to airport regulation as experience was gained, Australia being one such example. The Government privatised 11 Australian airports in 1997/98, accompanied by an RPI-X regulatory regime, including a dual till provision and quinquennium review. In 2002, however, this was replaced with a light-touch approach, initially temporary and then on a more permanent basis, with monitoring of aeronautical charges replacing the price caps at the four largest airports.[28] (The remaining 90 or so Australian airports are not subject to *ex-ante* regulatory review.) Three separate government bodies are involved in the revised regime: the Australian Competition and Consumer Commission (ACCC), the Productivity Commission (PC) and the Ministry of Infrastructure, Transport, Regional Development and Communications. It is the Minister who ultimately decides whether airports are to be regulated, based on advice from the PC. If regulation is imposed, it is implemented by the ACCC. Every five years the PC carries out a review of an airport's performance, in consultation with stakeholders and the ACCC. In its most recent review in 2018/19, clear differences of opinion emerged, similar to what has occurred in the UK, with the ACCC (and airline customers) arguing that the four airports (Sydney, Melbourne, Brisbane and Perth) had and exercised significant market power. The PC agreed that market power existed, but concluded that it had not been used against the public interest, a view with which the Minister agreed. Consequently, there was no reversion to a more interventionist regulatory regime.

The arguments advanced by the PC for reaching its decision reflect the widely held views of those who advocate a less interventionist approach. Specifically, the PC highlighted the risks of over-regulation, noting its "chilling effect on investment, leading to a long-term risk of increased congestion and falling quality of service" and the prospect of "incumbent airlines being able to use the system to stymie investment that would facilitate increased (airline) competition, potentially leading to higher air fares."[29] The Australian airlines took a very different view, of course. In a consultants' report[30] produced for their trade body, they argued that:

- Australia's light-touch regulatory regime does not constrain monopoly airports from exercising a high level of market power in the form of ever-increasing charges: and

– airport charges have not only increased far more than air fares over 10 years, but profit margins at the four main regulated airports have been significantly higher (in some cases more than double) than those of other airports around the world operating in competitive markets or with greater regulation.

Arblaster notes that the removal of price caps reduced risk substantially at the Australian airports concerned and shifted it towards airline customers, which at least partly explains airline opposition to such a move. She concludes that in practice price monitoring has limited effectiveness in providing a constraint on the use of market power.[31]

Thus, the intensity of the debate on Australian airport regulation shows few signs of declining. Academic studies, despite the conclusion reached by Arblaster, have tended to support a lighter-touch approach. Schuster[32], for example, concludes that: "The experience of the Australian airports demonstrates that a light-handed regime can work effectively." Starkie[33], addressing airport regulation more generally, also argues that airports are unlikely to exploit any market power they might possess because of the "unusual economic characteristics of the industry" and even where such incentives do not exist, "the adverse economic costs of exercising market power might be small …. [E]x-post regulation of conduct provided for under normal competition law is probably sufficient to curb monopolistic excesses." Similar arguments have been advanced by Thelle and Cour Sonne[34] and even by Stephen Littlechild[35], the author of the original RPI-X regulatory regime in the UK.

Finally, it is worth noting that despite considerable pressure from airlines, the EU has adopted only a superficial regulatory regime to control airport charges, whether *ex-ante* or *ex-post*. This may reflect the relative power of stakeholder political lobbying, with airports proving to be far more successful than airlines in this instance. (The role of governments as owners, and potential sellers, of airports may also be relevant here as well of course.) There are numerous EU regulations which apply to airports, such as those dealing with slot allocation, ground handling, passengers with reduced mobility, etc., but legislation to oversee pricing goes little further than the basic ICAO recommendations, as set out in the Organisation's 2004 principles on airport charges. The EU Airport Charges Directive was first adopted in 2009, and provides for a two-tier regulatory structure, distinguishing between small (handling up to five million passengers per annum) and larger airports. It aimed primarily to tackle two problems:[36]

- the existence of diverging charging systems in Member States that lack clear transparency in the way in which they are constructed; and
- the lack of effective competition among some airports resulting potentially in excessive prices and poor service quality.

The Directive stipulates that:

- Airport charges should not discriminate between users.
- Charges and how they are calculated should be transparent.
- There should be regular consultation with users.
- Each Member State should establish an independent supervisory authority.

The EU Commission's review of the Directive in 2019, based on a detailed consultants' study, found that while there had been some improvement in the regime for setting airport charges, the Directive had failed to meet all of its original objectives. Given that the original objectives were relatively limited, this is hardly an overwhelming endorsement. In particular, it was concluded, the Directive had failed to reduce disagreements between airlines and airports (the European airlines' trade body, Airlines for Europe, said the Directive had continued "to undermine Europe's competitiveness and thwarted the creation of more than 200,000 jobs"); nor had it succeeded in creating a single, harmonised regulatory regime for Europe. The latter point may not be surprising given the geopolitical environment in which airports operate. As Macário, Viegas and Reis[37] note, the development of airports is closely linked to their respective hinterlands, which means there is inevitably a need to "retain sufficient degrees of freedom to accommodate local and regional interests and different decision making processes."

Structure and Economics

There is no 'typical' airport. Not only do airports vary in ownership structure, as we have seen, but also in size (from the largest serving major conurbations to, in one case, a beach), prime purpose (e.g., hubs, all-freight, regional, etc.), profitability, and so forth. There are several ways of measuring airport size, but probably the commonest is passenger throughput as shown in Table 12.6 for the ten largest airports in the world in 2018. Four of the airports listed are located in the Far East, three in the US, two in Europe and one in the Middle East. In 2000, on the other hand, half of the top ten airports were located in the US, with four in Europe and just one in the Far East, a clear indication of the changing pattern of global aviation demand, seen especially in China's growing importance.

Of the airports listed in Table 12.6, over half of them can be regarded as traditional hub operations, dominated by a single airline. At the largest, Atlanta, for example, Delta accounted for some 78% of all passengers handled, with the second largest carrier, Southwest, accounting for just 11%. Chicago O'Hare also stands out as supporting two hub airlines, with American and United together handling 82% of total passenger traffic, split 48%/34%, respectively. (Tokyo's Haneda International is similar with a 50%/33% split between its two principal carriers.) Airports have also been impacted by the rapid growth of low-cost carriers, which in many regions took advantage of under-utilised and cheap secondary airports to establish themselves, sometimes with the added incentive of subsidies from airport owners. A study by Jimenez and Suau-Sanchez,[38] for example, showed that while primary, secondary and regional airports all gained from the expansion of LCCs in Europe, the main beneficiaries between 2001 and 2008 were the secondary airports. However, a significant change took place following the financial crisis, with a shift in LCC service towards primary airports between 2009 and 2019, as capacity became available at the larger locations. This not only had implications for the viability of smaller airports, but also served to exacerbate any capacity constraints at their larger counterparts once passenger demand recovered.

Table 12.6 Largest Airports in Terms of Passengers Handled, 2018

City	Airport	Country	No. of Passengers (000)	Largest Airline (% of Passenger Traffic)	Second Largest Airline (% of Passenger Traffic)
Atlanta	Hartsfield Int.	USA	107,394	Delta (78%)	Southwest (11%)
Beijing	Capital	China	100,983	Air China (39%)	China Southern (14%)
Dubai	International	UAE	89,149	Emirates (65%)	Flydubai (13%)
Los Angeles	International	USA	87,534	American (20%)	Delta (16%)
Tokyo	Haneda Int.	Japan	87,099	All Nippon (50%)	Japan Airlines (33%)
Chicago	O'Hare Int.	USA	83,400	United (48%)	American (32%)
London	Heathrow	UK	80,102	British Airways (46%)	Virgin Atlantic (5%)
Hong Kong	International	Hong Kong	74,688	Cathay Pacific (31%)	Cathay Dragon (16%)
Shanghai	Pudong Int.	China	74,054	China Eastern (28%)	Shanghai Airlines (9%)
Paris	Charles de Gaulle	France	72,230	Air France (51%)	easyJet (7%)

Source: Airline Business, May 2019.

As indicated in an earlier chapter, airports on average earn a superior rate of return than airlines do. (Then again, everyone in the aviation value chain is more profitable than airlines.) However, the average figure hides a wide variation in actual results. Tretheway and Markland,[39] writing in 2013, found that collectively airports have tended to barely cover their cost of capital. ACI data for 2019, a relatively good year, shows that on average airports earned a return on invested capital of 7.4%. Airports, whose charges account for some 7%–10% of airline costs, must finance 36% of the aviation value chain's capital, compared to 46% for airlines. On the other hand, most airline capital is far more mobile, suggesting a lower cost of capital and a lower financial risk.[40] Secondary and regional airports tend to perform significantly less well financially than their larger counterparts. 80% of all airports are classed as 'small,' handling less than one million passengers each year, and 94% of small airports are loss-making. Airports have large fixed costs, which means that viability usually requires a high level of traffic. This was always one of the arguments in favour of public ownership of airports, at least until they were able to become self-sustaining.[41]

One particular problem faced by airports, which was also highlighted in the previous chapter in relation to air traffic management, is that pricing can be counter-cyclical. Given the high level of fixed costs, if possible airports tend to raise their charges during economic downturns when traffic growth slows or even falls. This inevitably creates tension with airline customers, whose natural inclination is to reduce prices in such circumstances to stimulate demand. As Tretheway and Markhvida point out, from a value chain point of view, this is neither economically efficient nor financially desirable.[42] They suggest that a better approach would be to transfer the business cycle risk from airports to airlines, for example, by holding down airport charges in recessions and permitting higher-than-average returns in more prosperous years. Such an approach has been implemented in electric utility and ferry regulation, where fuel cost increases are temporarily banked during a period of higher energy prices, with increased charges for consumers accepted when fuel prices fall. A study by Zhang and Zhang, aptly partly called 'the long-run view,' came to a similar conclusion.[43] There is an inherent logic in such an approach, but it would require a degree of co-operation, and a longer-term perspective, than has so far proved to be achievable.

As Forsyth et al[44] have noted, the ownership and regulatory environments of airports across the world represent compromises between conflicting objectives. There are substantial variations between the different approaches adopted, a reflection partly of the different views taken by governments on the best way to pursue efficiency objectives. However, this outcome also reflects the different non-efficiency airport objectives pursued around the world. "Some governments are more keen to promote airline competition, some are more willing to become involved in detailed economic regulation than others and some take the view that the threat of regulation will be sufficient to discipline pricing behaviour." While in airline regulation, with a few exceptions, the clear trend over several decades has been towards a single objective of liberalisation, at least until recently, for airports there has been a lack of consensus on the best way forward.

Notes

1 David Starkie: *Aviation Markets. Studies in Competition and Regulatory Reform.* Ashgate, Aldershot, 2008.
2 Anne Graham: 'Airport management and performance.' In Lucy Budd and Stephen Isou (eds.): *Air Transport Management. An International Perspective.* Routledge, London, 2017.
3 See David Starkie: 'Testing the regulatory model: The expansion of Stansted airport.' *Fiscal Studies*, Vol. 25(4), 2004, pp. 289–413.
4 PwC: 'Airport Valuations Have Taken Off – The Question Is Where Will They End.' February, 2019.
5 Deloitte: 'Airport Ownership and Regulation.' Report for IATA, June 2018.
6 Anne Graham: 'Airport privatisation: A successful journey.' *Journal of Air Transport Management*, Vol. 88, 2020, pp. 1–9.

7 Robert W. Pool Jr.: 'Study: Leasing 31 US airports would generate $131 billion to fund other infrastructure and pay debt.' The Reason Foundation, Washington DC, August 2021.
8 Robert W. Poole Jr.: 'Annual Privatization Report: Airport Transportation.' Reason Foundation, Washington DC, May 2018.
9 Joseph Guinto: 'Privatizing Airports Is a No-Brainer'. The Atlantic, 18 August 2020.
10 David Gillen: 'The evolution of airport ownership and governance'. *Journal of Air Transport Management*, Vol. 17, 2013, pp. 3–13.
11 Tae H Oum, Jia Yan and Chunyan Yu: 'Ownership forms matter for airport efficiency: A stochastic frontier investigation of worldwide airports.' *Journal of Urban Economics*, Vol. 64(2), 2008, pp. 109–121.
12 Tae H. Oum, Nicole Adler and Chunyan Yu: 'Privatization, corporatization, ownership forms and their effects on the performance of the world's major airports.' *Journal of Air Transport Management*, Vol. 12(3), 2006.
13 Stephen X. H. Gong, Kevin Cullinane and Michael Firth: 'The impact of airport and seaport privatization on efficiency and performance: A review of the international evidence and implications for developing countries.' *Transport Policy*, Vol. 24, 2012, pp. 37–47.
14 Anne Graham (2020), op cit.
15 Andrew Charlton: 'The Plural of 'Anecdote' is not Data.' Aviation Intelligence Reporter, December/January 2019.
16 Mike Toms: 'UK-regulation from the perspective of the BAA plc.' In Peter Forsyth, David W. Gillen Andreas Knorr, Otto G Mayer, Hans-Martin Niemeier and David Starkie (eds.): *The Economic Regulation of Airports. Recent Developments in Australasia, North America and Europe*. Ashgate, Aldershot, 2004, pp. 117–124.
17 Rauf Gonenc, Maria Maher and Giuseppe Nicoletti: 'The Implementation and Effects of Regulatory Reform: Past Experience and Current Issues.' Economic Working Paper No. 251, OECD, June 20000.
18 Margaret Arblaster: 'Regulation in markets facing uncertainty: The case of Australia.' *Journal of Air Transport Management*, Vol. 67, 2018, pp. 249–258.
19 David Starkie (2008), op cit.
20 Ibid.
21 Volodymyr Bilotkach, Joseph A. Clougherty, Juergen Mueller and Anming Zhang: 'Regulation, privatization, and airport charges: Panel data evidence from European airports.' *Journal of Regulatory Economics*, Vol. 42(1), 2012, pp. 73–94.
22 UK Competition Commission: 'BAA plc: A Report on the Economic Regulation of the London Airports Companies.' London, 2002.
23 Virgin Atlantic Airways: 'Airport Regulation.' Submission to the UK Department for Transport Consultation, May 2009. (Note: this submission was largely written by this book's author.)
24 Financial Times: 'Who Will Pay for Heathrow Airport's £14bn Third Runway.' 22 June 2018.
25 Mike Toms, op cit.
26 UK CAA: 'Economic Regulation of Gatwick Airport Limited: Consultation on New Commitments.' CAP 1073, 2016.
27 Deloitte, op cit.
28 Margaret Arblaster, op cit.
29 Ibid.
30 Airlines for Australia and New Zealand: 'The Performance and Impact of Australia's Airports Since Privatisation.' Consultants' Report, May 2018.
31 Margaret Arblaster, op cit.
32 Dominic Schuster: 'Australia's approach to airport charges: The Sydney Airport experience.' *Journal of Air Transport Management*, Vol. 15(3), 2009, pp. 121–126.

33 David Starkie: 'Airport regulation and competition.' *Journal of Air Transport Management*, Vol. 8(1), 2002, pp. 63–72. See also Harry Bush and David Starkie: 'Competitive drivers towards improved airport/airline relationships.' *Journal of Air Transport Management*, Vol. 41, October 2014, pp. 45–49.
34 Ref Martin H. Thelle and Miela Cour Sonne: 'Airport competition in Europe.' *Journal of Air Transport Management*, Vol. 67, March 2018, pp. 232–240.
35 Stephen Littlechild: 'Regulation and the nature of competition.' *Journal of Air Transport Management*, Vol. 67, March 2018, pp. 211–223.
36 European Union: 'Commission Staff Working Document. Evaluation of the Directive 2009/12/EC of the European Parliament and of the Council of 11 March 2009 on Airport Charges.' Brussels, July 2019.
37 Rosário Macário, José M. Viegas and Vasco Reis: 'Impact of Low Cost Operation in the Development of Airports and Local Economies.' Workshop APDO-O, 2007.
38 Edger Jimenez and Pere Suau-Sanchez: 'Reinterpreting the role of primary and secondary airports in low-cost carrier expansion in Europe.' *Journal of Transport Geography*, Vol. 88, October 2020, pp. 1–12.
39 Michael W. Tretheway and Kate Markhvida: 'Airports in the Aviation Value Chain: Financing, Returns, Risk and Investment.' Discussion Paper 2013–15, Roundtable on Expanding Airport Capacity under Constraints in Large Urban Areas, Paris, Feb 2013.
40 Ibid.
41 David Starkie (2008), op cit.
42 Michael W. Tretheway and Kate Markhvida, op cit.
43 Anming Zhang and Yimin Zhang: 'Airport charges and cost recovery: The long-run view.' *Journal of Air Transport Management*, Vol. 7(1), 2001, pp. 57–62.
44 Peter Forsyth, David W. Gillen, Andreas Knorr, Otto G. Mayer, Hans-Martin Niemeier and David Starkie, op cit.

Annex

Vinci Airports 2019

Country	Airport	Vinci Ownership Share (%)	2019 Passenger Traffic (000)	End of Concession
France	Lyon Bron	31	11,754	2047
	Nantes Atlantique	85	7,272	2021[a]
	Rennes Bretagne	49	852	2024
	Toulon Hyères	100	507	2040
	Clermont-Ferrand Auvergne	100	431	2026
	Grenobles Alpes Isère	100	308	2026
	Chambéry Savoie Mont Blanc	100	204	2029
	Dinard Bretagne	49	96	2024
	Saint-Nazaire Montoir	85	20	2021[a]
	Pays d'Ancenis	100	Business Aviation	2025
Portugal	Lisbon	100	31,173	2063
	Porto	100	13,105	2063
	Faro	100	9,009	2063

(Continued)

Country	Airport	Vinci Ownership Share (%)	2019 Passenger Traffic (000)	End of Concession
	Madeira	100	3,370	2063
	The Azores	100	2,463	2063
	Beja	100	770	2063
United Kingdom	London Gatwick	50.01	46,568	Freehold
	Belfast Int.	100	6,285	2993
Sweden	Stockholm Skavsta	90[c]	2,277	Freehold
Serbia	Belgrade	100	6,159	2043
United States	Hollywood Burbank	MC[b]	5,908	2020
	Orlando Sandford	100	3,288	2039
	Atlantic City Int.	MC[b]	1,135	2021
	Middle Georgia	MC[b]	Business Aviation	2022
	Macon Downtown	MC[b]	Business Aviation	2022
Dominican Republic	Santo Domingo (Las Americas)	100	4,515	2030
	Puerto Plata	100	862	2030
	Samaná	100	170	2030
	La Isabela	100	84	2030
	Barahona	100	Business Aviation	2030
Costa Rica	Guanacaste	45	1,224	2030
Chile	Santiago	40	24,646	2035
Brazil	Salvador Bahia	100	7,784	2047
Japan	Kansai Int.	40	31,904	2060
	Osaka Itami	40	16,526	2060
	Kobe	40	3,363	2060
Cambodia	Phnom Penh	70	6,029	2040
	Siem Reap	70	3,926	2040
	Sihanoukville	70	1,680	2040

Source: Vinci Airports.
[a] "Termination for reasons of public interest decided on 24 October 2019, with effect from 15 December 2019 at the earliest."
[b] Management Contract.
[c] Sold to Arlandastad Group, early 2022.

13 Summary, COVID and the Future

Summary

This book has traced the evolution of the regulation of air transport from the end of the Second World War to the present day. It only remains to draw together the threads of that history and consider the lessons to be learned and where the industry might be heading in the future. Inevitably the global COVID epidemic will have a major influence on the latter, and we will return to that subject later in this concluding chapter. First, however, it is worth reminding ourselves how far the aviation industry has come since the allied Governments met in Chicago in 1944 to determine its future international regulatory regime. Despite initial tight regulation, stifling government involvement and the lack of real competition, airlines nevertheless experienced falling cost levels, almost wholly the result, at least initially, of technological improvements. Lower costs led to lower air fares and freight rates and therefore to higher demand, supported by increased wealth in many countries. Subsequently, other factors added to improved airline efficiency, and therefore to further traffic growth (see Table 13.1). In many ways, aviation experienced a genuine 'democratisation' as travel became far more readily available to the masses. Unfortunately, there are several reasons to question whether this trend will continue at the same pace, including the impact of the COVID epidemic, growing environmental pressures and, as we shall see, increased protectionism.

There may have been substantial progress in transforming the air transport industry over the past 70 or so years, but it is still far from being what might be regarded as a 'normal' business. It was inevitable that governments would play a leading role in the industry's early development, not least because of the perceived relationship between air transport and countries' strategic interests, as well as the struggle to achieve financial viability. What may be more surprising is that government involvement has remained such a key factor in the development of the industry up to the present day, despite repeated attempts to reduce it. For consumers, in particular, this has come at a significant price. The former Chief Executive of British Airways, Bob Ayling, once noted that States believe that to be a nation you need a flag, a national anthem and an

DOI: 10.4324/9780429448973-13

Table 13.1 Growth of Air Transport Since 1945

Year	Passengers (m)	Seat-km available (m)	Passenger Seat Factor (%)	Freight tonne-kms (m)	Total tonne-km performed (m)	Weight load factor (%)
1945	n/a	10,000	n/a	n/a	n/a	n/a
1950	n/a	58,624	61	1,012	4,426	58
1955	n/a	124,225	62	1,735	9,030	59
1960	n/a	233,225	59	2,839	15,650	55
1965	228	447,096	56	6,630	29,760	52
1970	400	880,364	55	14,635	60,655	50
1975	560	1,243,441	59	20,949	90,785	54
1980	784	1,817,977	63	31,789	140,099	58
1985	942	2,178,899	66	43,074	179,118	60
1990	1,232	2,939,581	68	63,632	252,006	60
1995	1,380	3,541,205	67	90,046	314,795	60
2000	1,753	4,484,092	71	127,798	429,784	61
2005	2,119	5,200,507	75	154,244	519,388	62
2010	2,705	6,299,370	78	186,631	645,596	67
2015	3,556	8,281,130	80	197,131	821,174	67
2018	4,322	10,105,144	82	230,967	1,004,763	69

Source: ICAO.

airline. "The first two come cheap, but the third is extremely expensive."[1] Sir Michael Bishop, Chairman of bmi (a UK airline now absorbed into British Airways), similarly described airlines as mainly being founded and expanded

> as a clone of the government – an unassailable symbol of prestige and sovereign virility… The intimacy of these airlines with their governments developed a long-standing acknowledgement that consumer and commercial considerations have been subordinated to national interest and political interference.[2]

Recent developments have shown that despite extensive privatisation and deregulation/liberalisation, this 'intimacy' remains very much a key factor in the industry's development today.

It is perhaps equally surprising that while the overall aviation industry has matured and, in many cases, achieved long-term viability, the core of the industry, the airlines themselves, has not done so. Airlines as a group failed to earn their cost of capital over many decades and have been sustained by a mixture of bankruptcy, refinancing and government bailouts. Nor have airlines consolidated to anything like the same degree as most other industries, particularly across borders. Restrictions on ownership and control have resulted in a failure to create truly global companies, despite the international focus of most carriers. Legacy airlines may face increased competition in many countries, but on the whole, they continue to dominate their national markets just as they have done for decades. Of course, these shortcomings should not disguise the fact that there has been considerable progress in many regulatory areas. The old bilateral restrictions on airline operations have been widely swept aside, privatisation has become far more common, and consumer rather than producer interests now feature more prominently (at least superficially) in the approach of many governments to aviation regulation. However, the fact remains that aviation is still characterised by a far higher degree of government involvement than most other industries and as a result the airline business especially cannot be said to have been 'normalised.' To that extent, nothing has fundamentally changed since 1944.

We have seen how the Chicago Conference established the basis for the regulation of international air transport for the following 70 years, particularly with respect to safety and, increasingly, security and the environment. However, it failed to achieve a consensus on the economic regulation of airlines, as a result of which there emerged a regime characterised by bilateral air services agreements negotiated between sovereign States. The focus was on the trading of rights; nothing could happen without the specific approval of the two governments involved, an approach that inevitably discouraged a competitive marketplace. Producer interests prevailed and collusion between airlines was not only tolerated but usually actually required. The result was inefficiency, high tariffs, reduced demand and financial losses, with an impact on the industry's structure that persists to the present day.

From a regulatory perspective, the development of the air transport industry since the Second World War has been characterised by the gradual dismantling of these restrictions and the creation of a far more competitive environment, with less direct government involvement and more focus on the interests of the consumer. Such progress, however, did not follow a smooth, uniform path. The industry has been subject to a series of disruptions, each of which had a dramatic impact and fundamentally changed the sector's structure. One of these disruptions was technology, which over the years has considerably improved airline efficiency. It was this improvement, continuing today, which more than countered the basic inefficiency of the traditional airline business model during the industry's early post-war decades and enabled costs and fares to be reduced.

Charter services had managed to avoid at least some of the post-Chicago bilateral restrictions, probably more by luck than design, and eventually began to provide a partial challenge to the established flag carriers during the 1950s and 1960s. The development of inclusive tour charters in Europe in particular had a significant market impact. Specialist IT airlines were sufficiently flexible to at least partly get around the market entry barriers erected to protect their more favoured competitors, and they had costs sufficiently low to present a real competitive threat to parts of the legacy carriers' route networks. The established airlines had little choice other than to try to adapt, which not all did successfully by any means. Subsequently, similar developments took place on long-haul routes, especially across the Atlantic, occasionally highlighting the farcical nature of regulatory regimes designed above all, and eventually unsuccessfully, to maintain the status quo.

By the 1970s, the international aviation regulatory regime was coming under increased pressure to change, despite what many regarded as the backward step of the UK/US Bermuda 2 agreement. However, it was domestic rather than international air services which first experienced the disruptive forces of deregulation. The US decision to move, virtually overnight, from a highly restrictive domestic regulatory regime to one characterised by open competition, initially created chaos in the largest aviation market in the world. During the first ten years or so of deregulation, between 1978 and 1989, 88 new jet-operating airlines were established in the US; no less than 83 of them failed before the decade was out. Another 164 carriers were planned but never got off the ground.[3] However, the whole structure of the market was changed. It may have taken some time to re-establish equilibrium, but few would disagree with the conclusion that, while there may have been winners and losers, overall the experiment was a huge success. Competition increased, fares were reduced and demand grew. Consumers were the main beneficiaries. Deregulation also saw the emergence nationally of a new airline business model, the low-cost carrier, whose *modus operandi* would have been largely impossible under the old regulatory regime. Perhaps most important of all, both deregulation and the LCC model set a pattern for much of the rest of the world to follow.

In Europe, deregulation became known as liberalisation and took far longer to evolve than it had in the US. Despite the creation of the EU internal market covering virtually all trade, aviation had continued to be treated differently and remained essentially the responsibility of individual Member States. It took a court case to confirm the European Commission's contention that air transport was subject to the Treaty of Rome's competition clauses, just like other sectors. This made reform inevitable, but even then it took several years to create the EU internal aviation market. Nevertheless, eventually, all the old bilateral restrictions between Member States were swept away and Community carriers were free to fly wherever they wished within the EU and charge whatever tariffs they chose. The extended period over which reform took effect meant that the immediate impact was nowhere near as dramatic as it had been in the US, but the long-term outcome was not dissimilar. In particular, liberalisation saw the emergence of several pan-European LCCs, presenting a major challenge to the established flag carriers, which were forced to adapt or downsize their short-haul operations. Partial or full privatisation became the norm within the EU, with a small number of legacy carriers disappearing and others effectively being absorbed by their larger competitors. The creation of the EU internal aviation market was also accompanied by the adoption of an extensive list of regulatory initiatives, some new and some replacing national rules, which represented a substantial transfer of responsibility from Nation States to a regional body.

The reform of aviation regulation seen in the US and Europe spread to numerous other countries, with a small number even going further, for example in opening up domestic markets to foreign competition. In practice, however, such reform was far from complete deregulation. It was certainly true that most of the old restrictions on airline operations were swept away within the relevant markets, but invariably they were replaced by other regulations designed primarily to protect the interests of consumers and promote competition. To this day, air transport remains as tightly regulated in several broad areas as it ever was. The second reason why the initial spurt of reform was limited was that it was restricted essentially to domestic/regional operations. International air services mostly remained constrained by protectionist bilateral agreements, although similar pressure for reform soon began to emerge in several markets. Again, the US took the lead with the promotion of its open skies policy which eventually saw over 120 liberal ASAs negotiated with countries around the world, and again the impact was overwhelmingly positive. It resulted in the disappearance of what one commentator aptly described as "the gentility of tacit collusion and avoiding head-on competition, which were typically working in the regulated era."[4]

In Europe, history repeated itself with a court case effectively giving the EU Commission the powers to negotiate aviation agreements with third countries on behalf of the whole of the EU. As a result, liberal agreements were reached with numerous States adjacent to the EU, and the Commission obtained a growing number of mandates to seek similar arrangements with countries further afield. There is little doubt, however, that when it came to negotiating aviation agreements with States beyond Europe's immediate sphere of interest, the Commission's main focus was the creation of an Open Aviation Area with the US. At the time, such an agreement would have covered almost 60% of global scheduled air services and potentially created a radical post-Chicago model for the world to follow.

The negotiating mandate agreed by EU Member States, with the support of their airline and airport sectors, essentially represented an extension of the EU internal aviation market across the Atlantic. It went far beyond the US open skies model, especially in providing for cabotage services and the reform of airline ownership and control rules, as well as seeking extensive regulatory convergence in a number of areas. To many, the EU/US negotiations represented a rare, possible unique, opportunity to change in particular the archaic airline ownership and control rules. Potentially it could have transformed the very structure of the industry by replacing imperfect alliances with consolidated, and more profitable, global companies. Unfortunately, the US negotiators were unable to overcome domestic legislative problems and could only go as far as acceptance of the concept of a Community Carrier, a modest step in the right direction but nowhere near as radical as Europe had wanted. The EU/US agreement which eventually emerged was, therefore, far closer to the US open skies model than the negotiating mandate initially granted to the Commission.

One of the ironies of the aviation industry is that airlines appear to be attractive to investors, yet as a group have an appalling record of profitability. As Sir Adam Thomson, founder and Chairman of British Caledonian Airways, once remarked: "When there's a recession, you tighten your belt. When there's a depression, you have no belt to tighten. When you lose your trousers, you're in the airline business."[5] This does not mean that there are no examples of profitable airlines, of course, but since its inception over a hundred years ago, the industry as a whole has repeatedly failed to meet its cost of capital. Such a record is not a prescription for a sustainable business. Some have even argued that the industry's fundamental economics prevent long-term viability, the so-called *empty core theory*. It is understandable that profitability was difficult, if not impossible, to achieve during aviation's formative years, stretching beyond the end of the Second World War. However, overall losses continued even as a level of maturity was achieved, very different from the experience of most other industries where maturity has been accompanied by sustainable viability. It is this record which led Warren Buffet to describe the airline industry as 'extraordinary,' noting that it has eaten up capital over the past century like almost no other business because people seem to keep coming back to it and putting fresh money in (including, of course, Mr Buffet himself).

It seems very likely that poor financial performance among airlines is associated in particular with the lack of global consolidation as a result of regulatory restrictions on ownership and control. The transformation of US airlines from the world's biggest loss-makers to the most profitable over a short period of time, following extensive domestic consolidation, would appear to lend some credence to such a hypothesis. The absence of reform of the airline ownership and control rules thus represents the most important single factor in preventing the 'normalisation' of the industry. Unfortunately, with the failure of the EU/US negotiations to make significant progress in this key area, the chances of widespread reform have receded and now seem very unlikely in the foreseeable future.

The regulation of airports has followed a different pattern from that of airlines. Since initially the vast majority of airports were either locally or centrally government owned, there was little official interest in regulatory intervention. It was assumed, perhaps slightly naively, that governments would act in the broader public interest. Certainly, there was appreciation of the economic benefits, both local and national, of airport development. Increased privatisation led to a different approach. The concern now was to protect airlines and their customers from abuse of a dominant position by certain airports, and the extent of airports' market power became the focus of a fierce debate which continues to this day. The challenge is to allow an airport to earn a return on capital invested and increase efficiency while limiting monopoly profits. Some countries have adopted a detailed, prescriptive approach to regulation, where intervention has been judged to be necessary, while others have preferred a lighter, *post hoc* approach. There is a marked absence of consensus among regulators, academics and governments on the 'correct' form of regulation. Air traffic management, on the other hand, remains firmly in the past with respect to regulatory progress, almost wholly unreformed. ANSPs are still overwhelmingly State owned, with initial experiments in forms of privatisation failing to find wider acceptance, despite persuasive arguments on the need for cross-border consolidation. Attempts at price regulation of State-owned air traffic control companies aimed at improving efficiency, such as that adopted within the EU, have been of only limited success, at least partly because of political interference.

The Impact of COVID

This book has been written in the middle of the global COVID-19 pandemic. It is very difficult to predict with any precision the impact the emergency will have on the aviation industry in even the short term. The only certainty is that the effect has been huge and will continue to be so for some time. It has been described as the biggest retrenchment in the history of aviation, in some ways even greater than the impact of the Second World War given the scale of the industry today. The size of the decline in passenger traffic has dwarfed what was experienced following the 9/11 disaster, SARS and the global financial crisis of 2008/09. The term 'Black Swan' has been increasingly heard in relation to what has taken place globally between 2020 and 2022. First appearing in a book of the same name by Nicholas Taleb in 2007, Black Swan refers to an event which is unpredictable and improbable, yet at the same time is inevitable.[6] A key factor is that while it may be impossible to forecast with any accuracy when a Black Swan event will take place, it is nevertheless important to prepare for it. The second, related key factor is, of course, that adequate preparation rarely actually takes place, as the COVID epidemic has only too clearly illustrated. Aviation has been no different from other industries in that respect.

Taleb himself was highly critical of forecasting, noting how easy it is to be complacent when all appears to be going well. (He uses the analogy of a turkey which predicts a contented future based on its experience of being well looked after and fed during the period leading up to Christmas.)[7] Nevertheless, it is possible to reach some, albeit tentative, conclusions on what the future will hold for the aviation industry:

- First, as already noted, the impact of the pandemic has certainly been without precedent since the end of the Second World War; it will have dramatic effects on the operation and regulation of the aviation industry for many years.
- Secondly, despite this, traffic *will* recover; the only question is, how fast? Some 80% of travel by air is for leisure-related purposes, and once the pandemic is under control globally, there is no reason to believe that such travel will not return and growth resume. Business travel may be

different, but again common sense would seem to indicate that predictions of a major collapse are likely to be wide of the mark. Past experience suggests that teleconferencing generates as much international travel as it replaces, and certainly does not fully remove the need to travel. As has been noted, Zoom calls are great until you see your competitor in the same room as your client. That does not mean, of course, that business travel will fully recover. For some countries, it has barely done so since the two previous downturns. But while intra-company travel may be particularly adversely affected, much of the rest is likely to reappear. Table 13.2 shows the latest (March 2022) forecasts produced by IATA.

- Finally, there will be a structural change in the industry. It could not be otherwise given the pressures exerted over a relatively short period of time. The good news is that the impact of the pandemic has created an opportunity for radical reform not seen since 1944. The bad news is that there is a real risk that rather than making progress towards the normalisation of the sector, the industry will actually go back to a more interventionist and protectionist regime. We will return to this debate in the final section of this chapter.

Table 13.2 IATA Traffic Forecasts, March 2022 Passenger Numbers, Share of 2019

	2021	*2022*	*2023*	*2024*	*2025*
Industry-wide	47%	83%	94%	103%	111%
International	27%	69%	82%	92%	101%
Domestic	61%	93%	103%	111%	118%
Asia Pacific	40%	68%	84%	97%	109%
Europe	40%	86%	96%	105%	111%
North America	56%	94%	102%	107%	112%
Africa	46%	76%	85%	93%	101%
Middle East	42%	81%	90%	98%	105%
South America	51%	88%	97%	103%	108%
Central America	72%	96%	102%	109%	115%
Caribbean	44%	72%	82%	92%	101%

The collapse in demand as a result of the pandemic is hardly difficult to identify. Table 13.3 shows that even with the partial recovery seen in 2021, global airline output, measured in terms of revenue passenger kilometres, was still over 58% down on 2019, with regional variations ranging from a 70% reduction in the Middle East to 39% for North America. Airlines were forced to reduce capacity substantially, but nevertheless experienced significant declines in average seat factors. Cargo, on the other hand, faired better (Table 13.4). Despite the reduced capacity available in the bellyholds of passenger aircraft, demand for freighters meant that globally cargo saw an increase in capacity tonne kilometres of almost 7% in 2021 compared with 2019, ranging from plus 20% in North America to a decline of over 15% in Latin America.

Actual capacity operated fell in all except one region, but utilisation, reflected in the capacity load factor, increased markedly.

Table 13.3 Regional Impact of COVID on Passenger Traffic, 2021 Compared with 2019

Region	Global Share in 2021(%)[a]	RPKs (%)[b]	ASKs (%)[c]	PLF (%)[d]	PLF[e]
Africa	1.9	−62.8	−55.1	−12.3	59.5
Asia Pacific	27.5	−66.9	−56.7	−19.2	62.6
Europe	24.9	−61.3	−51.9	−16.6	68.6
Latin America	6.5	−47.4	−43.9	−5.2	77.3
Middle East	6.5	−69.9	−55.5	−24.6	51.5
North America	32.6	−39.0	−29.9	−11.0	73.8
Total	100.0	−58.4	−48.8	−15.4	67.2

Source: IATA.
[a]Percentage of industry RPKs.
[b]Revenue passenger kilometres performed.
[c]Available seat kilometres.
[d]Year-on-year percentage point change in passenger seat factor.
[e]Actual seat factor.

Table 13.4 Regional Impact of COVID on Cargo Traffic, 2021 Compared with 2019

Region	Global Share in 2021 (%)[a]	CTKs (%)[b]	ACTKs(%)[c]	CLF (%)[d]	CLF(%)[e]
Africa	1.9	10.2	−16.1	11.4	47.6
Asia Pacific	32.4	0.2	−18.0	11.7	64.0
Europe	22.9	3.7	−16.5	12.5	64.4
Latin America	2.2	−15.4	−32.6	9.0	44.1
Middle East	13.4	10.5	−10.1	10.7	57.4
North America	27.2	19.8	4.0	6.0	45.5
Total	100.0	6.9	−10.9	9.3	56.1

Source: IATA.
[a]Percentage of industry CTKs.
[b]Capacity tonne kilometres performed.
[c]Available CTKs.
[d]Capacity load factor change, 2021 compared with 2019.
[e]Actual capacity load factor, 2021.

The decline in passenger numbers and yields had a dramatic effect on airlines, which almost universally incurred substantial financial losses. Many were bailed out by governments and almost all were forced to resort to additional borrowing. Airports, ANSPs, aircraft/engine manufacturers and support services – all were similarly affected, although aircraft leasing companies appear to have fared better than initially expected. According to ACI, over the first two years of the pandemic, the number of passengers at the world's airports was reduced by 11.3 billion. Global traffic in 2021 was only half of what it was in 2019. Annual airport revenue shortfall in 2021 was US$83.1 billion, with an additional US$60.8 billion shortfall forecast for 2022. Overall, airport revenues were reduced by over 45% in 2021 compared with 2019. It is more difficult to obtain an overview of the epidemic's global impact on ANSPs, but Eurocontrol has estimated that by early 2022, flights within Europe were still only 68% of their 2019 level. While it may be too early to judge the full impact of these developments, there is no doubt that it will certainly be dramatic. The aviation industry will not emerge from the pandemic in the same shape as it entered it.

Mark Twain commented that history might not repeat itself, but it often rhymes. There have been six identifiable global pandemics over the past 130 years, with estimated death rates ranging from 0.5m (Swine Flu, 2009/10) to 50m (Spanish Flu, 1918/19). To that extent, COVID is not so unusual. What all of these pandemics have done, however, as Mark Twain alludes to, is not so much cause new trends as accelerate existing ones, something which the airline sector has illustrated starkly during the COVID pandemic.[8] KPMG/Airline Economics identified 31 airlines which ceased operations during 2020, with a further 13 entering bankruptcy protection.[9] This was actually fewer casualties than in 2019, almost certainly reflecting the fact that the full impact of the pandemic was partly hidden by government financial support. Additional problems can be expected when that support is withdrawn and airlines have to service the enormous levels of debt they have accumulated. It was the financially weakest carriers which were the first to be forced out of business in 2020, as their underlying problems were revealed. To this extent the aviation industry's experience has not been radically different from that of many other sectors. However, the industry's record of poor profitability over many decades meant that it was in a particularly exposed position when disaster struck. The potential regulatory implications of this situation are discussed below.

The opacity and complexity of the actions taken by several governments in supporting their airlines have been such that drawing up a definitive list is almost impossible. Such aid has differed substantially from country to country, for example sometimes involving financial assistance available generally to all sectors and sometimes being airline specific. Support has taken numerous forms, from direct grants to loans to equity acquisition. The level of assistance has also varied considerably, with the US and some European nations being particularly generous.

It is worth noting as well the way in which what limited cross-border consolidation that has taken place, for example within Europe, has created difficulties in the provision of State aid. Governments have been reluctant to provide finance if there was a risk of the money being used to assist airlines in other countries. Thus, a carrier such as Lufthansa has had to enter into negotiations with several governments separately to attract support for each of its subsidiaries, adding greatly to the complexity of the process. Similarly, the airline subsidiaries of IAG have received very different levels of financial support from their home governments. Press reports suggested that the French Government had sought to use the recapitalisation of Air France/KLM to reform what it regarded as the company's dysfunctional governance, which would inevitably have meant a reduction in KLM's autonomy. This was never going to be acceptable to the Dutch authorities at a time when they were being asked for financial aid, and illustrates again the problems created by the complex and unusual company structures necessitated by the continued restrictions on airline ownership and control.

As already noted, airlines have not been alone in experiencing reduced demand as a result of the COVID pandemic. Airports, ANSPs and aviation support services have similarly suffered. On the whole, support services have tended to receive generic assistance where necessary. ANSPs are mostly government-owned monopolies and can therefore be relaxed about their survival, although it remains to be seen if and how they will recoup their losses in future years. To some extent, airports have been helped indirectly by the assistance given to airlines. If the latter are able to operate at least some air services, airports usually receive an income, albeit greatly reduced from normal levels. The mixture of public and private ownership in the sector has complicated financial bailouts, with some airports in the same position as ANSPs and others receiving State aid and/or resorting to increased borrowing.

The Future

Superficially at least, the aviation industry has witnessed a transformation from tight regulation and extreme State involvement to a far more competitive environment where governments have increasingly stood back from active involvement in the running of companies. As Lumbrosco has noted, there is ample research showing that liberalisation has produced positive economic benefits overall. He quotes a literature review covering the period beginning in 1992, which found that while theoretically there could be negative results, empirically this has not been the case. Most studies have shown a positive effect; at worst, a neutral impact was found.[10] As well as consumers, governments and the industry itself have all benefitted, and despite initial concern by some, continued growth has brought higher employment levels alongside improved productivity. The airline sector has experienced the most dramatic of the regulatory changes, but airports have begun to move in a similar direction, albeit at a slower pace. ANSPs, on the other hand, have seen little in the way of reform, with few prospects on the horizon.

It is easy to forget how pervasive government interference in the aviation industry was during its early decades. As we have seen, the straitjacket imposed by the Chicago regime affected business strategies, industrial organisation and market structures, and the resultant lack of effective competitive pressures led to high operating costs and restrictive growth. Where an element of competition did emerge, it tended to take the form of 'quality of service,' based on frequency, comfort and onboard service, rather than price, and even service quality was curtailed where possible.[11] Regulatory reform, starting with the deregulation of US domestic services, while far from complete, was sufficient to disrupt this cosy arrangement, to the benefit of all categories of air travellers.

Disruption has been the hallmark of the industry. Partly this was the result of external factors which dramatically affected aviation (see Figure 13.1), but it was also a reflection of internal reform as deregulation/liberalisation spread around the world. The problem is that for the past decade or so, evidence has grown of, firstly, a cessation in such disruptive reform, followed by a real risk of a reversal to the old protectionism, what one commentator has aptly called 'creeping Bermudaism.'[12] As long ago as 2014, the Chief Executive of a major European airline group commented that, regretfully, liberalisation had reached 'its high water mark' and that the trend towards a more open regime was going to unravel as reactionary forces regroup.[13] That forecast has proved to be prescient. Of particular note was the failure of the EU/US trans-Atlantic negotiations to create a fully liberal Open Aviation Area, including the abolition of airline ownership and control restrictions and the prospect of worldwide reform. The result was a growing pessimism that the airline industry could ever be 'normalised' and create the type of global companies typical of other industries.

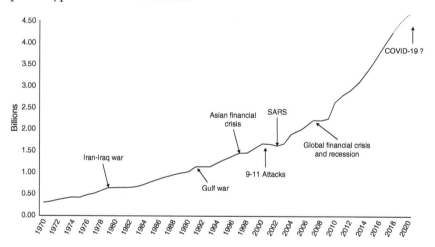

Figure 13.1 Impact of External Disruptions on Air Passenger Growth
Source: World Bank.

A second factor has been the reaction in many countries against globalisation in general. The Nation State, the core of the Chicago regulatory regime, has become a more acceptable concept again, not least in international trade, and as a result protectionism is seen as more attractive. Adam Pilarski of Avitas has even suggested that we are about to enter the 'era of deglobalization,' with the move away from globalisation accelerating and aviation inevitably affected negatively.[14]

The third factor in the slowdown of progress towards a fully liberalised global aviation regulatory regime has been the rapid growth of the Gulf sixth freedom carriers, and the reaction among some of their legacy competitors. By any measure, the scale of the growth of airline activity in the Middle East has been impressive in recent years. Dubai, for example, handled just 3 million passengers in 1981, which had increased to 10 million by 1998; by 2008 it was handling 37 million and no less than 90 million by 2019, replacing London Heathrow as the largest international airport in the world. Criticism of the business models and success of the likes of Emirates, Etihad and Qatar Airways (soon no doubt to be joined by Turkish Airlines with the development of its new hub at Istanbul Airport) first emerged in Europe, with airlines such as Air France/KLM and Lufthansa, in particular, urging the European Commission and their own Governments to either maintain or re-introduce market access restrictions. While the Commission resisted this pressure, supported by at least some other major European carriers and Member States, the battle lines were clearly established. With the further expansion of the Gulf carriers' route networks to North America, the US airlines launched their own attack, including a substantial lobbying campaign designed to persuade the US authorities to establish a 'level playing field' in bilateral aviation relations, a concept inevitably very difficult to define and even more difficult to implement. (As the Secretary General of the Arab Air Carriers Association once noted: "fair competition is like beauty, it is in the eyes of the beholder.")

The campaigns against the Gulf carriers became almost farcical at times. Airlines which had grown to success by using virtually the same business model as the Gulf carriers, including State subsidies, suddenly decided that this was unacceptable for others. Some legacy airlines argued publicly, with a straight face, that the Gulf carriers were stealing 'their' passengers in their home markets, while simultaneously seeking to attract sixth freedom traffic via their own hubs. Nevertheless, the lobbying campaigns certainly made an impression. There is no doubt that the expansion of the Gulf carriers in some markets was at least delayed. The public debate acted to encourage less liberally minded countries to resist further market opening and highlighted a resurgent resistance to further globalisation. It added to a growing feeling that regulatory reform had gone as far as was acceptable and may even need to be pushed back.

This is the background to the impact of the COVID epidemic, which as we have seen, served in many ways to exacerbate underlying trends. (The war in Ukraine has, of course, only added to the aviation industry's problems, but the full impact is impossible to determine at the time of writing.) The problem was not the fact that governments had to step in to save airlines; they did the same for many other businesses, some of far less strategic and political value than airlines. It was more the re-emergence of many of the protectionist, nationalist arguments which over the decades had gradually been disappearing from the debate about the regulation of the air transport industry. It soon became obvious that for many States, regulatory reform had been, at best, superficial and that fundamentally the aviation industry remained as fettered by anti-competitive government involvement as it had been in the 1940s. As James Forsyth commented in relation to the general emerging trend, COVID has changed the world; there is a realisation that in a crisis, borders reassert themselves.[15] The first wave of globalisation, which started in the 1870s, was ended by the First World War. By the 1930s autarky and self-sufficiency were being embraced by many major countries, a trend which ended in a global disaster.[16] The latest wave of globalisation, which started around the turn of the 21st century, may be ended by COVID.

Some have argued that the evidence of the past century points to each major global downturn being associated with a rise in discrimination against foreign commercial interests,[17] and aviation is probably more exposed to this development than most other industries, not least because it has always been characterised by more government involvement than found elsewhere. If, as this book has hopefully shown, there are sound reasons for 'normalising' the air transport industry, the recently revealed reversion to an almost Chicago mentality cannot be regarded as anything other than a backward step. As a result, it is difficult to be optimistic about the prospects for further regulatory reform. It is not even obvious, despite suggestions to the contrary by some, that the problems experienced by the airlines as a result of COVID will assist in the consolidation which, we have suggested, is clearly needed. As IATA has argued, the large stakes taken by many governments in carriers will make it more difficult for them to "sell this asset to any foreign actor and explain that to the taxpayer." In any event, the absence of global reform of the ownership and control rules, and any serious likelihood of such reform, will inevitably place a limit on progress.

Two further major challenges face the aviation industry once it emerges from the immediate COVID downturn. The first has been with us for a long time but is increasingly the focus of debate: the environment. One of the surprises of the COVID epidemic has been the fact that environmental issues have continued to attract so much attention among politicians and the general public, despite the economic problems encountered in almost every country. Prior to the 2008/09 financial crisis, the environment appeared towards the top of most lists of issues of public concern, especially in Europe, but following the economic downturn it attracted far less consideration as public attention was diverted to the economy and jobs. That does not appear to have happened this time to anything like the same extent. The resurgence of interest in environmental matters has been maintained, which has substantial implications for air transport. The industry simply has no choice but to face up to its responsibilities. Greenwash will no longer be sufficient or acceptable.

In Chapter 9, we discussed the size of the challenge facing the industry in this respect. There are no easy answers and it is impossible to forecast with any certainty what the outcome will be, especially because technology will inevitably have to play a key role and its development is always difficult to predict decades in advance. However, one outcome is clear: there will be growing pressure from governments to ensure that air travel pays for its environmental externalities. Whether imposed nationally, regionally or globally, we can expect to see more and higher taxes on the industry. Increased taxation means higher air fares, at least higher than they would otherwise have been, and therefore a lower rate of traffic growth. The technical innovations needed to reduce emissions, including the widespread adoption of sustainable aviation fuel, may also lead to higher costs. This is quite different from what the industry has experienced in the past; previously technology has almost always increased efficiency and reduced costs.

The second major challenge facing the air transport industry in a post-COVID world is the enormous financial support made available to airlines, airports and others in the form of loans, increased equity and especially direct State subsidy. We have seen in previous chapters how governments have repeatedly been forced to bear the financial burden of loss-making aviation companies, but this time the sheer scale of the support provided is wholly unprecedented over such a short period of time. IATA has calculated that financial losses in 2020 and 2021 amounted to some US$190 billion, with more to come in 2022, despite some US$130 billion government aid in the form of wage support, equity investment and direct grants. To put these losses into context, in 2019, a year marked by relatively good airline financial performance, only 30 international airlines were estimated to be sustainably profitable in earning more than their cost of capital. Analysis by Bloomberg showed that global airline debt, which stood at US$198 billion in 2019, had reached US$339 billion by September 2021.[18] The challenge in paying back the huge public and private debt accumulated is only too obvious. It will take many years to clear this debt, even in the unlikely event of no more profit-sapping surprises. The IAG Group, for example, has a debt repayment schedule totalling over €7.5 billion between 2022 and 2029, with some €2.8 billion due in one year, 2026. At the end of 2021, IAG's net equity stood at just €846 million.[19]

Given the scale of the problems facing the air transport industry during the COVID epidemic, there was no alternative to extensive government financial support. Airline veteran Bob Crandall has even suggested that governments have become an insurer, 'the lender of last resort.' However, the way in which this was done has created serious risks going forward, partly because of a likely return to greater government involvement in airline operations and partly because of the potential for competition to be distorted. The epidemic has affected countries in different ways and at different timescales, producing a recovery around the world that has been far from uniform. There remains at the time of writing substantial uncertainty about the final impact of the pandemic, but it is already clear that in future the aviation world, like much else, will be very different to what we have been used to. The key question is whether the outcome will be positive or negative for the industry and consumers. The omens unfortunately are not good.

Given the different forms of government support provided for airlines, there is a risk that the industry will split into the *'haves'* and the *'have nots.'* It is likely that those carriers which have predominantly received grants will be in a stronger competitive position than those which have had to rely to a greater extent on loans. This is even more true where support has taken the form of increased public ownership, in some cases including renationalisation. Greater government interest, either via loans or ownership, will almost inevitably result in more political involvement in the day-to-day running of companies, something which did so much harm during earlier decades of the industry's history. The Economist has drawn attention to the growing risk of 'cronyism,' "which ends up contaminating business and politics alike... [The] adherents [of State intervention] hope for prosperity, fairness and security. They are more likely to end up with inefficiency, vested interests and insularity."[20] Such a trend is also likely to have an adverse effect on future regulatory reform, at best slowing further progress and possibly worse. Under this scenario, governments are far more likely to pursue nationalistic objectives, taking the aviation industry further away from being a 'normal' business. History has surely shown that politically controlled and influenced airlines tend to be less efficient and consumer focused, with very few exceptions. There is a clear risk that governments will become more protectionist as they seek to immunise the carriers in which they have an increased direct interest from greater competition. They are far more likely to focus on protecting their investments than on pursuing a more liberal regulatory regime.

Early signs of such developments have already emerged, not least in Europe. Government loans to Air France, for example, have not only been accompanied by increased public ownership, but also by restrictions on the operation of domestic air services where rail provides an alternative transport mode, all carefully designed to protect Air France/KLM's hub at Charles de Gaulle Airport. The €600m bailout received by Austrian Airlines in the form of loans and grants provided an even more blatant example of protecting the interests of the flag carrier at the expense of competitors. One of the conditions of the aid was acceptance of a €40 minimum price floor, applicable to all airlines serving the country's airports. The main impact of this initiative, if fully implemented, would be felt by low-cost carriers, whose passenger share at Vienna Airport had increased from 5% to 24% since 2015, rather than by Austrian Airlines. (Across their networks, Ryanair's and Wizz Air's average fares were €37 and €38 respectively, excluding ancillary revenue.) The Austrian Government also proposed increases in taxes applicable to short and medium-haul air services, but a 30% reduction in long-haul taxes.[21] Again, it is difficult not to conclude that the main objective was to strengthen the relative competitive position of the flag carrier, in which the Government now had an increased financial interest. Further, similar examples can be found in other countries.

There are some positive signs. For example, both Air France/KLM and Lufthansa have been required to give up slots at some of their congested hub airports. Unlike most previous slot divestitures awarded in connection with alliance competition cases, these slots will not be tied to particular routes and therefore be more attractive to LCCs and more effective in increasing competition. However, the overall picture is not positive. One respected aviation commentator has suggested that the aviation industry resembles a hopeless drunk lurching towards the next crisis: "How can we expect a sustainable industry [to be] built on junk bonds?"[22] When recovery has finally fully arrived, the industry will be marked by a weakened and vulnerable airline sector, together with airports and ANSPs seeking to recover large losses. There will inevitably be more airline failures, although at the same time, and as ever, there seems to be no shortage of ambitious new entrants. But the key conclusion has to be that the final stages of regulatory reform, needed to transform the airline industry into a financially sustainable business, are no closer to being achieved and may be further away than ever.

Notes

1 Quoted in Simon Calder: *No Frills. The Truth behind the Low-Cost Revolution in the Skies*. Virgin Books, London, 2002.
2 Eugene Sochor: *The Politics of International Aviation*. MacMillan, London, 1991. Quoted in Thomas C. Lawton: *Cleared for Take-Off. Structure and Strategy in the Low Fare Airline Business*. Ashgate, Aldershot, 2002.
3 Sveinn Vidar Gudmundson: 'New-entrant airlines' life cycle analysis: Growth, decline and collapse.' *Journal of Air Transport Management*, Vol. 4(4), 1998, pp. 217–228. Quoted in Thomas C. Lawton, op cit.
4 David Jarach: 'Future scenarios for the European airline industry: A market-based perspective.' *Journal of Air Transportation*, Vol. 9(2), 2004, pp. 23–39.
5 Adam Thomson: *High Risk: The Autobiography of Adam Thomson – The Politics of the Air*. Sidgwick & Jackson, London, 1990.
6 Aviation Strategy: 'Aviation Ingests a Huge Black Swan.' March 2021.
7 Ibid.
8 Tom Smith, CEO Fundsmith LLP, Fundsmith Annual Report, 2021.
9 KPMG/Airline Economics: 'The Airline Industry Leaders Report: Route to Recovery.' 2021.
10 Alain Lumbrosco: 'Aviation liberalisation: What headwinds do we still face?' *Journal of Air Transport Management*, Vol. 74, 2019, pp. 22–29. See also InterVISTAS: 'The Economic Impact of Air Service Liberalisation. Updating the Landmark 2006 Study to Reflect the New Realities of Commercial Passenger Aviation.' June 2015, Vancouver.
11 G. Gönenç and Giuseppe Nicoletti: 'Regulation, Market Structure and Performance in Air Passenger Transportation.' *OECD Economic Studies*, No. 32, 2001.
12 Andrew Charlton, Aviation Advocacy.
13 Willie Walsh, CEO of IAG. CAPA: 'Protecting the fortress.' *Airline Leader*, April/May, 2014.
14 Adam Pilarski: 'Pilarski Says – Are we about to Enter the era of Deglobalization?' *Avitas*, 17 September 2020.
15 *The Times*, London, 19 March 2021.
16 Simon Nixon: 'History Warns that Retreat from Globalisation Can Lead to Disaster.' *The Times*, London, 1 April 2021.

17 Simon J. Evenett: 'What's next for protectionism? Watch out for state largesse, especially export incentives.' In Richard E. Baldwin and Simon J. Evenett (eds.): *COVID-19 and Trade Policy: Why Turning Inward Won't Work*. Centre for Economic Policy Research, London, 2020.
18 'Cash is King but Debt Rules OK?' *Aviation Strategy*, Issue No. 264, October/November 2021.
19 'IAG: Delicately Balancing its Finances.' Aviation Strategy, March/April 2022.
20 The Economist (Leader): 'Welcome to the era of the Bossy State.' 15 January 2022.
21 Linnea Ahgren: 'EU Concerned about Austria's Minimum Air Fare Policy.' *Simply Flying*, 4 February, 2021.
22 Peter Harbison speaking at the CAPA Live Summit, April 2021.

Index

AAAVTAG *see* ENAV
Aberdeen Airport 214
Abra Group 133
Aden Airways 152
Advanced Booking Charters (ABCs) 35, 126
Advanced Purchase Excursion (APEX) fares 35
Advertising Standards Authority (UK) 168
Aegean 119
Aer Lingus 122, 140, 152
Aerial Navigation Act 11
Aeroflot 15, 119
Aerolineas Argentinas 123
Aeromexico 126, 152
Aeroports de Paris 217
Aerothai 202–203
affinity/closed group charters 33
African Union (AU) 104–105, 134
Agenda for Freedom 142
Aigle Azur 153
Air Afrique 134, 152
Air Asia 124, 134
Air Asia Japan 124
Air Asia Malaysia 125
Air Berlin 152
Air Canada 116, 185
Air Commerce Act (US) 130
Air France 19, 66, 90, 99–100, 119, 139–140, 147, 152, 162, 169, 248; Air France/KLM 74, 116, 119, 123, 139, 152, 162, 243, 245, 248
Air Gabon 152
Air India 29, 141
Air Italy 152
Air Mail Service (US) 192
Air Navigation Service Providers (ANSPs) 192–211, 214, 239, 241–243
Air New Zealand 29, 119
Air Portugal/TAP 147, 153
Air Serbia 152
Air Services Agreements (ASAs) 6, 15, 17, 23–24, 28–29, 38, 42, 50, 62, 81–88, 131–132, 139, 141–142, 237
Air Seychelles 152
Air Southwest 109
air traffic control/management (ATC/ATM) 74, 179, 192–211, 239
Air Tran 138
Air Transport Action Group (ATAG) 1, 187
Air Transport Advisory Council 31
Air Transport Regulatory Reform Act 49
Air Union 147
Airboat Line 187
Airbus 2, 126, 128, 156–157, 161–164, 166
Airline Clearing House (ACH) 21
Airline Deregulation Act 54
The Airline Group (AG) 202–204
Airlines for Europe 227
Airport and Airways Trust Fund (AATF) (US) 198
Airport Charges Directive (EU) 226–227
Airport Improvement Program (US) 218–219
Airport Privatization Pilot Program (US) 219
airport slots 70–72
Airports Council International (ACI) 70, 216, 228, 241
Alaska Airlines 112–114, 116, 138, 185
Alcazar Alliance 147
Alitalia 66, 74, 119, 147, 152
Allegheny 146
Allegiant 114
Amadeus 66
America West 138
American Airlines 48, 53, 66, 99, 113–114, 137–138, 145, 150, 152, 162, 185, 227

Index

American Depository Receipts 133
Anchorage Airport 158
Ansett/Ansett International 133
Arab Air Carrier Association 245
Asia-Pacific Economic Cooperation (APEC) 102–103
Association of European Airlines (AEA) 93, 195
Association of Southeast Asian Nations (ASEAN) 100–101, 103, 133–134
Atlanta Airport 52
ATLAS 147
Austrian Airlines 139, 141, 147, 248
Avianca 133
An Aviation Strategy for Europe 99
Azul 112, 116, 126, 153

Bailey, Elizabeth 49
Baliles Commission 82, 86
Beijing Capital Airlines 153
Berlin Airlift 30
The Bermuda Agreement 21–24, 28–29, 36–45, 82, 90–92, 95, 98, 131, 235, 244
Big Bang 50
Bishop, Sir Michael 234
Black Swan 239
Blackrock 137
Blair, Tony 202
bmi 141, 234
BOAC 28–29, 31, 35, 39, 152
Boeing 27, 33, 36, 53, 109, 156–157, 160–162
Bonderman, David 110, 125
Borealis Alliance 209
Borneo Airways 152
Braniff 109
Branson, Sir Richard 96, 144, 182
Brattle Group 97–98, 143
Breeze 112
Brexit 179
Brisbane Airport 225
Britannia Airways 32–33, 132
British Airports Authority (BAA) 203, 214–217, 221, 223
British Airways 19, 43, 66–67, 95–96, 119, 123, 140–141, 147–148, 150, 169, 173, 185, 203, 233–234
British Caledonian Airways 33, 43, 238
British European Airways (BEA) 19, 20, 28, 31, 39; BEA Airtours 33, 35
British Overseas Air Charter 35
British United Airways 33
Brussels Airlines 139, 141; see also Sabena
Brussels Airport 217

Buffet, Warren 138, 187, 238
Buzz 122–123

Caledonian Airways see British Caledonian Airways
Callaghan, Jim 39
Cameroon Airlines 152
Carbon Offsetting and Reduction Scheme for International Aviation (CORSIA) 173–174
Cardiff Airport 217
Cathay Pacific 19, 136, 147, 152
Cebu Pacific Air 125
Central European ATM System (CEATS) 208
Channel Island Air Transport 31
Chapter 11 bankruptcy 137
Charles de Gaulle Airport, Paris 248
Chicago Conference 6, 11–17, 21, 235
Chicago Convention 6, 13, 15, 25, 27, 43, 102, 108, 130, 170, 192, 195, 221, 237, 243–244, 246
China Eastern 152
China Southern 153
China West Air 153
Churchill, Winston 3
Cities Program (US) 82, 85, 87
Citilink 125
Civil Aeronautics Act 46
Civil Aeronautics Board (CAB) 18–19, 30, 33, 35, 46–50, 53, 85–86, 96, 109, 146
Civil Aviation Act (UK) 224
Civil Aviation Authority (UK) 35, 39, 43, 47, 60, 69, 72–73, 91, 97, 117, 134, 136, 202–204, 223–224
Civil Aviation Authority (US) 46
Civil Reserve Air Fleet (CRAF) 135
codeshare 145–146
Comair 153
Comité des Sages for Air Transport 86
Community Carrier 74, 92–93, 97, 103, 141, 143–144, 236
Competition and Consumer Commission (ACCC) (Australia) 150, 225
Competition and Markets Authority (UK) 150
Competition Commission (UK) 215, 223–224
Computer Reservation Systems (CRS) 55, 66–68, 146, 185–187
Condor 35
contestability 54

Continental Airlines 47, 109, 114, 138, 152–153
Continental Lite 113–114
Convention on Air Navigation 11
COP26 174
Copenhagen Airport 217
Cosmos Holidays 32
Council of Member States (EU) 59, 61–62
Court of Appeal (US) 47
Crandall, Bob 48, 162, 247
Croydon Aerodrome 192
Cypress Airlines 152

Darwin Airline 152
De Havilland 160, 177
dehosting 67
Dell, Edmond 38, 41–42, 45
Delta Air Lines 53, 113–114, 116, 137–138, 144, 147, 152, 165, 185, 227
Delta Express 114
Department of Defense (US) 135
Department of Justice (DOJ) (US) 90, 113, 148
Department of Transportation (DOT) (US) 18, 44, 46, 50, 53, 87, 90, 96, 112, 145, 148, 150–151, 198
DGVII (EU) 59
Director General/Directorate for Mobility and Transport 99, 143
dual till 222–223
Dubai Airport 245
Dusseldorf Airport 245

easyJet 116–117, 119–122, 169, 185; easyJet Switzerland 120; *see also* TEA
economics of scope 52
Edinburgh Airport 214–215
Edwards Committee/Report 8, 39, 182, 202
Edwards, Sir Ronald *see* Edwards Committee
EEC Treaty 58
Embraer 122
Emirates Airlines 20, 116, 159, 177, 245
Emissions Trading Scheme (ETS) 170, 172–174, 179
empty core 189–191, 238
Ente Nazionale di Assistenza al Volo (ENAV) (Italy) 205
environment 156, 165–179, 246–247
Equity Alliance 152
Essential Air Services (EAS) program 48

Etihad 152, 159, 245
Etihad Regional *see* Darwin Airline
EU/US Agreement 82, 94–97, 99, 143, 237–238, 244
Euratom 59
Euravia 32
Eurocontrol 206, 211, 242
Eurocontrol Convention 206
European Aviation Safety Agency (EASA) 8, 68–69, 167, 208
European Civil Aviation Conference (ECAC) 19, 57, 60, 68, 70, 86
European Commission 58–75, 91–93, 95–96, 98, 100–101, 103, 141, 143–145, 150–151, 158, 168, 170, 176, 179, 209–210, 227, 236–237, 245
European Common Aviation Area (ECAA) 93
European Court of Justice (ECJ) 59, 61, 91–92
European Economic Community 59
European Union (EU) 8–9, 16, 23, 57–75, 81, 91–105, 133, 136, 141, 143–144, 158, 168–172, 204, 206–210, 226, 236–237
Eurowings 119, 123, 169

fatality risks 7
Federal Aviation Administration (US) 46, 69, 197–199, 201, 206, 209
Ferrovial 214
Fiji Airways 152
Finnair 119
Fit for 55 (EU) 170, 179
flag carriers 5, 30, 57, 82–83, 213, 235, 248
flags of convenience 23, 136
flight shame 165
Franke, Bill 125
Frankfurt Airport 217
freedoms of the air 14, 15–16, 130
frequent flyer programme (FFP) 55, 145–146, 150–151
Frontier 114–115, 126
Functional Airspace Block (FAB) 209

Galileo 66
Garanair 140
Gatwick Airport 91, 95, 99, 120, 214–215, 221, 224
General Agreement on Trade and Services (GATT) 102
Germanwings 123
Ghana World Airways 153

254 *Index*

Glasgow Airport 214–215
Global Distribution System (GDS) *see* computer reservation systems
Global Excellence Network 147
Global Infrastructure Partners 215
globalisation 246
Go 123
GOL 126, 133, 152
Government Accountability Office (GOA) (US) 198
grandfather rights 70
Gulf Air/Aviation 134, 152
Gulf carriers 100, 159, 245

Hainan Airlines Group 153
Haji-Ioannou, Stelios 119
Hamburg Airport 217
Haneda International Airport, Tokyo 227
Harbour Air 177
Havana Convention 12
Heathrow Airport 42, 71–72, 82, 85, 91, 95–96, 99, 120, 168, 203, 214–215, 221, 224, 245
Hong Kong Airlines 152–153
Hong Kong Express 116, 153
Horizon Holidays 31
House of Commons (UK) 69
hubs/super hubs 51–53, 82, 135, 159, 227, 245; hub-and-spoke 145; hub-bypassers 161; hub premium 52

IAG 74, 116, 123, 139–140, 153, 242, 247
Iberia 66, 119, 133, 140–141
inclusive tour charters 29–33, 118, 235
Indigo Partners 114, 125–126; Indigo Airlines 125
Intergovernmental Panel on Climate Change 177
Interjet 126
interlining 145
International Air Services Transit Agreement (IASTA) 15, 130, 159
International Air Transport Association (IATA) 9, 16–21, 24, 33–36, 65, 70, 74, 85–86, 137, 141–142, 145, 150, 168–170, 173, 175–176, 178, 184, 186, 203, 211, 216, 220–221, 224–225, 240, 246–247; IATA Clearing House 20–21; IATA Resolution (045)/ Provision 1 31, 33
International Air Transportation Competition Act (US) 82, 84
International Air Transportation Policy (US) 82, 83

International Aviation Climate Ambition Coalition 174
International Chamber of Commerce 134
International Civil Aviation Organisation (ICAO) 2, 5–9, 14, 16, 27, 57, 101, 142, 169, 172–174, 192, 195, 198, 200, 221; Provisional ICAO 14; ICAO Standard Rules and Procedures (SARPS) 192
International Commission on Air Navigation (ICAN) 12
International Maritime Organisation 172
International Monetary Fund 37
International Operational Safety Audit (IOSA) 9, 20
Inter-Regional Air Services Directive (EU) 60, 62
Iraq Airways 152
Irish Supreme Court 122
Istanbul Airport 245

Japan Airlines 185
Jet Airways 152
Jet Smart 126
Jet2 116, 120, 123
JetBlue 112–113
Jetstar 116, 124, 134; Jetstar Japan 124
Joint Airworthiness Authorities (JAA) 68–70
Junker 178

Kahn, Fred 18, 49, 54, 84, 87, 187, 189
Kangaroo route 29, 160
Kelleher, Herb 109, 111, 122–123
King, Rollin W. 109
KLM 61, 66, 100, 119, 123, 139–140, 147–148, 151, 152, 243
Korean Air 152
KSSU 147
Kuwait Airways 152
Kyoto Protocol 172

Labour Government (UK) 37, 39
Laker, Sir Freddie 32, 39, 60, 108, 126; Laker Airways 43, 127
LAN 153
LATAM 126, 133, 153
Lauda/Laudamotion 123
Lend Lease Agreement 21
Level 123
Levine, Michael 49, 52, 54, 145
Levitas, Representative Elliott 50
LFV (Sweden) 197
Lion Air 125; Thai Lion Air 125

London Stock Exchange 214
long-haul charters 33–36
low-cost/no-frills carriers (LCCs) 108–128, 149–151, 164, 228, 236, 248–249; ultra low-cost carrier (ULCC) 115
Lucky Air 153
Lufthansa 35, 66, 74, 116, 119–120, 123, 139, 141, 147, 162, 169, 242, 245, 248
Luis Muñoz Marin International Airport (San Juan) 219
Lundgren, Johan 122

Maastricht Upper Area Control Centre 208
Malaysia Airways 152; Malaysia-Singapore Airlines 29
Malta Air 123
Manchester Airport 215, 221, 224
Mandala Airlines 126
Market-Based Measures (MBAs) 173
mercantilism 38, 45, 83
Meridiana *see* Air Italy
Messina Intergovernmental Conference 59
Metrojet 114
Middle East Airlines/MEA 152
Midway Airport, Chicago 219
Ministry of Infrastructure, Transport, Regional Development and Communications (Australia) 225
Monarch Airlines 32, 132
Monet, Jean 59
Montreal Convention 65
Morris Air 112
Most Favoured Nation (MFN) 102
Multilateral Agreement on the Liberalization of International Air Transport (MALIAT) 102–103
Muse, Lamar 110–111

Narita Airport, Tokyo 85
National Air Traffic Services (NATS) (UK) 197, 201–205
National Airlines 37, 52
NavCanada 197, 199–201, 204, 207
New Generation Air Transportation System (NextGen) 208–209
9/11 203, 239
Northwest Airlines 138, 147–148, 150, 152
Norwegian Airlines 119, 169; Norwegian International 99–100
Nouvelles Frontières 61

O'Hara Airport, Chicago 227
O'Leary, Michael 122
OECD 173, 184
off-setting *see* Emission Trading Scheme
Oman Air 70
oneworld 145, 149, 153
Open Aviation Area (OAA) 96–98, 100, 143, 237, 244
open skies 15, 49, 81–105, 143, 147–148, 237

Pacific Southwest Airlines 48, 110
Pan Am 18, 37, 43, 52, 82, 160
Paris Agreement 172
Paris Peace Convention 12
Parkinson, Cecil 44
passenger rights (EU) 64
Peach 124
Pegasus 116, 119
Pension Protection Fund (PPF) (UK) 204
People Express 126–127
Performance Review Board (PRB) (EU) 210
Perth Airport 225
pooling agreements 29
Port Authority of New York and New Jersey 219
Porter's competitive advantage 109
President (US): Bush 87, 131; Carter 42, 47, 49, 82, 84; Clinton 82, 86–87; Ford 18, 47; Hoover 3; Nixon 47; Reagan 199; Trump 100, 199
Prestwick Airport 217
Productivity Commission (PC) (Australia) 225
Public-Private Partnership (PPP) 202–203

Qantas 20, 29, 124, 160
Qatar Airways 152–153, 159, 245

Regulated Asset Base (RAB) 222, 224
Rifkind, Malcolm 44
Ritz, Vladimir 31
Royal Air Maroc 152
RPI-X 203, 209, 221
RwandaAir 152
Ryanair 59, 64, 110, 116, 118, 122, 133, 168–169, 173, 182, 188, 248; Ryanair Sun 122–123

Saab 197
Sabena 18, 74, 147; *see also* Brussels Airlines
Sabre 66
safety regulation 6–9
SARS 239
SAS 17, 66, 71, 119, 123, 134, 147, 152, 169
Schiphol Airport 141
Scoot 124
Seaboard 37
SEAMA 147
Senate Committee on Commerce (US) 3
Senate Sub-Committee on Aviation and Space (US) 199
Senator (US): Cannon 48–49; Kennedy 48–49; Pearson 48–49
Shannon Airport 27, 158
Show Cause Order (US) 18, 85
Silk Air 124
Singapore Airlines 19–20, 124, 144, 147, 152, 161, 163; *see also* Malaysia-Singapore Airlines
Single African Air Transport Market (SAATM) 104, 134
Single European Act (EU) 59
Single European Railway Area 208
Single European Sky (SES/SES-II) 207, 210; Single European Sky ATM Research (SESAR) 208–209
single till 222–223
Skyteam 145, 149, 153
Skytrain 39, 60, 126
Slot Allocation Regulation (EU) 70
Song 113–114, 116
Southampton Airport 214
Southwest Airlines 48, 53, 109–116, 120–123, 137–138, 182, 185, 227; Southwest effect 53, 112
Spaak Report 59
SpiceJet 125
Spirit 113–115, 126
Spring Air Lines 125; Spring Airlines Japan 124
Stansted Airport 214–215, 221, 224
Star Alliance 141, 145, 147–150, 153
State Department (US) 44
Statement of International Aviation Policy (US) 84
Statement on International Air Transport Policy (US) 41
Stewart Airport, New York 219
Sustainable Aviation Fuel (SAF) 170, 173, 175–178

Sutherland, Peter 60
Swiss 139, 141; Swissair 66, 74, 120, 147, 152
Sydney Airport 225

TACA 133
Taleb, Nicholas 239
TEA 120; *see also* easyJet Switzerland
Ted 113–114; *see also* United Airlines
Terminal Air Navigation Services (TANS) 197
Texas International 109
Thai Air Asia 125
Thai International 147
Thatcher, Margaret 43, 60, 95, 200
Thomas Cook 32
Thomson Airways *see* Britannia Airways
Thomson Industrial Holdings 32
Thomson, Sir Adam 238
Tianjin Airlines 153
Tigerair/Tiger Airways 124–125
Trans-Atlantic Aviation Area (TAA) 93, 98–99
Transavia 123
trans-Siberia route 15, 159
Travel Group Charters 35
Treaty of Rome 58–59, 61, 91, 236
Tui Group 122
Tunis Air 152
Turkish Airlines 119, 245
TWA 18, 37, 43, 52, 82
Twain, Mark 242

U-FLY Alliance 124, 150
Ukraine war 245
United Airlines 99, 113–114, 116, 137–138, 162, 185, 227; *see also* Ted
Universal Sky Tours 32
Urumqi Airlines 152
US Congress 3
USAir/US Airways 48, 114, 138, 146–148, 152–153
UTA 147

Value Alliance 124, 150
Vanguard 137
Vanilla Air 124
Vienna Airport 248
Vietjet Air 116, 125
Vinci Airports 215, 217, 229–230
Virgin: Australia/Blue 124, 152–153; America 96, 112, 138; Atlantic Airways 43, 95, 127, 144, 152, 175, 182, 203; Galactic 144; Group 96, 112, 124, 144

Viva Aerobus 116, 126
Volaris 116, 126
Vuelling 119, 123, 140, 169

Warsaw Convention 65
Webster, Ray 119
Wells, H. G. 6
Westjet 112
Wheatcroft, Stephen 39
Whittle, Frank 177
Wilson, Harold 39
Wizz Air 116, 118–119, 123, 126, 133, 168–169, 248

World Airways 47
World Trade Organisation (WTO) 5, 102
Worldwide Airport Coordination Group 70
Worldwide Slot Guidelines 70, 72
Wright Brothers 1, 4, 137, 156, 182

Yamoussoukro Declaration (YD) 104–105, 134

Zurich Airport 223

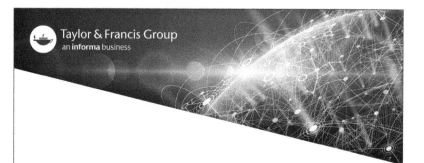

Milton Keynes UK
Ingram Content Group UK Ltd.
UKHW052010170624
444208UK00016B/265